Ethnic Conflict

For Bob and Cesiek
For Maximilian Alexander

Ethnic Conflict

Causes – Consequences – Responses

KARL CORDELL AND STEFAN WOLFF

polity

First published in 2009 by Polity Press

Polity Press
65 Bridge Street
Cambridge CB2 1UR, UK.

Polity Press
350 Main Street
Malden, MA 02148, USA

ISBN-13: 978-0-7456-3930-7
ISBN-13: 978-0-7456-3931-4 (pb)

A catalogue record for this book is available from the British Library.

Typeset in 9.5 on 13 pt Swift Light
by Servis Filmsetting Ltd, Stockport, Cheshire
Printed and bound by MPG Books Group, UK

The publisher has used its best endeavours to ensure that the URLs for external websites referred to in this book are correct and active at the time of going to press. However, the publisher has no responsibility for the websites and can make no guarantee that a site will remain live or that the content is or will remain appropriate.

Every effort has been made to trace all copyright holders, but if any have been inadvertently overlooked the publishers will be pleased to include any necessary credits in any subsequent reprint or edition.

For further information on Polity, visit our website: www.polity.com

Contents

Acknowledgements

There are many people to whom we owe a debt of gratitude with regard to this volume. In particular, our thanks go out to Louise Knight at Polity, who commissioned this work, for her patience, encouragement and advice, to Rachel Donnelly and Emma Hutchinson at Polity for their help and support, and to Caroline Richmond for her professionalism and patience at the copy-editing stage. Thanks are also due to Jenny Hedström for her assistance in preparing the case study on Burma, and to Annemarie Peen Rodt, Martin Ottmann and Ana-Maria Anghelea for assistance with some of the theoretical chapters. Credit must also be extended to those too numerous to mention who helped us with their own insights into ethnic conflicts around the world, challenged us to question our own assumptions, and encouraged us on this long intellectual journey. Without all of you, this work would not have seen the light of day. We believe the text to be accurate as of 31 March 2009. Nevertheless, we freely acknowledge that any mistakes and infelicities are entirely our responsibility.

We do not consider this book the end point of our work on ethnic conflict, but it does mark a significant milestone in more than ten years of collaboration and synthesizes the knowledge and understanding that we have accumulated over this period of time. While the book as a whole is an original endeavour, we draw, in part, on individual and joint work, both published and forthcoming, including Cordell and Wolff (2004, 2005, forthcoming), Schneckener and Wolff (2004) and Wolff (2003c, 2004a, 2006, 2007a, 2008a, 2008b, 2009).

1

Introduction

Ethnic conflict is a phenomenon in international affairs that is almost equally difficult to understand as it is to define. Who fights in ethnic conflicts, and why do they do it? Why do ethnic conflicts cause often seemingly random and excessively cruel violence to civilians? What drives people to inflict such suffering, or at least support those who do? Why are international organizations and powerful states often indifferent to the security threats that ethnic conflicts pose until a major crisis has developed? What is it that makes many an ethnic confict so difficult to settle? These are pressing questions, and satisfactory answers to them are few and far between.

However, these are not the only questions one may want to ask about ethnic conflict. In addition to finding out about its causes, it is equally important for our understanding to investigate when, how and where people kill each other. These are questions about mobilization processes, the strategy and tactics of inter-ethnic warfare, and whether there are specific environmental factors that facilitate conflict rather than coexistence. Equally, international involvement raises questions beyond what can be done about ethnic conflicts. Again, there is a question of timing: when is it best to intervene – before, during or after a conflict? It is also important to consider the various means of intervention, i.e., to decide whether non-coercive or coercive means are most appropriate. Finally, there is a question about where to intervene. Should intervention occur in conflicts that affect the intervener's own strategic interests, in conflicts that cause particular suffering for innocent civilians, or in conflicts in which there is a reasonable chance of doing more good than harm? These are all questions of great significance, and they are closely connected. Only once we understand the reasons that lead people to continue to rely on violence, despite its costs, will we be able to devise appropriate policies that help them to renounce violence.

These questions have exercised academics and policy-makers, civil society activists and businessmen, politicians and their voters in different parts of the world for many decades. As a consequence, over the past twenty or so years, the literature on ethnic conflict has grown exponentially, and with it disagreement among its authors about what the causes and consequences of such conflicts are and how one should best respond to them. It would be foolish to attempt to resolve these debates or provide the ultimate and all-encompassing answer to even one of the questions raised above. While this book does, of course, investigate a number of ethnic conflicts over time and across continents, our main aim is not to develop a completely new theory that can explain some, carefully chosen, ethnic conflicts. Rather, our long engagement with the subject, both academically and through our practical involvement in conflict settlement attempts, has taught us that what is needed is an analytical model that can be applied to specific conflict situations and that is not biased for or against any of the existing theories.

After developing this analytical model in the first chapter, the next two chapters address existing theories of ethnic conflict. We recognize that over the past two decades a vast range of explanations for the existence of ethnic conflict – both individual instances and more epiphenomenal studies – have been put forward by academics. While it is not possible to examine each individual theory in detail, we will provide some order to this vast literature by examining a number of particularly significant contributions and authors that can be located in two broad schools of thought. On the one hand, there are those scholars who adopt a rational choice approach to the study of the causes of ethnic conflict and explain it in terms of a security dilemma or economic opportunities. The other broad school of thought includes academics who seek causal links by utilizing psychological theories, such as realistic group theory, social identity theory and psycho-cultural/psychoanalytic theories. Chapter 3 will, thus, undertake a detailed overview of these theories and their advantages and limitations, assessing their explanatory value not only for the causes of ethnic conflict but also for their duration and intensity.

Based on the theoretical survey provided in chapter 3, chapter 4 demonstrates how different theories of ethnic conflict can be integrated into a multi-level analysis of the phenomenon, showing that different theories have different utility at different levels of analysis. That is, we put some flesh on the bare bones of the analytical model we propose in chapter 2 and reiterate our point that it is empirically unlikely that there can be a single general theory of ethnic conflict as such. Rather, we argue, and provide evidence, that a proper analytical framework that draws on several theories is the most useful approach, as it allows thorough and comprehensive case-by-case analysis that relies on a broad understanding of the nature and dynamics of ethnic conflict in general and leaves room for the specific context of individual cases. This allows us to examine the ways and means through which such conflicts are generated and sustained, considering a variety of endogenous and exogenous factors.

Understanding the causes and consequences of ethnic conflict, while intellectually rewarding in itself, is also important from a policy perspective. Without such an understanding it is difficult to imagine how it would be possible to negotiate, implement and operate sustainable solutions within the context of any conflict. Hence, the second half of the book is devoted to the politics of ethnic conflict regulation[1] and begins with a conceptual exploration of this notion, focusing in particular on the role of the international community. Following from that, chapter 5 argues that different objectives require different policies for their successful implementation, as well as a prior proper analysis of opportunities and limitations faced by different actors involved in such conflicts. Having thus offered some conceptual background on the politics of international intervention as a common approach to conflict regulation, chapter 6 offers an empirical test of the utility of our overall approach to the study of ethnic conflict in the context of conflict regulation, pointing to recent failures and successes and offering explanations both as to why international actors choose particular courses of action and why these sometimes succeed but at other times fail.

While chapters 5 and 6 thus deal primarily with procedural aspects of conflict regulation, the next two chapters address its more substantive elements. In chapter 7 we consider the theory and practice of conflict regulation by engaging with three main theories of conflict settlement – power sharing, centripetalism and power dividing.

Chapter 8 examines and illustrates 'alternatives' to the approaches discussed in the preceding chapter: majoritarian control, forced assimilation, ethnic cleansing, secession and partition, and ultimately genocide. While we do not consider any of these approaches as real alternatives to the kind of accommodation examined in chapter 7, it is important not to deny that such practices have occurred throughout more distant and more recent history. Showing the often horrendous consequences of the policies associated with them, this chapter also strengthens and substantiates the arguments put forward in the preceding chapter about the value and possibility of accommodation. In chapter 9, which concludes our volume, we revisit the questions we originally posed and the beginning of chapter 1 and draw some broader empirical and analytical conclusions concerning the study of ethnic conflict.

2

The Study of Ethnic Conflict

1 Introduction

Our approach to the study of ethnic conflict is informed by one fundamental premise: ethnic conflicts, while complex political phenomena, can be understood. Their complexity must not be confused with a difficulty, let alone an impossibility, to understand them. Rather, what it means is that there are lots of different things to understand. This understanding can be facilitated by the help of an analytical model that allows us to identify, categorize and group together a wide range of different factors that are relevant in explaining the origin, duration and intensity of ethnic conflicts. In order to construct such a model, we proceed by several steps. First, we develop the 'shell' of our analytical model, drawing on an existing body of international relations literature where the so-called levels-of-analysis approach has been developed and used since the late 1950s. Second, we argue that there are three sets of theories that can provide useful insights into how it is possible to establish causal relations between the independent variables categorized within the levels-of-analysis model and specific outcomes, namely the occurrence (or lack thereof), intensity and duration of ethnic conflict and the success or failure of policies aimed at its prevention, management and settlement. The three bodies of literature we discuss are theories of international relations, of ethnicity and of inter-ethnic relations.

2 Ethnic conflict: a definition

Before embarking on this intellectual journey, it is necessary to define as precisely as possible the subject of this inquiry. Ethnic conflict is a term loaded with often legitimate negative associations and entirely unnecessary confusions. The most important confusion is that ethnic conflicts are about ethnicity – 'ethnicity is not the ultimate, irreducible source of violent conflict in such cases'.[1] Alternatively, ethnicity may provide the mobilizational basis for collective action, with violence being used as a tactic. It often forms an important part of the explanation, but we do not know of any conflict that can be explained solely by reference to ethnicity, which is itself a hotly contested term, as we shall see later on.

Generally speaking, the term 'conflict' describes a situation in which two or more actors pursue incompatible, yet from their individual perspectives entirely just, goals. An ethnic conflict is one particular form of this: that in which the goals of at least one party are defined in (exclusively) ethnic terms, and in which the primary fault line of confrontation is one of ethnic distinctions. Whatever the concrete issues may be over which conflict erupts, at least one of the parties will explain its dissatisfaction in ethnic terms. That is, at least one party to the conflict will claim that its distinct ethnic identity is the reason why its members cannot realize their interests, why they do not have the same rights, or why their claims are not satisfied. Thus, ethnic conflicts are a form of group conflict in which at least one of the parties involved interprets the conflict, its causes and potential remedies along an actually existing or perceived discriminating ethnic divide. In other words, the term ethnic conflict itself is a misnomer – it is not the conflict that is 'ethnic' but at least one of its participants. To put it differently, an ethnic conflict involves at least one party that is organized around the ethnic identity of its members.

Empirically, it seems easy to determine when conflicts are ethnically driven: one knows them when one sees them. Few would dispute that Northern Ireland, Kosovo, Cyprus, Rwanda, the Democratic Republic of Congo (DRC), Kashmir and Sri Lanka, to name but a few, are the locus of ethnic conflicts. That is so because, in each of these cases, organized ethnic groups confront each other and/or the institutions of the states in which they live. All of these conflicts have been violent, yet violence in each of them was of different degrees of intensity. Leaving aside, for the moment, considerations of relativity (Cyprus is, after all, smaller and has fewer inhabitants than the DRC), some 3,500 people were killed in Northern Ireland in thirty years of violence, there were roughly the same number of fatalities during three months of conflict in Kosovo after the commencement of NATO's air campaign, and during the genocide in Rwanda a single day could have easily seen that many people killed in just one town.

In contrast to these examples, relationships between Estonians and Russians in Estonia and the complex dynamics of interaction between the different linguistic groups in Canada, Belgium and France are also based predominantly on distinct ethnic identities and (incompatible) interest structures, yet their manifestations are less violent. These and similar situations are more correctly described in terms of tension or dispute. Finally, there are cases in which various ethnic groups have different, and more or less frequently conflicting, interest structures, but hardly ever is the term 'tensions', let alone 'conflict', used to describe them. An example is Switzerland, where fairly stable and legitimate political institutions provide a framework in which different interests can be accommodated. Thus, the way in which we use the term 'ethnic conflict' is related to the fact that organized ethnic groups have systematically used violence for strategic purposes.[2]

3 The levels-of-analysis approach

In 1961, J. David Singer published an article in *World Politics* entitled 'The level-of-analysis problem in International Relations', in which he made a strong case for distinguishing between systemic (global) and subsystem (nation-state) levels for the analysis of various processes in the international system (Singer 1961). In addition, he made some broader general remarks about the use and usefulness of analytical models, requiring them to 'offer a highly accurate *description* of the phenomena under consideration', 'to *explain* relationships among the phenomena under investigation', and to hold the 'promise of reliable *prediction*' (ibid.: 78f.). Maintaining this standard is absolutely essential in the development of analytical models, both to gain a better (scholarly) understanding of specific phenomena and to be able to make dependable and effective policy recommendations.

While Singer offers good general guidance on the levels-of-analysis approach, his counsel is geared primarily towards deciding which one of his two identified levels should be chosen, rather than giving scholars and analysts a choice of combining the two in their analysis. Two years earlier, Kenneth N. Waltz had offered a consideration of three images (i.e., levels of analysis) in accounting for the occurrence of war, and had suggested that what led to war was neither human nature nor the aggressive behaviour of states alone, but rather the nature of the international system and the expectation of violence within it (Waltz 1959). As Jack Levy has pointed out, the levels-of-analysis approach, in the tradition of Singer and Waltz, was subsequently used in IR scholarship mostly to classify 'independent variables that explain state foreign policy behaviour and international outcomes' (Levy 2001: 4). Levy also emphasizes that '[i]t is logically possible and in fact usually desirable for explanations to combine causal variables from different levels of analysis, because whether war or peace occurs is usually determined by multiple variables operating at more than one level of analysis' (ibid.). Despite the traditional focus on states and their relations with one another, there is nothing inherently prohibitive in the levels-of-analysis approach to extend its application to non-state actors and structures and to a range of 'issues' that fall somewhere outside the actor and structure dichotomy yet remain important independent variables when accounting for the causes and consequences of ethnic conflicts and for the success or failure of specific policies adopted to prevent, manage or settle them.

Implicitly or explicitly, earlier models for the analysis of ethnic conflict have drawn on a levels-of-analysis approach (e.g., Brubaker 1996; Wolff 2001). Most notably among them, Michael Brown, synthesizing the state of the discipline some ten years ago, suggested a two-stage model accounting for so-called underlying and proximate causes of ethnic conflicts. This was in itself a significant advance, as it brought into focus a shortcoming of much of the literature up to that point which had done 'a commendable job of surveying the underlying factors or permissive conditions that make some situations particularly prone to violence, but [had remained] weak when it [came] to identifying the catalytic factors – the triggers or proximate causes – of internal conflicts' (Brown 1996: 13). Among the underlying causes, he identified structural, political, economic and social, and cultural and perceptual factors, individually or in various combinations, as necessary but not sufficient conditions for the outbreak of ethnic conflicts. He then used a variation of the levels-of-analysis approach to account for the impact of proximate causes. Presenting a 2-by-2 matrix, Brown (ibid.: 13–17) distinguishes between internal and external elite and mass-level factors that he argues are responsible for triggering ethnic conflicts.

This two-level approach is consistent with the traditional neo-realist distinction between the system level and the unit level, but it deprives us of a more nuanced analysis. The terminology used by Brown to describe external-level factors ('bad neighbours', 'bad neighbourhoods') emphasizes the regional level, which is undoubtedly of great importance, but he does so at the expense of the global level.[3] While he makes some reference to broader international developments, such as 'sharp reductions in international financial assistance' and 'sharp declines in commodity prices', more recent literature has identified a range of other factors well beyond a (potential) conflict's immediate neighbourhood. These include diaspora communities (e.g., Adamson 2005; Sheffer 2003), international human rights norms and their use in the justification of outside intervention into ethnic conflicts R2P (Holzgrefe and Keohane 2003), the moral hazard that intervention precedents create (Crawford and Kuperman 2006; Kuperman 2008), and links between ethnic conflict and organised crime (Williams 2001). Since September 2001 there has also been an emerging body of evidence that local ethnic conflicts, especially those involving Muslim minorities, have been instrumentalized by al-Qaeda and its local offshoots in their pursuit of global jihad (Abuza 2003; Frost et al. 2003; P. J. Smith 2005).

Equally, at the internal level, Brown subsumes national-level and local-level factors into one single category, which is potentially problematic. For example, it is entirely plausible to attribute a significant share of the blame for the violent escalation of the conflicts in Northern Ireland in the late 1960s and in Kosovo in the second half of the 1990s to deplorable political leaders (i.e., to internal elite-triggered factors in Brown's terminology). Yet, this glosses over differences that are both significant and policy-relevant, apart from the fact that the United Kingdom was a democracy in the late 1960s, while the former Yugoslavia in the 1990s was at best in a state of arrested transition between communist regime and liberal democratic market economy. The situation in Northern Ireland was very much a local affair between two communities with very different and incompatible conceptions of national belonging, exacerbated by economic decline and, at the time, a central government in London that showed negligible concern. Kosovo, on the other hand, was a conflict primarily between a local secessionist movement and the increasingly repressive institutions of the central government in Belgrade. Thus, while Northern Ireland in the late 1960s had a realistic chance of effective conflict management and settlement by way of a central government acting as an arbiter,[4] this was an opportunity that did not exist in the Kosovo case.

Therefore we propose an analytical model that disaggregates the traditional two levels of analysis into four. At each of these levels, analysis should concern itself with the behaviour and impact of both actors and structures on the onset, duration and termination of ethnic conflicts. The four levels are:

1. The local (or substate) level: existing scholarship[5] suggests that, among state actors and structures, local elites/leaders, authorities and representatives of the central government, established institutional arrangements and socio-economic structures play a decisive role, while among non-state actors and structures it is the locally resident communities/ethnic groups/religious groups and their elites/leaders and locally operating NGOs, rebel forces, private-sector interest groups and criminals whose actions and effects are likely to have an impact. For example, for rebel forces with a clear territorial base in part of the state affected by conflict (e.g., South Sudan, Darfur, the Lord's Resistance Army in northern Uganda, Albanians in Kosovo, South Ossetians, Abkhaz), specific local dynamics would need to be considered alongside those at the national level of analysis, regardless of whether the overall aim of the movement is secession, control of local resources or state capture. The same holds true for conflicts that are relatively locally contained or where the stakes are of a more localized nature (e.g., Northern Ireland, eastern DRC, Niger delta).

2. The state (or national) level: this level of analysis contains essentially the same kinds of actors and structures as exist at the local level, and it is difficult to imagine situations in which there would be no relevant factors at the state level of analysis. The conflict in Kosovo in the late 1990s, for example, had a very clear local dimension, but at the same time could not be fully explained without reference to political, social, economic and cultural dynamics at the state level in Serbia – the balance of power and influence of different political parties, the strength of national sentiment among Serbs in Serbia, the social and economic impact of war over Kosovo and of the potential loss of the territory, etc.

3. The regional level: scholarship on regional security and regional conflict would suggest that relevant neighbouring states and their institutions, regional powers and regional international organizations (IOs), as well as their respective elites/leaders, and established structures of political and economic cooperation are the key variables to consider among state structures and institutions, while cross-border/transnational networks (ethnic, religious, civil society, business, organized crime, rebel groups, etc.) and their elites/leaders are the relevant non-state equivalents.

4. The global level: this level benefits from a large body of existing scholarship, suggesting that powerful states and IOs of global reach and their elites/leaders are the relevant state actors and structures, while international non-governmental organizations (INGOs), diaspora groups, international organized crime networks, and transnational corporations (TNCs), as well as their respective elites/leaders, are those worthy of consideration among non-state actors and structures.

In addition to structures and actors, we consider it worthwhile to examine the impact on ethnic conflicts of a range of issues that cannot easily be classified as either actor- or structure-related. These include environmental degradation, resource scarcity, energy security, food security, communicable diseases, etc., all of which by their very nature cannot easily be 'assigned' to one particular level of analysis, but rather straddle the boundaries between several levels.

To summarize thus far, the levels-of-analysis approach that we are proposing uses a framework of distinct levels to categorize and classify a range of independent (i.e., potentially causal) and intervening variables to account for the causes of ethnic conflicts and the success or failure of specific policies adopted to prevent, manage or settle them (see table 2.1). The identification of these factors, however, is only the first step towards a comprehensive understanding of ethnic conflict. As a second step it is now necessary to draw on various existing theories of ethnic conflict and conflict settlement to establish causal relationships between these factors (the independent variables) and specific outcomes (dependent variables, i.e., ethnic conflict and its prevention, management and settlement). We consider three such bodies of literature: theories of international relations, theories of ethnicity and theories of inter-ethnic relations.

4 Theoretical foundations for the study of ethnic conflict and conflict settlement

4.1 International Relations theories

Drawing on International Relations theory makes sense for several reasons. IR theory is concerned primarily with issues of war and peace. While one has to be cautious and avoid a straightforward translation of findings from the realm of inter-state relations to those of inter-ethnic/inter-group relations, it is equally important to bear in mind that some of the units of analysis are of course the same, not least if one subscribes, as we do, to the idea that it is after all individuals – leaders as well as followers – who have choices to make about war and peace or conflict and coexistence. Even though theories of international relations are concerned with the role and behaviour of states in the international arena, they nevertheless start by making fundamental

Table 2.1 The levels-of-analysis approach

	State structures and actors	Non-state structures and actors	'Issues'
Local	Local elites/leaders, authorities and representatives of the central government, established institutional arrangements and socio-economic structures	Locally resident communities/ethnic groups/religious groups and their elites/leaders and locally operating NGOs, rebel forces, private-sector interest groups and criminals	Environmental degradation, resource scarcity, energy security, food security, communicable diseases, etc.
State	National elites/leaders, central government, established institutional arrangements and socio-economic structures	Communities/ethnic groups/religious groups and their elites/leaders and statewide-operating NGOs, rebel forces, private-sector interest groups and criminals	
Regional	Neighbouring states and their institutions, regional powers, and regional IOs, as well as their respective elites/leaders; established structures of political and economic cooperation	Cross-border/ transnational networks (ethnic, religious, civil society, business, organized crime, rebel groups, etc.) and their elites/leaders	
Global	Powerful states and IOs of global reach and their elites/leaders	INGOs, diaspora groups, international organized crime networks, and TNCs, as well as their respective elites/leaders	

assumptions about human nature. Realism and liberalism both consider human beings as self-interested and rational actors concerned with their own survival. In an anarchical world – the Hobbesian state of nature – this translates readily into a complete reliance on self-help: acquire as much power as you possibly can in order to defeat any threat to your survival. Where proponents of the two traditions and their various subschools differ is the extent to which this is not only the natural state of affairs, but one that exists in perpetuity. Realists are generally pessimistic about human nature, while liberalists are optimistic (some would say idealistic) about human beings being capable of learning from experience.[6]

A second reason for drawing on IR theory for a better understanding of ethnic conflict is empirically informed. While it is true that wars between states have dramatically decreased in frequency since 1945, the often drawn conclusion that wars within states are now one of the predominant challenges to international security is at best an oversimplification of a much more complex matter. So-called internal wars, of which ethnic conflicts are but one form, may not be inter-state wars, but they are often not internal wars either in the sense that they are frequently not confined within the borders of just one state. The conflict in Chechnya has involved Georgia, used as a supply base and route for Chechen rebels, and has destabilized neighbouring regions in Russia. In turn, Georgia's two ethnic separatist conflicts – South Ossetia and Abkhazia – are marked by significant Russian involvement and support for the separatists, including their recognition as independent states by Moscow in August 2008. The conflict in the eastern part of the Democratic Republic of Congo has, over time, involved regular and irregular forces from almost all of the country's neighbours, earning it the title of Africa's first world war. The still lingering conflicts in the Balkans are inseparably linked. The conflict in and over the Nagorno-Karabakh area has involved Azerbaijan and Armenia, and will not be resolved unless the two states find a mutually acceptable solution to their territorial dispute that also has the backing of three major regional powers – Russia, Turkey and Iran. Similarly, the disputed territory of Kashmir has been partitioned between China, India and Pakistan, and the latter two have gone to war with each other four times since 1947. India, in the meantime, has also been dragged, at times willingly, into the conflict in Sri Lanka, partly because of its own large Tamil population, who are ethnic cousins of the Sri Lankan Tamils, which initially led the Indian government to lend de facto support to Tamil separatists. Then, having reversed its position, if only out of fear that Tamil secessionism in Sri Lanka could create a precedent that would threaten the territorial integrity of the Indian state itself, India devised an ill-conceived peacekeeping mission to Sri Lanka in an attempt to resolve this long-lasting conflict. As a final example, the conflict in the Solomon Islands escalated, in part, because of an ongoing conflict in neighbouring Bougainville, itself part of Papua New Guinea.

Relations between states, thus, continue to matter in the understanding of ethnic conflict. Yet there are important differences, too: rather than being fought exclusively between regular armies of recognized states, ethnic conflicts also involve non-state armed groups, defined on the basis of ethnic identities, that straddle state boundaries and give many of today's ethnic conflicts a distinct regional dimension.[7]

This leads us to a third reason why IR theories are relevant for the study of ethnic conflict: external intervention by states and their regional and international organizations remains the predominant approach to conflict prevention, management and settlement (Weller and Wolff 2008). Its forms vary, and success stories are far and few between. UN peacekeepers were sent to Bosnia and Herzegovina with no peace to keep and a weak mandate. In addition, there were too few of them and they were not well equipped.

With close to 40,000 military personnel and at a cost of over $4.5 billion, the UN Protection Force in the former Yugoslavia managed to break the siege of Sarajevo in 1995 only with the help of NATO. The UN safe area of Srebrenica was overrun by Bosnian Serb forces in 1995, leading to the massacre of several thousand Bosnian Muslim men and youths despite the presence of a Dutch troop contingent in the town. In the end, only massive air strikes by NATO in support of Bosnian and Croat ground forces brought Serbs to the negotiation table in Dayton, Ohio. Spending $1.6 billion and involving some 22,000 military personnel, the UN Mission to Somalia from March 1993 to March 1995 did not even see a negotiated end to the clan warfare in the country but left with most of its mission unaccomplished. In another example, $450 million was the price for failing to prevent the genocide in Rwanda.

To the credit of international organizations, there have also been some successes of late, which means that something can be done, at least about some ethnic conflicts. The Australian-led UN intervention in East Timor in 1999, following the fighting that broke out between pro- and anti-Indonesian forces after a majority of East Timorese voted for independence in a referendum, must be judged as one of the few relatively unambiguous success stories.[8] Similarly, a UN-authorized and again Australian-led Regional Assistance Mission to the Solomon Islands in 2003 has been able to bring about a large measure of stability to this country. The United Nations office in Burundi, established after a 1993 coup which killed the first democratically elected Hutu president in a country traditionally controlled by its Tutsi minority, succeeded in preventing a civil war of similarly genocidal proportions to the one in neighbouring Rwanda. The UN Mission in Cyprus, created in 1964, may have failed to prevent the partition of the island in 1974, but has at least been able to maintain peace there for over three decades since, even if it has so far been unable to achieve a resolution to the conflict. Following the NATO intervention in the Kosovo conflict in 1999, the UN, the Organization for Security and Cooperation in Europe (OSCE), the European Union (EU) and NATO have undertaken the tremendous task of rebuilding the conflict-torn territory – not as unambiguous a success as the mission in East Timor, but so far clearly less of a failure than earlier efforts in Bosnia and Herzegovina. Finally, decisive EU and NATO intervention in Macedonia prevented a significant escalation of the conflict between ethnic Albanians and Macedonians in this other successor state of the former Yugoslavia. The aftermath of the violence in 2001 and the difficult implementation of the EU and NATO-brokered Ohrid Agreement of August in that year have not been free from problems, but Macedonia has embarked on a path to peace and stability, rather than teetering on the brink of civil war. In all these cases, successes and failures alike, core issues of concern to the discipline of International Relations were at stake: the principles of sovereignty, non-intervention and territorial integrity, as well as international standards of human and minority rights and their enforceability.

A fourth reason, closely related to the above, is not without a certain irony.

IR theory generally acknowledges that a main difference between the systemic level of analysis and the state or unit level is that the anarchic state of nature is brought under control at the unit level through the institution of government, making it possible for people to rely on government rather than themselves for protection from any threats to their physical security. If such a government is missing or fails to perform this function, people will naturally have to revert to their own devices. This realist perspective is concerned primarily with security, whereas (neo-)liberalism puts greater emphasis on the importance of economic factors and the need to regulate economic interaction within and beyond state borders. Especially the advocates of complex interdependence theory, such as Keohane and Nye (1977), argue that complex transnational connections between states and societies, particularly in the economic sphere, have increased and created new dependencies complementing, but not replacing, those based on military power. In order to regulate such systems of economic and social interdependence, avoiding the free-rider and defector problems common in anarchical systems, participating states establish so-called regimes to regulate and facilitate cooperation.[9] Similarly, collective security approaches to international relations rely on the observation that states, as a result of growing interdependence, have a wider range of options available about how to respond to threats – options that extend beyond military means to diplomatic and economic measures. The more recent social constructivist approach to international relations gains significance in this context, too. Norms and values, emerging from and consolidating shared knowledge among actors over time, motivate human behaviour in a similar way to purely material interests and can ensure that 'actors follow a logic of appropriateness rather than a logic of consequentiality' (Boekle et al. 2001: 105). Translated into the context of inter-ethnic relations, this means that pure rational choice accounts of ethnic conflict will not be able to present a complete picture of the phenomenon, and especially why individuals and groups oftentimes pursue seemingly irrational courses of action – be it in accommodating far weaker opponents or confronting far superior enemies. In other words, the concern of IR theories with institutions (or lack thereof) at the global level leads many IR-informed approaches to conflict settlement to emphasize the paramount importance of institution-building and good governance (e.g., Paris 2004; Walter 1999, 2002; Weller and Wolff 2005). While there is disagreement on the nature of institutions to be designed to achieve successful conflict settlement,[10] there is virtually no dissent from the general assumption that functioning institutions are essential for successful conflict settlement and that they are best established with outside assistance.

Our final point about the relevance of IR theory for the understanding of ethnic conflict relates back to the levels-of-analysis approach outlined earlier in this chapter. The local, state, regional and global levels of analysis postulated as relevant in this approach are at the same time governance levels, that is, levels within a vertical system of layered authority at which decisions are being made on a range of different issues, varying from case to case. Power is a coveted resource both vertically (i.e., between these levels) and horizontally (i.e., at these levels) in such a system of multi-level governance. This is important for the understanding of ethnic conflict in two ways. First, ethnic conflict occurring at one particular level in this system cannot be seen in isolation from its consequences at other levels; ethnic conflicts are partly shaped by the responses that actors at all levels adopt. These actors, in turn, are constrained by structural factors that determine their behaviour. Second, the levels-of-analysis approach emphasizes again the crucial role that institutions play in ethnic conflicts by guiding the conduct of relevant actors at each level of analysis. Well-functioning institutions can generally provide mechanisms within which the interests of different actors can be accommodated. If these institutions break down at the local and/or state level and peaceful accommodation is no longer guaranteed, violent conflict is more likely to ensue. At the same time, poorly functioning institutions at a regional and/or global level may create uncertainties as to the responses that actors at these levels will adopt in a specific case of ethnic conflict. Inability or unwillingness to mandate and resource an effective intervention may encourage stronger parties in ethnic conflicts to pursue their objectives by violent means and with fewer inhibitions (the cases of Rwanda and Chechnya serve as a powerful reminder), while the promise and precedent of intervention on behalf of weaker parties may well create incentives for them to provoke stronger opponents, such as in Kosovo and Darfur (cf. Crawford and Kuperman 2006; Kuperman 2008).

In conclusion so far, then, theories of international relations offer useful tools and insights in the study of ethnic conflict and conflict settlement. Yet, for a comprehensive analytical model to emerge, we need to integrate them with theories of ethnicity and inter-ethnic relations. After all, as we have argued above, ethnic conflicts are distinct forms of conflict in which organized *ethnic groups* have recourse to the systematic use of violence for strategic purposes. Understanding the implications of this requires a more detailed engagement with the nature and characteristics of ethnic groups.

4.2 Theories of ethnicity

Theories of ethnicity provide an obvious starting point when thinking about the nature of ethnic groups. There is general agreement among most scholars that there are two ideal types of theories of ethnicity – primordialism and constructivism.[11] It is also generally agreed that constructivism has developed into the more prominent discourse on ethnicity and that there is no longer much debate questioning which of the two schools offers the more credible approach to the study of ethnicity. Yet, in the same way as there are virtually no 'pure' primordialists left, there are also only very few 'pure' constructivists around.[12] The reason for this degree of convergence – albeit a convergence with strong constructivist tendencies – is easy to see if one considers the core

assumptions of the ideal-typical versions of primordialism and constructivism. The former holds that 'ethnicity is so deeply rooted in historical experience that it should properly be treated as a given in human relations', while
constructivists argue that 'ethnicity is not a historical given at all, but in
fact a highly adaptive and malleable phenomenon' and that it is 'primarily
a practical resource that individuals and groups deploy opportunistically to
promote their more fundamental security and economic interests and that
they may even discard when alternative affiliations promise a better return'
(Esman 1994b: 10–11). In other words, both individual and collective identities are seen as fluid; individuals are said to be able to choose them more or
less at will and to instrumentalize them opportunistically for themselves, as
well as manipulate the identities of others because they either feel a heightened need of cultural identification or seek to pursue specific political mobilization agendas.[13]

There are, of course, schools of thought that seek to overcome the
primordialist/constructivist dichotomy, with ethnosymbolism the most
prominent among them. Initially developed by Crawford Young (1976), it
then became associated primarily with Anthony D. Smith (1991) and Walker
Connor (1994), as well as more recently, in the form of symbolic politics
theory, with Stuart Kaufman (2001).[14] The essence of the ethnosymbolist synthesis is well captured in Smith's (1991: 20) description of an ethnic group
as 'a type of cultural collectivity, one that emphasizes the role of myths of
descent and historical memories, and that is recognized by one or more
cultural differences like religion, customs, language, or institutions.' As self-
defined communities, ethnic groups are distinguishable by a collective proper
name, a myth of common ancestry, shared historical memories, one or more
differentiating elements of common culture, the association with a specific
homeland, and a sense of solidarity for significant sectors of the population
(ibid.: 21). This link between tangible and intangible aspects is key to understanding the political implications of ethnic identity and of the formation
of conflict groups based on ethnicity. Connor has noted that tangible characteristics are important only inasmuch as they 'contribute to this notion or
sense of a group's self-identity and uniqueness' (Connor 1994: 104). In turn, a
threat to, or opportunity for, these tangibles, real or perceived, is considered
as a threat to, or opportunity for, self-identity and uniqueness. Confronting
this threat or taking this opportunity leads to the ethnic group becoming a
political actor by virtue of its shared ethnic identity. As such, ethnic identity
'can be located on a spectrum between primordial historic continuities and
instrumental opportunistic adaptations' (Esman 1994b: 15).

Such a definition that draws on both tangible and intangible aspects of
ethnic identity and emphasizes both their objective and subjective elements
is particularly useful for the study of ethnic conflict. This synthetic definition, therefore, allows meaningful comparative research. It sees ethnicity as a
quasi-universal phenomenon, despite certain contextual differences, in terms

of which criteria may be more relevant in specific cases precisely because it leaves room for subjective interpretation on the part of those who ascribe a certain ethnic identity to themselves (and often also to others with whom they feel to be in competition). Including both the tangible (e.g., customs, traditions, language or religion) and intangible (e.g., sense of solidarity among group members, feeling of uniqueness) aspects of ethnicity, as well as their social and political implications, makes it possible to explain the intense emotions that 'ethnic issues' generate and to account for the often excessive violence and wilful humiliation that can be observed in many of today's ethnic conflicts.

It is important at this stage to pause and not jump to hasty conclusions about the inevitability of conflict between different ethnic groups. It is neither theoretically logical nor empirically correct to assume that the mere existence of two or more different ethnic groups – i.e., two or more groups of people who respectively share an ethnic identity with one another – automatically leads to the onset of ethnic conflict (as defined here) between them. For that to happen, certain patterns of interaction are required, which themselves occur only under specific circumstances. This is the reason why theories of inter-ethnic relations need to be considered on the way towards developing a comprehensive analytical model of the study of ethnic conflict and conflict regulation.[15]

4.3 Theories of inter-ethnic relations

Theories of inter-ethnic relations are inevitably informed by theories of ethnicity – it is only possible to think about the nature and dynamics of inter-ethnic relations based on a sound understanding of the characteristics of one's units of observation. A proper understanding of the sources and processes of identity formation is essential to develop and test hypotheses about their impact on inter-ethnic relations, and thus ultimately about the occurrence, duration and intensity of ethnic conflict and the likelihood of its successful resolution with specific policies. While we will return to these theories in greater depth in the second half of this book, we present here only a brief outline of two prominent sets of theories – rational choice accounts and social-psychological approaches – in order to illustrate how they can be utilized in our analytical model.

Rational choice theories assume that the individual actors in ethnic conflicts choose to be involved on the basis of rational cost–benefit calculations. In one subset of theories, focused on security, the primary explanation for the occurrence of ethnic conflict is that the choice of violence is predicated on the fear of an imminent violent attack by an opponent who threatens the very survival of the group and its members thus coming under attack. In other words, offence is considered to be the best defence of the group's vital interests. If the focus, however, is on individual economic gain, rather than security, the rationale for violence is found in the opportunity to profit from conflict. Social-psychological approaches to ethnic conflict take inequality between groups as their main explanatory variable. Where groups feel entitled to status or goods that they are objectively denied, or where their continued enjoyment of this status or these goods is coming under threat, they will be prepared to use violence to attain what they claim to be rightfully theirs. Both sets of theories, thus, provide distinct but valuable insights into the dynamics of ethnic conflict, into how and why ethnic identity is a useful and usable resource to mobilize groups for conflict and hold them together during conflict. While we do not question that these theories individually account for important dimensions of the occurrence, intensity and duration of specific ethnic conflicts, we challenge their claim to universality. First of all, ethnic conflicts involve individuals – leaders and followers alike – and these individuals make personal choices. While some may be motivated by personal concern for their own and their families' security, others may be motivated by the desire to obtain more social justice for their group, and yet others again may seek to satisfy rather more personal interests of enrichment or the gratification of other needs.

Moreover, it is important, in the context of our analytical model, to bear in mind that motive alone is not enough to explain ethnic conflict. Equally important, including from the perspective of rational choice and social-psychological theories, is the presence of means and opportunity. For example, ethnic Albanians in Kosovo had very long-standing grievances about their situation. Yet only with the changing regional and international situation in the 1990s did they have the means and opportunity to engage Serbia in an armed conflict with a realistic prospect of 'victory'. A combination of factors was at work here. First, in the summer of 1998, the shadow Albanian government ceased its condemnation of the Kosovo Liberation Army (KLA) and increasingly turned a blind eye to its activities. This in turn enabled the KLA to strengthen its support networks, particularly in northern Albania, where the reach of Tirana was weaker than that of ancient kin networks, many of whom engaged in economic activities that were both illegal and beyond the reach of the state. In essence, the KLA was able to re-equip itself and embarked upon a strategy of liberation that was predicated on involving NATO in the war as its de facto ally.

5 Theories of ethnic conflict settlement

Each theory of inter-ethnic relations offers not only different accounts of the causes of conflict but also different prescriptions for how to respond to it. Again, we examine different theories of ethnic conflict resolution in greater detail later on in this book, but here we want to demonstrate primarily how they fit into our analytical model. The aim of *conflict settlement* is to establish an institutional framework in which the conflicting interests of the different principal conflict parties – ethnic groups and/or the state with which they are in dispute – can be accommodated to such an extent that incentives for cooperation and the non-violent pursuit of conflicts of interest through compromise outweigh any benefits that might be expected from violent confrontation. Thus, using the term conflict resolution, as is often the case in the literature, is in fact not always completely accurate: in many cases the conflict itself may continue to exist for a shorter or longer period of time after a peace agreement has been reached – or at least some of its underlying aspects will – but the conflict parties have found non-violent, sometimes even democratic ways in which they can address their differences. To achieve this is obviously difficult, as is proved by so many different ethnic conflicts around the world – from the Middle East to Kashmir and from Sri Lanka to the Darfur region in western Sudan. Other cases, however, for example Northern Ireland, Bosnia and Herzegovina or Bougainville, show that resolving ethnic conflicts is not impossible either, but rather that it depends on the timing of initiatives and the skill, resources and determination with which they are pursued.

To be sure, there are many other ways in which conflicts can be managed and resolved. John McGarry and Brendan O'Leary (1993: 4) suggest a very simple and useful distinction between methods that aim at eliminating differences between conflict parties and methods that try to manage them. Elimination of differences can be achieved through genocide, ethnic cleansing, partition and/or secession and integration and/or assimilation. Differences are managed through control regimes,[16] third-party arbitration, federalism and other forms of territorial organization giving conflict parties greater autonomy over their own affairs, and through various forms of power sharing. Ulrich Schneckener (2004) presents a slightly more refined classification, distinguishing between methods of elimination, of control and of recognition. While operating with a similar set of conflict settlement methods, Schneckener takes an approach that is more clearly driven by normative judgements, that is, by a distinction between acceptable and unacceptable policies aimed at resolving ethnic conflicts. As with McGarry and O'Leary, elimination strategies comprise genocide, ethnic cleansing and forced assimilation, while control regimes include coercive domination, coopted rule and limited self-rule. In contrast to these two categories of unacceptable approaches to conflict management and resolution, Schneckener endorses so-called policies of recognition, such as minority rights, power sharing, territorial solutions and bilateral and multilateral regimes.

Different ways of classifying the wide range of existing approaches to conflict management and resolution approaches to one side, McGarry and O'Leary and Schneckener, between them, cover all known and applied policies. Rather than debating the merits of the one or other classification, we intend to show how certain proposals for conflict settlement are directly related to underlying assumptions about the nature of ethnic groups and the causes of ethnic conflict, and thus how a more complementary approach to theories of inter-ethnic relations can help devise more comprehensive and balanced settlements of ethnic conflicts.

Take, for example, elimination strategies. The perceived need to eliminate ethnic differences rests on two assumptions – that ethnic identities are basically fixed and that peaceful coexistence between different groups is virtually impossible. In other words, a security dilemma will inevitably emerge between different ethnic groups living in the same state. There are, of course, different gradations of this view, but the essential policy recommendation of this discourse is to find ways and means to eliminate the threat allegedly posed by ethnic differences, including ethnic cleansing and genocide, forced assimilation, and secession and partition. The fact that these 'solutions' have a poor track record of success does not mean that they no longer have any attraction. Partition and population exchanges (i.e., ethnic cleansing) continue to enjoy a certain degree of support among some scholars (e.g., Mearsheimer and Pape 1993; Kaufman 1996a, 1996b, 1998), despite evidence to the contrary (Sambanis 2000; Wolff 2004b).[17] Genocidal policies, too, remain in the repertoire of ethnic extremists, as tragically shown in Rwanda and in Bosnia and Herzegovina in the mid-1990s and in Darfur ten years later. Secession is what many so-called self-determination movements aspire to – from Sri Lanka to the post-Soviet periphery of Chechnya, South Ossetia, Abkhazia, the Nagorno-Karabakh area and Transdniestria, from Kosovo to the Basque Country. While states are generally determined to prevent secessions (Weller 2005b), they nevertheless often support it on a selective basis according to their interests. Thus, Kosovo enjoyed a degree of direct or indirect support for its drive towards independence from various Western countries (the US, the UK and Switzerland among them), while Russia, opposed to independence for Chechnya, first argued that wide-ranging autonomy for Kosovo could be considered a 'model' for other cases in its neighbourhood,[18] but subsequently, while rejecting Kosovo's unilateral declaration of independence in February 2008, also argued that a clear precedent had been set, and exploited it practically with the recognition of South Ossetia and Abkhazia some six months later.

Solutions aimed at integration are the only elimination strategy that subscribes to a version of constructivism in terms of the nature of ethnic identity. It therefore seeks not to eliminate differences as such, but rather to mitigate the political consequences of these differences. Prominent scholars (and practitioners) in this tradition include Donald Horowitz ([1985] 2000) and Benjamin Reilly (2001), who emphasize the value of electoral systems designed to achieve moderation among group-based elites and a gradual transformation of identity-based politics. Seeking to encourage pre-election cross-community coalition-building, such a model implicitly advocates a form of majoritarian democracy, even though it is one in which majority–minority relations are no longer defined in ethnic terms.

Another, albeit more extreme, version of constructivism underlies claims that ethnic identities are all but accidental vehicles of convenience to mobilize people where economic opportunity beckons. Findings by Collier and Hoeffler (1998, 2001) and Fearon and Laitin (2000) that civil wars, including ethnic conflicts, are far more prevalent in low-income countries lead these scholars to advocate policies of economic development as fail-safe mechanisms to deal with conflict. In other words, the argument here is that ethnic identities will become politically less salient once economic development takes away the motive and opportunity to mobilize groups for economic gain.

Solutions to ethnic conflicts that are aimed at managing ethnic differences are distinct in their assumptions from those proposing the elimination of differences, in that they are generally more optimistic about the prospects of ethnic groups being able to live together peacefully – provided appropriate institutional mechanisms exist that allow for conflicts of interest and identity to be accommodated. Apart from that, there is wide disagreement about possible solutions, rooted partly in different conceptions of ethnicity and the nature of inter-ethnic relations. Advocates of consociational power sharing in the tradition of Arend Lijphart, most prominently John McGarry and Brendan O'Leary (McGarry and O'Leary 2004; O'Leary 2005b), base their model of conflict settlement on the assumption that 'collective identities . . . based on nationality, ethnicity, language and religion are generally fairly durable once formed' (O'Leary 2005b: 8). They do not claim consociationalism as a universally applicable solution 'in every country or every possible policy sector where identity politics may manifest itself' (ibid.), but as one that can be usefully applied in many cases where insecurities and inequalities need to be addressed. Other scholars embrace consociationalist designs for power sharing as well, albeit to different degrees. Philip Roeder and Donald Rothchild (2005) see power sharing as a short-term transitional mechanism that can address concerns about security and equality, especially of weaker groups, and entice them to participate in, rather than fight against, state institutions. In their view, power sharing can provide the basis for parties to end violence, but is unlikely to offer stable institutions of governance in the long term. Weller and Wolff (2006) offer another view on consociational power sharing that considers the transformative capacity of such settlements – they are less pessimistic than Roeder and Rothchild about the potential for long-term stability generated by consociational democracy, but more optimistic than McGarry and O'Leary about the possibility that, over time, ethnic identities will become politically less salient and allow for more traditional forms of democratic governance to emerge.[19]

The second type of solutions for managing difference consists of proposals for autonomy and/or federalism (e.g., Coakley 2003; Lapidoth 1997; McGarry and O'Leary 1993; O'Leary 2005b; Weller and Wolff 2005; Wolff 2009). These are also meant to address concerns over security and equality and recognize, similarly to consociational arrangements, the specific identity needs of territorially based ethnic groups, such as the desire to exercise a level of self-governance in what they consider their homeland. Their critics allege that autonomy and federalism are but the first step towards the eventual break-up of existing states, and there is considerable, albeit superficial, evidence that this is indeed the case. Yet at the same time there is also a remarkable trend in the practice of ethnic conflict settlement that sees the granting of territorial autonomy as an integral part of many recent peace settlements facilitated by international assistance (Weller and Wolff 2005).

The feasibility and sustainability of any solution adopted on the basis of any one or more of the theories examined briefly above depends on a variety of factors. Without discussing 'success conditions' in any great detail in the context of this chapter, it is important to point out that these factors exist at different levels of analysis. Local commitment to sustainable peace is obviously the most important, but very often not sufficient: international security guarantees may be as necessary as economic aid to create conditions in which people feel safe and can begin to appreciate that 'peace pays', and often does so better than war. Regionalized conflicts, such as in the Western Balkans, the Caucasus or the African Great Lakes region, are unlikely to enjoy sustainable solutions without a clear commitment of regional actors to any peace process. Thus, analogous to understanding the causes of ethnic conflict as located in the complex interplay of different factors at local, state, regional and global levels of analysis, we must contextualize the success or failure of conflict settlement in the same way in order to explain why some policies work and others fail, and, crucially, to be able to make credible recommendations about how to respond to very specific conflicts.

6 Conclusion

We have introduced in this chapter a levels-of-analysis model that will enable us to classify and categorize a range of factors identified in various academic and policy debates as contributing to, or inhibiting, ethnic conflict and its successful prevention, management and settlement. Such factors figure in different ways in existing theories of ethnic conflict and conflict settlement, which in turn are informed by assumptions about the nature of ethnic identity and inter-ethnic relations. These theories are normally presented in relatively exclusive ways. Using a levels-of-analysis model enables us to employ simultaneously different existing theories in a non-exclusive manner in order to develop more comprehensive accounts of ethnic conflicts. This, however, is not a new theory of ethnic conflict itself; rather, it is a specific approach to its study, one that also offers important insights into conflict settlement theory and practice.

From a policy perspective, this levels-of-analysis approach to ethnic conflict also enables us to identify the causes why people *keep fighting* each other at a given point in time, i.e., what issues need to be addressed in order to enable conflict parties to stop the fighting. These are not necessarily the issues over which fighting *starts*, but this is beside the point. More importantly, it allows us to reassess our dependence on the linear logic that is often involved in advocating particular solutions to specific conflicts based on the (over-) reliance on a single theory of ethnic conflict and rather embrace explanations that rely on multiple factors significant at different levels of our analysis.

Part I

The Causes and Consequences of Ethnic Conflict

3

Theories of Ethnic Conflict

The apparent 'explosion' of ethnic conflicts onto the international policy agenda after the end of the Cold War drew a great number of scholars of different disciplinary and methodological persuasions to the study of this phenomenon. While a range of earlier studies existed from as far back as the 1950s, these were concerned predominantly with nationalism per se (e.g., Deutsch 1953; Gellner 1983; Kedourie 1960; Smith 1971, 1981), or focused on particular cases of minorities (such as various German communities resident outside of Germany and Jewish minorities in Europe). It was only from the late 1970s onwards that scholars began to explore the phenomenon of ethnic conflict more systematically, including analytically rigorous examinations of its causes (e.g., Rabushka and Shepsle 1972; Esman 1994b). The most influential among these was Donald Horowitz's *Ethnic Groups in Conflict* ([1985] 2000), which remains an important reference point even today, some two decades after its original publication.

What further distinguishes the analyses of the early 1990s from earlier endeavours is that they sought to illustrate the relevance of rational choice and international relations theories for the study of ethnic conflict, and, at least during the last decade of the twentieth century, established their dominance. At the same time, more social-psychologically informed approaches remained relevant (especially in the shape of social identity theories) and new lines of research were developed (for example, psychoanalytically informed approaches, such as in the work of Marc Howard Ross 2007). Several theorists, most prominently among them Stuart Kaufman (2001) and David Lake and Donald Rothchild (1996), began to work on more integrated theories drawing on findings of rational choice and social-psychological approaches, while still operating predominantly within a framework prioritizing (in)security as the main explanatory variable. Since the late 1990s, a third strand of theories, also grounded in the rational choice approach, has emerged in the shape of an economic theory of ethnic conflict, which is associated predominantly with Paul Collier (e.g., Collier 2001; Collier and Hoeffler 1998).

In this chapter, we will introduce these various theories by exploring their main tenets and illustrating their strengths and weaknesses with some occasional references to a number of cases of ethnic conflict. We begin by looking at approaches that focus on the security dilemma and 'greed' as causal mechanisms and then turn to theories that prioritize inequality. Finally, we will consider theories that systematically incorporate factors outside the domestic context into their explanation of ethnic conflict, including Kuperman's (2005, 2008) theory of moral hazard, Brubaker's (1996) triadic nexus, and David Smith's (2002) further development of this theory towards a 'quadratic' nexus. Thus, our discussion is not informed primarily by epistemological or ontological distinctions, even though these are reflected inasmuch as most of the theories examined are either rationalist or constructivist in nature and use methodologies related predominantly to either positivist or empiricist ontologies. Rather, we focus on the different conceptual tools scholars employ in their efforts to explain ethnic conflicts.

1 Insecurity

Theories focused on insecurity derive their insights from a concept common in realist IR theory, the so-called security dilemma (e.g., Jervis 1976, 1978; Waltz 1979; Mearsheimer 2001). The IR theory version of the security dilemma, as formulated by Kenneth Waltz in 1979, is that the ordering principle of the international system is anarchical rather than hierarchical, requiring states in their quest for survival to seek security through the accumulation of (military) power (Waltz 1979). More than twenty years later, realist reasoning had essentially not changed. John Mearsheimer explains that there are three features in the international system that force great powers to compete with each other for supremacy: the absence of a central authority which can protect states from one another, and the facts that states invariably have some offensive military capability and that they can never be certain of other states' intentions (Mearsheimer 2001). This means not only that states will constantly compete with each other for (access to) greater resources, and strive to develop ever more powerful armaments systems, but also that at some stage a strategic advantage might be gained from a pre-emptive attack.

  Informed especially by the ethnic conflicts in the context of the dissolution of Yugoslavia and the Soviet Union, Barry Posen published an article in 1993 in which he drew a parallel between the anarchy of the international system and the anarchy that emerges in states as a consequence of regime change (Posen 1993). He argued that two conditions that are often present in transition states heighten perceptions of the security dilemma among ethnic groups. The first of these is what he refers to as 'groupness' of ethnic groups, which provides a readily mobilizable army for either offensive or defensive purposes. As groups, like states in realist IR theory, are said to be unable to be certain of each other's intentions, they will judge each other's actions through the lens of history – i.e., whether the other group's military preparations are more likely to be for defensive or offensive purposes, given past inter-ethnic relations. The second condition Posen identified was political geography: whenever segments of an ethnic group are geographically isolated and/or potentially vulnerable to small bands of fanatics, their sense of insecurity will be heightened, leading them to take measures which they might intend as purely defensive, but which might easily be perceived as offensive from the perspective of another group. Using the example of Croats and Serbs in what is now the Republic of Croatia, Posen demonstrates how the security dilemma takes hold. Both parties identified the other as a threat because of a previous history of inter-group conflict, especially during the Second World War. For both sides, offensive actions were considered as strategically advantageous because there were a number of pockets of Serbian settlements on Croat territory (Krajina and Eastern Slavonia). This combined with a perception of incentives for preventative war because the two sides were not evenly matched. Once small bands of fanatics began to terrorize members of the other group, and especially after ethnic cleansing had begun, both sides preferred war to seeking a peaceful settlement.

Since the publication of Posen's article, security-dilemma explanations of ethnic conflict have remained prominent and have seen considerable refinement. In the opening chapter of a collection of essays on the topic, Barbara Walter (1999: 1) set out to identify the 'conditions under which high levels of fear and uncertainty emerge . . . lead to war, and how outside intervention might or might not help manage these issues', thus posing questions that straddle different levels of analysis, from the local to the global. In answer to the first two of these questions, Walter (ibid.: 4–8) established that there were five so-called fear-producing environments for ethnic groups in which war was more likely to be seen as a rational course of action: government breakdown (e.g., Azerbaijan, Moldova, Georgia, Chechnya, Yugoslavia, Kashmir, DRC), geographic isolation or vulnerability (Abkhazia, South Ossetia, the Nagorno-Karabakh area, Transdniestria, Serbs in Bosnia and Herzegovina and in Croatia, Muslims in Kashmir), changing balances of political/demographic power (i.e., actual or potential regime change, as in Lebanon, Yugoslavia, the former Soviet Union, Rwanda, Burundi, Sri Lanka, Aceh), redistribution of (economic and/or military) resources (Yugoslavia), and forced or voluntary disarmament (Northern Ireland, Rwanda).

To this, one needs to add one particular condition that builds on insights from international relations theories, but also on empirical observation: fear and uncertainty among groups may also emerge if there is a change in external patronage or in the balance of power between rival patrons. This affects internal power balances either directly or through the redistribution of resources. It occurs in the context of imperial collapse (e.g., the Balkan Wars in the second decade of the twentieth century, the dissolution of the Soviet Union) and during major shifts in regional or world order (e.g., the Soviet Union's appearance on, and withdrawal from, the world stage as a sponsor of 'national liberation movements', the rise of China as a strategic player, the emergence of the Organization of the Islamic Conference as a supporter of Muslim minorities, etc.). This observation is also conceptually important: the regional and global levels of analysis are essential to understanding the genesis of ethnic conflict.

Walter, however, is careful not to infer from these conditions an automatic and inevitable onset of ethnic conflict. Rather, she contests that violence is triggered primarily by unscrupulous and predatory leaders who portray the leaderships of other groups as incorrigibly predatory rivals (Walter 1999: 9). This is an observation that is shared widely among authors who otherwise consider the security dilemma as a useful explanatory variable. Laitin (1999) and de Figuero and Weingast (1999) in the same volume share the belief that elites play such a crucial role, which is more generally reflected also in Snyder and Jervis's argument that the intra-state security dilemma is the outcome of a social situation, not simply of a strategic situation. That is, certain expectations about how rival groups are likely to behave determine one's own behaviour (i.e., the expectation of an opponent defecting increases the incentive of trying to defect first – which in turn intensifies expectations of opponent defection). The crucial role of leaders is then linked to how historical memories are used to construct defection as likely, not merely as theoretically possible, thus portraying the other as 'historically proven' aggressor (Snyder and Jervis 1999: 24–6).

Probably the most comprehensive analysis of the role of the security dilemma in the violent escalation of ethnic conflicts is contained in an article by David Lake and Donald Rothchild, published originally in 1996.[1] The three strategic dilemmas arise on the basis of individual group members' fear for their physical safety. These are information failures (groups cannot obtain the information necessary to bridge the bargaining gap between them and have incentives to misrepresent their intentions and capabilities), problems of credible commitment (at least one group cannot sufficiently reassure the other that it will not defect from an agreement in the future when the balance of power might shift) and the security dilemma which results from the former two (one or more parties have incentives to resort to the pre-emptive use of force). Additionally, the dilemmas are exacerbated by ethnic activists and political entrepreneurs, whose activities polarize societies by creating and reinforcing a climate in which memories, myths, emotions become crucial guidelines for groups' decision-making processes focused on fears of physical security and cultural domination (ibid.: 128ff.). On the basis of this more complex picture, Lake and Rothchild (ibid.: 130) correctly assert that (assessment of the) competing policy preferences of ethnic groups alone cannot explain recourse to violence.

The two additional strategic dilemmas that Lake and Rothchild (2001) identify – credible commitment and information failure – have also been discussed by other scholars. Fearon's (1995, 1998) work was path-breaking in terms of introducing credible commitment problems into the study of ethnic conflict. He argues that ethnic war 'arises when two groups find themselves without a third party that can credibly guarantee agreements between them' (Fearon 1998: 109). In his two related studies, Fearon explores the link between commitment problems and ensuing ethnic war by applying game-theoretic tools to analyse the relations between ethnic groups. His model encompasses majority and minority groups – both treated as unitary actors – who are confronted with the task of renegotiating their relationship in a new state in the wake of the collapse of a superior authority (ibid.: 116ff.). The majority group, however, cannot credibly commit to treat the minority group in a fair way (ibid.: 117). Given that, the minority group considers secession as the only viable way to secure its interests (ibid.: 117).

Information failures (or asymmetric information problems) are the second additional strategic dilemma considered by Lake and Rothchild in their integrated approach. More detailed studies of information failures, on their own, are also well worth considering. The model presented by Fearon and Laitin (1996) partly identifies asymmetric information as a major factor in precipitating outbreaks of ethnically based violence. Their starting point is the question why, in the majority of cases, inter-ethnic interaction tends not to erupt into ethnically based violence (Fearon and Laitin 1996: 715). In their opinion, ethnic groups rely on informal networks to enforce cooperation within their group (ibid.: 718f.). These informal networks between different ethnic groups, however, are not as dense as the networks within a group (ibid.: 719). This results in asymmetric information between the groups: the first group does not know if the second group is willing or able to sanction members of its own group when these offended members of the first group (ibid.). Depending on the degree of asymmetric information, there are two possible outcomes to this dilemma. First, it is possible that the attacked group holds the other group in its entirety responsible, and violent conflict erupts (ibid.: 722). Second, potential tensions between different ethnic groups can be resolved rather quickly when the offended group can rely on the effectiveness of in-group policing of the other ethnic group (ibid.). From this perspective, information failures clearly contribute to credible commitment problems and, in turn, to an evolving security dilemma (as examined in Lake and Rothchild 2001) at the local and/or state level.

A second relevant study dealing with problems of asymmetric information is de Figueiredo and Weingast's contribution in Walter and Snyder's (1999) volume on *Civil Wars, Insecurity and Intervention*. They concentrate on the asymmetric information that exists between elites and masses within and across ethnic groups to explain the ethnification of politics and subsequent ethnic war. Their starting point is the question 'why do citizens whose primary interest is in peace choose to support bloody ethnic wars?' (de Figueiredo and Weingast 1999: 261ff.). Their focus lies on assessing the impact of incomplete information on the part of citizens about the preferences of their elites. De Figueiredo and Weingast (ibid.: 263ff.) identify such gaps as constituting a key variable in explaining the onset of ethnic conflict. Elites are thereby able to create a perception of increased risk of victimization among the members of their own ethnic group. Incomplete information of elite preferences (of both their own and rival groups) creates a situation in which the risk of 'being wrong' (i.e., assuming peaceful intentions on the part of the rival group and their elite) is too great to take and violence becomes a rational strategy for dealing with this uncertainty, and hence inter-ethnic violence breaks out (ibid.: 271–81).

Similar to Lake and Rothchild's more nuanced approach, Stuart Kaufman (1996) offers a comprehensive explanation of how the security dilemma, combined with elite and mass interaction within and between ethnic groups, operates in causing the onset of ethnic conflict. To be sure, Kaufman's approach is, unlike Lake and Rothchild's (2001), not a rational choice approach – he uses the concept of symbolic or emotional choice to emphasize the power of symbols and emotions in ethnic relations. Yet the security dilemma remains as a central explanatory variable in his theory. Instead of focusing solely on the structural level, Kaufman, by incorporating elite and mass behaviour in his analysis (Kaufman 1996: 150–7), moves beyond the assumption of ethnic groups as unitary actors and offers a more fine-grained analytical focus. He argues that, ultimately, it is the interaction between the elites, the masses and the structural dynamics of the security dilemma that leads to conflict (ibid.; 157).

Kaufman's emphasis on the role of elites and masses in determining the role of ethnic identities creates a link to the constructivist strand of ethnic conflict theories (Kaufman 2001). This is evident in his view of ethnicity as constructivist rather than instrumentalist and his assumption that human motivation is based on emotion rather than rational cost–benefit calculations. As noted above, this sets him apart from rational choice informed applications of the security dilemma (e.g., Lake and Rothchild 2001; Posen 1993; Walter 1999), even though the overall reasoning among most scholars is fairly similar: fear of the future makes security the top priority for ethnic groups and their members.[2] In Kaufman's view, '[e]ach ethnic group is defined by a "myth-symbol complex" that helps single out those elements of shared culture and an interpretation of common history that ties members of one group together and binds the group together while distinguishing it from others.' Importantly in this definition, ethnicity is historically and culturally rooted: it enables and simultaneously constrains the political instrumentalization of ethnic identities. Consequently, according to Kaufman, the more a group's myth–symbol complex emphasizes hostility towards a particular (actual or potential) adversary group, portraying it and its individual members as enemy and/or inferior, the greater is the probability of ethnic conflict. Thus, the symbols that define a group and to which its members respond reflect both interests and 'values': a struggle for security, status and ultimately group survival is at the same time a struggle against hostile, evil or subhuman forces (Kaufman 2001: ch. 2).

Similar to Donald Horowitz ([1985] 2000), Kaufman assumes that 'the sources of ethnic conflict reside, above all, in the struggle for relative group worth' and identifies three preconditions for ethnic conflict (Kaufman 2001:

ch. 2): first, there must be a group mythology that justifies hostility towards *means* at least one other group; second, a group must fear that its very physical exist- *motive* ence is threatened (in this, it is the individual group members' perception *opportunity* that matters most, though this perception need not be an accurate reflection of reality); third, ethnic groups require opportunities to mobilize. These can manifest themselves in political space, for example political freedom, state failure/regime collapse, support from a third party, and/or demographic concentration of a group within the state and/or a territorial base in a third, often neighbouring country, thus also emphasizing the need to look beyond local and state-level environments to understand escalation towards violence. All these are, according to Kaufman, necessary but not sufficient conditions for the occurrence of violent conflict. For escalation towards violence to occur, which can be either elite- or mass-led, three additional factors are necessary: mass hostility, chauvinist political mobilization, and a security dilemma. *RW* Analysis of the various Yugoslav wars of secession tends to lend credence to these claims.

While still using the security dilemma as a central explanatory variable in his theory, Kaufman's approach at the same time serves as a fundamental critique of rational choice uses of this concept. Even though one might argue that Kaufman's own theory of symbolic choice does not completely resolve all of the problems it identifies with rational choice approaches, it goes to some considerable length in so doing. For Kaufman, four fundamental problems exist with the rational choice use of the security dilemma. The first is the assumption that both sides want to avoid war and are willing to compromise, but cannot because they do not trust each other. Yet, empirically, we would be hard pressed to find even a single example in which violent ethnic conflict has not resulted from the openly propagated intentions of one or both conflict parties of aggression. From the hatred propagated by Hutus in the Rwandan genocide, to the clearly stated intentions of the Serbs, Croats and Bosniaks in the disintegration of Yugoslavia, to the aggressive rhetoric of both parties in the conflict in Sri Lanka, it is difficult to square one of the core assumptions of rational choice theorists with the reality of ethnic conflicts. Second, while the logic of information failures and commitment problems is quite persuasive at one level, hostile perceptions between ethnic groups are normally far too deeply rooted in long and often antagonistic group narratives. It is thus unlikely that more symmetric and full information and credible commitment could assure groups of their individual security.

A third assumption made by rational choice applications of the security dilemma is that a security dilemma is the consequence of (domestic) anarchy rather than its cause. That, too, is empirically questionable, at least in some cases. Take the disintegration of Yugoslavia, for example, especially the case of Bosnia and Herzegovina, where an argument can be made that it was the perception of existential threat by different communities in that Yugoslav Republic, and their response (arming themselves, increasing hostile rhetoric, initial episodes of ethnic cleansing, etc.), that led to the destruction of public order and an anarchic situation without any government being able to guarantee the security of all communities. This does not mean that the security dilemma does not help us understand the processes of ethnic mobilization and violent conflict escalation, but it does mean that we may have to look elsewhere to discover what caused the emergence of a security dilemma in the first place, for something other than anarchy.

Fourth, the focus on the security dilemma as a main explanatory variable of ethnic conflict must not make us lose sight of other dimensions that need also to be explained. One of these dimensions is the emergence of (violent) group norms, another is the factors that hold groups together, and a final one is the replacement of individual self-interest with collective group interests. Kaufman's use of the security dilemma in combination with a focus on elite and mass behaviour, as well as Lake and Rothchild's strategic dilemmas of inter- and intra-group relations, goes some way in addressing these concerns. However, as we shall see below, a focus on social-psychological motivations for ethnic conflict generally has greater currency when it comes to explaining these group-level dynamics.

2 'Greed'

Since the late 1990s, a number of scholars have sought to expand the debate on the causes of ethnic conflicts beyond the traditional grievance (insecurity and inequality) paradigm, maintaining that violence may be more economically motivated than previously assumed. Particularly prominent in this debate have been Paul Collier, an economics professor at the University of Oxford and for a number of years also affiliated to the World Bank (e.g., Collier and Hoeffler 1998, 2001) and the Stanford-based political scientists James Fearon and David Laitin (2000). The main argument in this discourse is that civil war occurs if the (economic) incentive for rebellion is sufficiently great relative to the costs (Collier and Hoeffler 1998; Fearon and Laitin 2000). In the following section we will discuss primarily the work of Collier and Hoeffler (1998, 2001), as theirs is the more explicitly economic explanation of ethnic conflict.

In their first major contribution to the field, Collier and Hoeffler (1998) assume that there are two primary but mutually exclusive objectives of rebellion: to capture the state or to secede from it. They further assume that the incentive for rebellion is the product of the probability of victory and its consequences, with the probability of victory depending upon the capacity of the government to defend itself. In other words, the incentive for rebellion is conditional upon there being a real prospect of victory and is determined by the capacity of a future rebel government to reward its supporters. This can be clearly related to the costs of rebellion, which can be determined in two dimensions: opportunity cost of rebel labour (i.e., whether people lose out on other income by becoming rebels) and the disruption to economic activity caused by warfare (and hence the reduction of gains to be made from a victory). This means that these costs of rebellion increase with the duration of the conflict. Theoretically, this implies that the probability of war is diminishing to both the expected duration of conflict (lowering gains) and the per capita income of the population (increasing opportunity costs of rebel labour). At the same time, according to Collier and Hoeffler, the probability of civil war and its duration are also linked in the sense that both are a function of the gains from rebellion, made up of the probability of rebel victory combined with the potential gains from such a victory (state capture or secession), and the costs of rebellion, made up of the opportunity costs of conflict and the cost of coordination (maintaining cohesion among the rebels and preventing the government from infiltrating them).

Testing these theoretical propositions on a large data set of civil wars, Collier and Hoeffler (1998) have four main findings. First, civil war is overwhelmingly a phenomenon of low-income countries (i.e., where the opportunity costs of rebel labour are low). Second, usually, the presence of natural resources makes things worse (i.e., natural resources are easily lootable commodities which are attractive for rebels to seek to control in order to gain materially), unless there are so many of them that there is no real need for competition. Third, countries with larger populations have higher risks of war, and these wars last longer (i.e., in these countries there is a greater attraction of secession). Fourth, it is not ethno-linguistic fractionalization which is damaging to societies but rather that specific degree of fractionalization which most facilitates rebel coordination (i.e., clear and obvious distinctiveness of the rebels from the rest of the population, which inhibits government infiltration).

In a further paper three years later, Collier and Hoeffler (2001) specifically aim to test the explanatory value of different greed- and grievance-based models. They accept that rebellion needs both motive and opportunity, but contest that opportunities are more important than motives in explaining conflict. In their view, political science and economic approaches to rebellion have assumed different motivations and different explanations of rebellions. While political scientists focus predominantly on grievances as motivation and favour atypically strong grievances as an explanation for the occurrence of rebellions, economists favour greed as the basic motivation of rebels and atypically good opportunities as the main cause of rebellions.

In order to prove their assumption that opportunity is the more viable explanation, Collier and Hoeffler (2001) develop a set of quantitative indicators for different types of opportunity for rebellions. First, they discuss opportunities for financing rebellions that arise from the extraction of natural resources (one of the findings from their earlier study; see above), from diaspora donations, and from subventions for rebels from governments hostile to their own. Also consistent with their earlier study is the focus on opportunities arising from atypically low costs. For these, they use three different (proxies) for foregone income: mean income per capita (the lower this figure, the lower the cost, as the loss of low income is less costly than that of high income), male secondary schooling (again the lower this figure, the lower the cost, because low levels of education will diminish career and earnings prospects), and the growth rate of the economy (the lower the growth rate, the lower the cost, because income is unlikely to increase for those who are in paid employment – or profitable self-employment – and opportunities are unlikely to occur for those without jobs). A range of further opportunities arise from unusually cheap conflict-specific capital (availability of weapons, military skills and organizational structures), which will decrease over time (hence, Collier and Hoeffler use the time since the last civil war as a proxy for this); atypically weak government military capability (i.e., an inability of the government to defend itself); terrain favourable to rebels, such as forests and mountains which provide safe havens and operational bases; and geographical dispersion of the population, which inhibits government capability, alongside low population density and low urbanization.

In contrast to these opportunity-focused propositions, Collier and Hoeffler (2001) also test four grievance-based models: ethnic or religious hatred, political repression, political exclusion and economic inequality.

The findings that Collier and Hoeffler (2001) come up with on the basis of a large quantitative study of civil wars are quite unequivocal in favouring opportunity as an explanation of rebellion, which in turn is consistent with the economic interpretation of rebellion as greed- rather than grievance-motivated. Specifically they find the following. First, primary commodity exports (as a proxy for easily lootable resources) are highly significant for explaining rebellion. Second, foregone earnings (low rebel labour cost) are also significant, which is demonstrated by the fact that higher rates of secondary schooling and growth both reduce the risk of rebellion (as they increase the cost of rebel labour). Third, the cost of conflict-specific capital is another indicator for the strength of opportunity-based explanations of rebellion: the shorter the time period since any previous conflict (dating back to 1945), the higher the likelihood of rebellion. Conversely, the longer this time period, the lower the likelihood, which suggests that 'time heals'.[3] The only grievance-based variable that turns out to be significant is ethnic dominance, which nearly doubles the likelihood of rebellion.

Obviously, these findings have important implications for conflict settlement, the two most important of them being the need for poverty reduction (i.e., development) and good governance (i.e., promotion of democracy).

Several criticisms have been levelled against the approaches and findings of Collier and Hoeffler (1998, 2001) (and, to a lesser extent, those of Fearon and Laitin 2000).[4] Their arguments are substantiated by quantitative analyses of a large number of cases, but this in itself poses a significant problem, as there is no sufficient distinction in these data sets between ethnic and non-ethnic conflicts, which inevitably biases findings against specifically 'ethnic' explanations: the fewer cases there are that involve ethnic groups and their specific grievances, the less significant these become in the overall picture of explaining civil war. Other critics have questioned the usefulness of the proxy variables employed in these large quantitative tests and have noted possible ambiguity in how one might interpret the resultant findings (Ballentine and Sherman 2003; Pugh and Cooper 2004). Equally importantly, there is also an empirical argument that can be made: it is difficult to see why and how grievances, fears and hatred cannot be significant in explaining individual and group behaviour in the conflicts in Bosnia and Herzegovina, Kosovo, Rwanda, Sri Lanka, Kashmir or the Nagorno-Karabakh area. This, however, does not mean that economic motivations did not play a role: control over territory and populations is lucrative for rebel movements and their local and external supporters, it means easier access to valuable resources (gold, diamonds, oil, coltan), control of transport routes (for gun running, people trafficking and drugs smuggling, piracy), and an opportunity to exploit a local population (taxation, enslavement, forced recruitment into rebel forces).

A very useful, empirically grounded critique of economic theories of ethnic conflict is Karen Ballentine and Jake Sherman's *The Political Economy of Armed Conflict: Beyond Greed and Grievance* (Ballentine and Sherman 2003). They contend that qualitative studies can capture the influence of economic factors and their interplay with non-economic factors far better than the statistical analysis of large data sets of civil wars. Studying the cases of Colombia, Nepal, Bougainville, Kosovo, Sri Lanka, Burma, DRC, Sierra Leone and Angola, Ballentine and Sherman and their contributors include in their examination of the causes of conflict three other sets of factors: socio-economic and political grievances, inter-ethnic disputes and security dilemmas. They analyse the impact of both these and economic factors on three dimensions of conflict in each of their case studies: incidence, duration and intensity.

In terms of the incidence of conflict, the findings presented in Ballentine and Sherman (2003) are that economic factors are never the sole cause for the outbreak of conflict. In Kosovo, Sri Lanka and Bougainville, grievances and insecurity bred by systematic exclusion of minorities from political and economic participation were the most important factors, while in Nepal it was landlessness and the caste system. In Colombia and Angola, in contrast, an ideological battle – i.e., the Cold War-influenced struggle for state capture – was the predominant cause of conflict. Only in Sierra Leone and the Democratic Republic of Congo were conflicts primarily economically driven, but even here political misrule, corruption, socio-economic deterioration and institutional decay played an important role.

While there was no question that opportunities (or proxy indicators thereof), such as economic gain, favourable terrain, poverty and unemployment, matter, Ballentine and Sherman (2003) emphasize that it is far less clear *how* they mattered: by reducing the relative costs for individuals of joining a rebellion or by fuelling their grievances and thus increasing their motivation to do so. A similar problem exists in relation to diasporas, who generally have very different views towards conflicts 'at home', which in part are determined on the opportunities they have in their new host country (for example for political organization, fund-raising, maintaining contacts with their former home, etc.). In this context, Ballentine and Sherman (2003) highlight the example of the Kosovo Albanian diaspora, whose members first and for a long time supported the peaceful movement for independence led by the Democratic League for Kosovo (LDK), and only after more than fifteen years of a fruitless peaceful struggle began to back the KLA. Another important lesson of the Kosovo case is that high levels of social capital within ethnic communities can make rebellions viable (and thus likely to succeed) despite an otherwise unfavourable opportunity structure, determined, for example, by the government's capacity to defend itself and defeat the rebellion.[5]

The findings of Ballentine and Sherman (2003) as to the impact of economic and other factors on the duration of conflicts are equally ambiguous. Clearly, access to lucrative economic resources is a more important factor here, but the question is how to interpret this: as self-enrichment by rebels being an end in itself, or instrumental for funding a rebellion motivated by social, economic and/or political grievances? Equally important, especially in the context of conflict settlement, is the type of access to resources that rebels have. Direct access by combatants can create disciplinary problems and prolong conflicts: in these cases, individual greed may sooner or later replace other motivations. By way of contrast, where access to resources by combatants is indirect and through their command structure, compliance with and commitment to peace agreements may be more readily enforceable.

Finally, Ballentine and Sherman (2003) find little conclusive evidence of a direct correspondence between resource availability and the higher intensity of conflicts: in Colombia and Sri Lanka such a connection could be established, but in three other cases – Angola, Sierra Leone and DRC – it could not.

These and other critical findings highlight some of the limitations of greed-based explanations. First, there is a certain selection bias in Collier and Hoeffler's (1998, 2001) data sets in that they do not differentiate between different subsets of conflict, yet exclude all anti-colonial liberation wars. Second, there is a question mark over some of the interpretation of certain findings (e.g., no consideration of instrumental use of 'greed': funding for a politically/ethnically/ideologically motivated campaign). Third, there are, moreover, clear incompatibilities of interpretations based on similar findings in different data sets; for example, commodity export dependency for Collier and Hoeffler indicates opportunity and thus likelihood of conflict, whereas for the State Failure Task Force (2000) it indicates a high level of incorporation into the international economy and thus reduced conflict risk. A final point of criticism is that Collier and Hoeffler (1998) and Collier (2001), as well as Fearon and Laitin (2000), rely predominantly on country indicators that do not account for substate variation, for example in income or resource availability (cf. Pugh and Cooper 2004). In other words, a failure to distinguish between local and state-level factors weakens the analytical power of existing economic theories of ethnic conflict. At the same time, the incorporation of economic factors, including diaspora remittances and access to global markets to finance war, highlights the importance of regional and global factors for our understanding of ethnic conflict.

3 Social-psychological motivations

Theories of social-psychological motivations for ethnic conflict locate the sources of conflict in the way in which individuals perceive their environment, locate themselves in it, and on that basis form the individual and group identities that guide their behaviour and actions.

The most important social-psychological theories of conflict are realistic group conflict theory, social identity theory and psychoanalytic/ psychodynamic theories. All of these theories were developed in their earliest forms in the 1960s. The first to emerge was realistic group conflict theory (Sherif et al. 1954). Social identity theory has its origins in the 1970s and 1980s (Billig 1976; Tajfel 1981; Horowitz [1985] 2000). In turn, psychoanalytic and psychodynamic theories of inter-group conflict have been developed mostly from the late 1980s onwards (Volkan 1979, 1988, 1997, 2006; Montville 1990; Ross 1993a, 1993b. We shall now consider each sub-group in turn.

3.1 Realistic group conflict theory

This theory was first formulated by Muzafer Sherif in 1954. It adopts basic premises of the rational choice approach in assuming that inter-group conflict originates in the perceptions of group members with regard to real competition for scarce resources, thus suggesting that hostility between groups results from real or perceived conflicting goals because they generate inter-group competition. In other words, the dynamic that evolves when groups are engaged in competitive zero-sum competitions leads to each group developing negative stereotypes about, and enmity towards, the other group(s) with which it competes.

Sherif et al. (1954) verified these basic premises in the so-called Robbers' Cave experiment involving boys in a summer camp who had never met before. When they were split into two groups engaging in competitive activities with conflicting goals (i.e., goals that can be achieved only at the expense of the other group, such as sports tournaments), inter-group hostility emerged very quickly and almost automatically. These findings are in turn extrapolated as a means of understanding group behaviour in broadly analogous situations.

3.2 Social identity theories

The most important theorists in the social identity approach are Henri Tajfel (1981), Michael Billig (1976) and Donald Horowitz ([1985] 2000). According to this theory, every individual divides his or her social world into distinct classes or so-called social categories and locates themselves and others in relation to them. On the basis of a cumulative process of locating oneself, individuals can constitute their social identity, i.e., define themselves in terms of social categories such as gender, geographic location, class, profession, ethnicity, etc.

The basic assumption is that people strive for a positive social identity. As social identity is derived from membership in groups, a positive social identity is the outcome of favourable social comparisons made between the in-group (i.e., the group to which one belongs) and other social groups. As long as membership in a group enhances one's self- esteem – that is, as long as social comparisons remain (on balance) favourable – one will remain a member of that group. However, if the group fails to satisfy this requirement, the individual may try to change the structure of the group (social change), seek a new way of comparison which would favour his or her group and hence reinforce his or her social identity (social creativity), or leave/abandon the group with the desire to join a 'better' one (social mobility).

For individuals who are members of a minority group to achieve a positive social identity is very difficult because minorities almost always have an inferior status in comparison with the majority. Thus, for members of minorities, different strategies are required to confront the challenge of achieving a positive social identity. First, if the social system is perceived as legitimate and stable and there are no visible alternatives to the status quo, or there is no conceivable prospect of any change in the nature of the system (such as in a feudal society), they just accept their inferiority and acquiesce. Second, if the system is perceived as illegitimate by the minority, very soon alternatives begin to be envisioned. The system loses its stability, and oppression and terror by the majority-controlled state become the only way to maintain the status quo. Third, if majority–minority relations are perceived as illegitimate and the system is no longer stable, the minority group members will tend towards a rejection of their inferior status. They then may reinterpret and redefine their group's characteristics and, thus, try to transform their social identity into a positive one.

Donald Horowitz ([1985] 2000) offers the best-known application of social identity theory to cases of ethnic conflict. It focuses on the comparison between backward and advanced groups in which members of the backward groups must decide whether to emulate out-group behaviour in order to compete or adopt different coping strategies, such as claiming preferential treatment or compensation if backwardness is perceived to have emerged from past injustices and discrimination. Backward groups harbour fears of extinction if they cannot catch up with advanced groups or if preferential treatment is limited, and their anxiety flows from diffuse danger of exaggerated dimensions, limits and modifies perceptions, and produces extreme reactions to modest threats. Horowitz also stipulates a relationship between self-esteem, anxiety and prejudice in relation to conflict. Self-esteem is raised by aggression, especially if aggression is projected on others as justification for one's own actions – i.e., prejudices about other groups' aggressiveness produces and intensifies anxiety and justifies aggression (as self-defence).

Comparisons between ethnic groups centre on their relative group worth and relative group legitimacy and merge easily into a politics of ethnic entitlement in which the quest for power is both instrumental (power as a means to an end, e.g., averting the threat of group extinction) and symbolic (power as a confirmation of status). This means that, in unranked systems, groups will make efforts to dominate and avoid domination by others. What may thus have initially been a conflict over needs and interests becomes subordinate to conflicts over status and concerning the rules of the political system (citizenship, electoral systems, official languages, constitution, etc.). The intensity of ensuing conflict is, according to Horowitz, a function of the relative strength of group claims: the more invidious the group comparison and the larger the area of unacknowledged claims to group legitimacy, the more intense the conflict.

3.3 Psychoanalytic/psychodynamic theories

The most important representatives of the psychoanalytic approach to intergroup conflict are Vamik Volkan (1979, 1988, 1997, 2006), Marc H. Ross (1993a, 1993b, 2007) and Joseph Montville (1990). Their theories seek mainly to explain how people form images about themselves and others. Volkan argues that there are suitable targets of externalization either determined by culture (familiar objects of a child's environment) or shown to the children by parents and other adults. Suitable targets of externalization are symbols such as flags, songs, special dishes, places of worship, religious icons, memorials and certain animals (Ross, 1993b), but also people and groups of people (Volkan 1988), and they can have both positive and negative connotations. Yet this is not sufficient for the definition of group identity. In addition to cultural symbols and rituals, a group identity needs enemies (who help the group members define who they are not), chosen glories (important, usually mythologized and idealized achievements that took place in the past), chosen traumas (losses, defeats, humiliations – also mythologized – that are usually difficult to mourn) and borders (physical and/or mental) that facilitate a clear distinction between in-group and out-group.

Minorities, Volkan (1988) argues, especially if they are considered impossible to assimilate into the majority, can easily become suitable targets for externalization of the majority's negative feelings and self-images. In this case,

minorities not only attract the hatred, suspicion and opprobrium of the majority because of the characteristics they allegedly have, but they also serve as res-
ervoirs of the majority's negative self-images whose very existence is blamed
on the minority (e.g., majority aggressiveness is necessary as a self-defence
against minority aggressiveness). Relations between minority and majority
communities may become even more strained if that minority is linked to
a state or nation that in the past inflicted a deep trauma upon the majority
group (e.g., favoured/ruling majorities in colonial regimes). In that case, and
after the balance of power changes in favour of the majority, the minority
often becomes a target of ethnic cleansing, massacres and genocide.

Starting from the assertion that the dominant theories on ethnic conflict
pay too little attention to the importance of culture and identity, Ross (2007)
formulates a social psychological theory explaining the incidence and intensity of ethnic conflicts. This approach is based on his earlier studies (Ross
1993a, 1993b), which link psycho-culturally based identities, social processes
and structural interests in order to explain conflict and conflict management.
Ross's basic assumption is that identity issues are at the heart of any ethnic
conflict (Ross 2007: 14). Identity is understood as a process which 'connect[s]
individuals through perceived common past experiences and expectations
of shared future ones' (ibid.: 22). Furthermore, this connection results in the
strengthening of 'social categories that organize a good deal of behavior'
(ibid.). Consequently, culture is seen as a common system of shared beliefs
and meanings which is used by people in order better to interpret reality
(ibid.: 17).

Given the extraordinary importance attached to identity and culture, it is
essential to explore the particular group identities, cultural systems and symbolic actions and how they link psychological processes to social actions (Ross
2007: 2). Ross claims that cultural enactments and performances constitute
the causal factors because these 'refer to behavioral expressions that evoke
central meanings, images, and metaphors rooted in collective memories'
(ibid.: 21). To explore these causal factors, he places psycho-cultural interpretations and narratives at the centre of the analysis (ibid.: 18). The first concept
describes the shared cultural views that provide a group with essential psychological accounts of the world. This is then aggregated by psycho-cultural
narratives into a particular account of 'a group's origin, history, and conflicts
with outsiders, including its symbolic and ritual behaviors' (ibid.: 24). In
order to understand the underlying identities of an ethnic conflict as well
as its given intensity, it is therefore essential to explore how these identities
are constructed by culture and the dominant discourses. It must, however, be
mentioned that Ross emphasizes that adherence to differing cultural identi-
.ties does not necessarily result in conflict and violence but can also create
opportunities for conflict mitigation (ibid.: 319ff.).

The strength of these different social-psychological explanations of ethnic
conflict lies in their ability to give a fairly comprehensive account of group

motivations, something that is generally found missing in greed-based explanations and in the rational choice strand of security dilemma applications. Their corresponding weaknesses, however, are threefold, in that they fail to explain elite motivations in full, there is little in terms of an account of opportunity structures, and they define interests primarily in relation to grievances. To be sure, not every conflict can be reduced to the manipulative, power-seeking behaviour of elites who instrumentalize ethnicity for their own purposes, but the disintegration of Yugoslavia, and especially the war in Bosnia and Herzegovina, would be difficult to explain in full without accounting for the role of individual leaders (cf., for example, Caspersen 2004; Woodward 1995). Likewise, had it not been for very specific opportunity structures, in particular access to the arsenal and expertise of the Yugoslav People's Army, the Serbs in Croatia and Bosnia and Herzegovina would not have been able to make the gains they did in the early days of the war, nor would Croatian and Bosnian government forces have been able to defeat them without the support of the international community (NATO air and ground forces, the imposition of a sanctions regime on Serbia, etc.). Finally, and looking beyond the Balkans, grievances alone fail to explain the motivation of ethnic groups to resort to violence at a specific time and the intensity of the violence that ensues. For example, the Darfur rebellion coincided with the conclusion of the North–South peace agreement in Sudan and the discovery of large oil deposits, rather than with a sharp worsening of the situation in the Darfur region, which had been dismal for decades as a result of neglect by the central government, which in turn coincided with growing desertification and an increasingly futile competition for scarce agricultural resources. Similarly, grievances about economic deprivation, political exclusion, and/or cultural marginalization cannot explain the use of rape, torture, mutilation, etc., as tactics in ethnic conflict that have become the norm in many of Africa's civil wars. Moreover, such developments are by no means confined to Africa, as the existence of rape and torture camps in the war in Bosnia and Herzegovina illustrates.

4 The international dimension of ethnic conflict

One of the most influential studies of the 1990s that addressed the issue of external factors in ethnic conflict is Rogers Brubaker's *Nationalism Reframed* (1996). Brubaker develops a 'triadic configuration' of national minorities, nationalizing states, and external national homelands in order to establish a model of the 'relational field [of the elements of the triadic configuration] and its interactive dynamics' (1996: 55ff.). His discussion of the complex relationship between these three elements is very elaborate. He emphasizes that the 'relations between the three fields are closely intertwined with relations internal to, and constitutive of, the fields' (ibid.: 67). Brubaker describes the general features of the triadic nexus as '(1) the close interdependence of relations within and between fields; (2) the responsive and interactive character of the triadic interplay between the fields; and (3) the mediated character of this interplay' (ibid.: 69). Yet what he does not consider is a fourth component that has almost identical 'functional' characteristics and relates to the three elements identified by him in the same way as they relate to one another. This additional component is the international context (or the state, and to some extent non-state, actors within it, including international governmental and non-governmental organizations).[6] Adding this factor into the analysis is crucial not only in explaining events such as in Bosnia and Herzegovina, Kosovo or East Timor but also in accounting for less explosive situations in other parts of Europe. Expanding the analytical framework such as to include an international component (be it single or collective state actors, regional or extra-regional actors) will allow assessment of the viability and implications of political strategies employed by all actors in this now enlarged relational field (minority, host state/nation, kin state/nation, international actors). Empirically, the importance of external actors to processes of conflict escalation and de-escalation has been studied by a number of authors and in relation to a broad range of cases.[7]

Theoretically, but not devoid of empirical backing, David Smith has also highlighted this shortcoming in Brubaker's triadic approach. He argues that 'Brubaker neglects the crucial role of international organisations such as the EU, NATO, the OSCE and the Council of Europe in shaping post-communist identity politics of Central and Eastern Europe' and suggests instead that 'it would be more apt to talk of a quadratic nexus linking nationalising states, national minorities and external national homelands to the institutions of an ascendant and expansive "Euro-Atlantic space"' (D. Smith 2002: 3). The role of these institutions, Smith maintains, has been to limit the opportunity structures that give rise to the violent clash of rival ethnic nationalisms. Smith is careful not to attribute too much causal power to the role of international institutions, but his and other research (e.g., that of Barany and Moser 2005; Kemp 2001; McGarry and Keating 2006; Weller and Wolff 2008) illustrates that any attempt to explain why violent conflict in post-communist Central and Eastern Europe at least has been the exception rather than the norm cannot but take into account the role of external actors, especially regional and international governmental organizations.

A slightly different argument about the role of international organizations is made by Alan Kuperman, who demonstrates convincingly how the promise (or precedent) of humanitarian intervention on behalf of a minority against a state might increase the risk of ethnic conflict by offering an otherwise inferior conflict party a credible prospect of victory (Kuperman 2008; also Janus 2009). Kuperman argues, with reference to Bosnia and Herzegovina and Kosovo, that an emerging norm of humanitarian intervention 'may exacerbate some violent conflicts and thereby cause precisely the human tragedies it is intended to avert' (Kuperman 2008: 50). Kuperman had already argued that the norm of humanitarian intervention, 'intended as a type of insurance policy against genocidal violence, exhibits the pathology of all insurance systems by creating moral hazard that encourages risk-taking' and specifically 'encourages disgruntled sub-state groups to rebel because they expect intervention' (Kuperman 2005: 150).

While it may thus be possible to attribute some degree of causality to external actors and their actions, it is important to bear in mind that Kuperman does not argue for mono-causality, but rather draws our attention to the fact that existing models, especially those that apply rational choice approaches, do not fully explain instances of apparently suicidal rebellion, and in fact deviate from their own assumption of rational actors by implying that 'vulnerable groups are driven by the frustration of prolonged discrimination to launch violent challenges against state authorities without necessarily calculating their chances of success or the consequences of failure' (Kuperman 2005: 153). Admittedly, cases of apparently suicidal rebellions are relatively few among ethnic conflicts in general, but even so Kuperman's argument highlights a gap in many existing theories of ethnic conflict, caused by their neglect of regional and global actors and factors.

What is significant about the work of Brubaker, Smith, Kuperman and others when considering external aspects of ethnic conflict is that they remind us of the multi-dimensionality of the phenomenon. The resultant degree of complexity, in our view, is only insufficiently addressed by any single theory of ethnic conflict that we have presented in this chapter. As we stated at the beginning, our aim is not to create another theory of ethnic conflict, but rather to develop an approach for its study in which there is room for several such theories, none of which can explain every conflict, but all of which can contribute to our understanding of different aspects of specific conflicts. In the following chapter, we therefore use our levels-of-analysis approach to demonstrate empirically how these different theories can be used to create a more comprehensive picture of the causes of ethnic conflict.

4

Motive, Means and Opportunity:
A Framework for Understanding the
Causes of Ethnic Conflict

1 Introduction

In the previous chapter we presented a broad overview of relevant theories of
ethnic conflict and discussed their strengths and weaknesses. In particular,
we emphasized that, in our view, no single theory exists that can comprehensively explain the multitude of ethnic conflicts across time and space. This is
not only an issue of some exceptional cases deviating from broadly acknowledged 'norms' or of the way(s) in which ethnic conflict is defined. Rather,
we argue that the complexity of ethnic conflicts requires us to integrate the
findings of different theorists into a framework that allows us to analyse
individual conflicts in their specific context. We are thus not proposing a new
'super-theory' of ethnic conflict, nor do we take refuge in saying that every
case is different and no regularities can be found about the causes of ethnic
conflict.

The underlying premise of this book is that ethnic conflict – its causes and
consequences, and the responses to it – is best understood in terms of four
different layers of analysis: the local, state, regional and global levels. On,
and between, each of these levels, different actors and structures interact and
create a specific context in which ethnic conflicts escalate or de-escalate, in
which they can be resolved or become protracted. In addition, we contend
that there are certain issues, such as food and energy security, communicable
diseases, etc., that are difficult to attribute to any one particular level but
rather cut across these levels.

In general, we subscribe to the idea that ethnic conflicts are not natural
disasters that simply happen, but that they are man-made; that is, they are
the consequences of deliberate choices made by individual human beings,
be they leaders or followers. Regardless of whether these choices are based
on emotions or on economic cost–benefit calculations, they are grounded on
people's motivations. Hence, the first conceptual element of our framework is
the set of motives that drive people to opt for conflict. Motive alone, however,
is insufficient to account for the occurrence of ethnic conflict. Most existing
theories also emphasize that, for ethnic conflict to happen, its participants
need to have both the means and the opportunity. These three elements,
then, taken together, can help us make sense of the relationships between
the different actors and structures at and across our four levels of analysis.[1]

Importantly, if our framework is to be viable, these relationships need to be able to explain both the occurrence of conflict and its absence.

The rest of this chapter is structured as follows. First, we offer a broad-brush application of our approach to understanding the causes of ethnic conflict, drawing on three cases that illustrate how factors at different levels of analysis constrain and enable actors to pursue ethnic conflict; that is, how they enable or deny access to the means of, and open or close opportunities for, engaging in the systematic use of violence for strategic purposes. In a second part of the chapter we focus on just one case of ethnic conflict – Macedonia[2] – to substantiate our ideas at a greater level of empirical detail and at the same time show how our framework for understanding the causes of ethnic conflict can be applied to specific individual cases.

2 Ethnic conflict as a function of motive, means and opportunity of its protagonists: evidence from Georgia, Rwanda and the Philippines

In this section we will draw on evidence gleaned from three case studies: Georgia, Rwanda and the Philippines. These examples have been chosen for a variety of reasons. First, they enable us, through the application of the levels-of-analysis approach, to assess the interplay of forces affecting the incidence, duration and intensity of conflict. Second, by choosing examples beyond our major case study of Macedonia, we are able to illustrate the relative similarity of such conflicts on a global scale. Third, by establishing the broad parameters of the issues under consideration, the brief case studies of Georgia, Rwanda and the Philippines prepare the ground for the in-depth analysis that follows with regard to Macedonia.

2.1 Georgia

The conflicts related to the two separatist regions in Georgia – Abkhazia and South Ossetia – have their origins in Soviet and pre-Soviet politics in the (South) Caucasus. In total, over 80 ethnic groups live in Georgia, the largest, and politically most significant, ones being Georgians, Armenians, Russians, Abkhaz and South Ossetians (Cornell 2001: 63). Since 1988, Georgia has experienced two violent ethnic conflicts, as well as a short two-phase civil war, the latter between different political factions struggling over control of the Georgian state, the former essentially the result of increasingly aggressive Georgian nationalism during, and after, the dying days of the Soviet Union. Both Abkhazia and South Ossetia had enjoyed substantial autonomy after their incorporation into the Soviet Union and, even though the population of both regions was ethnically mixed, it was not until the intensification of Georgian nationalism from the late 1980s onwards that tensions emerged. The nationalist movement in Georgia became further radicalized after Soviet troops crushed a pro-independence demonstration in April 1989. Calls for independence, the legal proclamation in August 1989 of Georgian as the only official language, and a referendum on independence and the subsequent election in May 1991 of the nationalist leader Zviad Gamsakhurdia provided the background against which these tensions escalated into full-scale violent conflict. Abkhaz and South Ossetians, considering their survival as ethno-cultural communities distinct from the Georgian majority to be in acute danger in an independent Georgian state, wanted to preserve, and remain within, the Soviet Union (Cohen 2002; Coppieters 1999; Wennmann 2006). Georgians, on the other hand, for precisely the same reasons of identity preservation and development, were keen to seize the opportunity of breaking free from the Soviet yoke, while considering everyone opposed to this aim an enemy of the Georgian nation. Steps by both sides towards the realization of these goals further increased mutual suspicion and allowed the dynamics of the security dilemma to take hold of Georgia – with devastating consequences for all three groups involved. Over the past two decades, the combination of economic devastation and political uncertainty and instability has created opportunities for various local and transnational crime networks and fostered an environment in which, without proper government control, corruption can thrive, additionally aided by low living standards and weak law enforcement on all sides. Abkhazia has become a heroin transit point, and is thus primarily connected with transnational organized crime, while poverty-stricken South Ossetia, one of the most heavily armed regions of Georgia, suffers predominantly from low-level local criminal activity, such as robbery, kidnapping and smuggling. The local dynamics in South Ossetia and Abkhazia are characterized by kin ties and Russian post-imperial ambitions and security concerns. In turn, these concerns are prompted partly by the long-standing involvement of international bodies in attempts to resolve the two conflicts in Georgia (and a third one in neighbouring Nagorno-Karabakh). All of these territitories lie in the Caucasus, an area that both Russia and the West consider as geostrategically significant and in which they have competed for influence and control since the break-up of the Soviet Union.

Despite overall similarities and close links between the conflicts in South Ossetia and Abkhazia, there are nonetheless important differences in detail. South Ossetians belong to the same ethnic group as the people of North Ossetia (now an autonomous republic of Russia which is considered to be the indigenous homeland of Ossetians). A (South) Ossetian presence in contemporary Georgia dates back only a few hundred years (Cornell 2001: 96), and is often used by Georgian nationalists to dispute any rights of South Ossetians to the territory in which they live, despite the fact that, before the outbreak of conflict, levels of intermarriage between Ossetians and Georgians were quite high and many of the local residents had developed a sense of regional belonging alongside their ethnic identity. In 1989, South Ossetians made up just over two-thirds of their autonomous region's population, roughly

65,000 out of a total of 98,000. Yet at that time there were around another 100,000 Ossetians in other regions of Georgia. Tensions grew in the last years of the Soviet Union and escalated into full-scale conflict initially between November 1989 and January 1990. In August 1989, the 'March on Tskhinvali', the South Ossetian capital, of between 20,000 and 30,000 Georgian nationalists, supposedly to protect the city's Georgian population, prompted violence which led to the deaths of six people and injury to an additional 140 (ibid.: 101). Subsequently, South Ossetians not only boycotted the political process in Georgia, including the September 1990 elections, but also declared their region's independence, while Georgians effectively abolished South Ossetia's autonomy with the proclamation of Georgia as an independent, unitary state with no internal borders.

Tbilisi initially responded only with an economic blockade, but 1991 saw a significant escalation of hostilities, leading initially to the Georgian occupation of Tskhinvali. On several occasions in March, June and September, Gamsakhurdia, who tried to use South Ossetia to strengthen his own grip on power in Georgia (Wennmann 2006: 14), failed to restore full Georgian control over the region in the face of well-organized, highly motivated and Russian-backed resistance. The conflict lingered on for another year, but, with the disposal of Gamsakhurdia in December 1991 and the former Soviet foreign minister Edvard Shevardnadze's ascent to the Georgian presidency in March 1992,[3] it took only one final defeat of Georgian forces to pave the way towards the OSCE-mediated Sochi Agreement of June 1992, which established a permanent ceasefire and a military exclusion zone. It was followed by the deployment of an OSCE Observer Mission and a Russian-led Commonwealth of Independent States (CIS) peacekeeping force, as well as the creation of the so-called Joint Control Commission, meant to facilitate cooperation between the sides on a day-to-day basis.

This arrangement worked relatively well during the presidency of Edvard Shevardnadze, driven primarily by pragmatic considerations that assured all sides of benefits as a result of relative stability based on an acceptance of the status quo (cf. Lynch 2004). Mikhail Saakashvili's ascent to power in 2003 changed this configuration significantly, as the new president had made restoration of full sovereignty across the entire territory of Georgia a key campaign promise. The success he had in reining in Adjara in April 2004 emboldened Saakashvili to move on South Ossetia in summer that year, under the pretext of abolishing the (illegal) Ergneti market. While there is little doubt that trading in this market was connected to smuggling, it also presented one of the few opportunities for direct interaction between Georgians and South Ossetians. The violence during and after the closure of the market destroyed much of the confidence that had been built between the sides and threw into jeopardy ongoing peace talks. In fact, violence got so bad in early August that a formal ceasefire was agreed between Georgian and South Ossetian authorities, only to be broken within days. Violence continued through much of the summer, with Georgian forces making some strategic gains, but then withdrawing and agreeing to a further round of formal demilitarization measures with South Ossetia in Sochi in November. Nonetheless, the 2004 events contributed to further polarization and radicalization on all sides, increasing the frequency and intensity of clashes along the ceasefire line up until the full-scale war in August 2008. They also sent an important 'message' to Abkhazia about the intentions and resolve of the new Georgian president – a message received in Russia and the West as well.

The conflict in South Ossetia led to around 1,000 people being killed, 100,000 being forced to flee, and extensive damage being done to homes and infrastructure (ICG 2004: 4). In addition to ethnic Georgians and South Ossetians leaving the region for Georgia proper and North Ossetia, respectively, a very large number of South Ossetians were driven from their homes in Georgia. Within South Ossetia, segregation between the two communities increased significantly as a result of the conflict, with members of each ethnic group taking refuge in the areas controlled by 'their' side.

The background to the conflict over Abkhazia is somewhat different. Historically, the Stalinist period saw the persecution and destruction of the political and cultural elites of the Abkhaz population in Georgia. Abkhazia, during this period, additionally experienced a massive influx of Georgians, decreasing the proportion of ethnic Abkhaz among the resident population to around one-third between the late 1930s and the early 1950s, and to under 18 per cent by 1989. This policy of Georgianization continued after the Stalin years, and triggered several short spells of violence in 1957, 1967, 1978 and 1981 (Cornell 2001: 155ff.) The resurgence of Georgian nationalism under Georgia's first post-independence leader, Zviad Gamsakhurdia, could not but be seen as a precursor of worse things to come by the Abkhaz, leading them to conclude that establishing their own state was all the more necessary to ensure their ethnic survival (ICG 2004: 3).

Following Georgia's declaration of independence in 1991, and the simultaneous abolition of Abkhazia's autonomy, the Abkhaz immediately reinstated their 1925 constitution, which defined Abkhazia as an independent state united with Georgia on the basis of a special union treaty, and proceeded to declare their desire to leave Georgia. This quickly escalated into open violence, with Georgian forces taking over the Gali region in August 1992, thereby cutting Abkhazia off from Russia. However, the pretext for the attacks was the alleged abduction of Georgians by supporters of Gamsakhurdia, who had been ousted in a coup in December 1991 by three Georgian warlords, who subsequently asked Shevardnadze, a native of Georgia, to lead the country through this difficult period.

As a result of Georgian advances, the Abkhaz leadership was forced to retreat from Sukhumi but immediately regrouped and organized guerrilla-style resistance. Backed by North Caucasian, in particular Chechen, fighters, as well as Russian air support (Sabanadze 2002: 11), the Abkhaz quickly recaptured most of the territory initially lost, with Georgian control being reduced to the Khodori gorge and Gali. Ceasefires were agreed and broken time and again until May 1994, when the Moscow Agreement established a permanent ceasefire line with military exclusion zones on either side. In parallel, the UN Security Council passed Resolution 854, establishing the UN Observer Mission in Georgia (UNOMIG). The Russian-dominated CIS also dispatched a peacekeeping force to the region. Until August 2008 violations of the ceasefire were rare, even though the general security situation, especially in the Kodori gorge, deteriorated sharply in 1998, 2001 and 2006, bringing both sides to the brink of new war. Around 10,000 people in total are believed to have been killed in the fighting; in addition, around a quarter of a million Georgians have been displaced from Abkhazia. In August 2008, in the midst of the war between Georgia and South Ossetia, Abkhaz forces seized the opportunity to complete the expulsion of Georgian forces from Abkhazia.

Two things therefore make the Georgian case particularly interesting to study. First, both conflicts indicate the importance of different actors in processes of conflict escalation: driven by local anxieties among the different groups over their post-Soviet future, regional actors played a major catalytic role in fuelling and sustaining the violence. Second, what were initially first and foremost identity conflicts have become deeply entangled with local and transnational organized criminal agendas and geopolitical power games that make it hard, if not inconceivable, to see how a solution acceptable to the three ethnic groups (Georgians, Abkhaz and South Ossetians), Russia and the West can be found now, following the recognition of Abkhazia's and South Ossetia's independence by Russia – in turn a move that cannot be seen in isolation from Kosovo's Unilateral Declaration of Independence in February 2008, its recognition by the US and all but five EU member states, and the increasingly close links between Georgia and NATO.

2.2 Rwanda

In the public consciousness, Rwanda is synonymous with genocide and inter-ethnic violence. Inevitably, the genocide of 1994 forms the backdrop to much of this section, but, if we are to account for why the killing occurred, we need first to establish some basic facts about Rwanda and examine the nature of Rwandan society.

Approximately 85 per cent of the population of the Republic of Rwanda is Hutu and around 14 per cent is Tutsi. Approximately 57 per cent of the population is Roman Catholic, a further 37 per cent belongs to various non-Catholic Christian denominations, and around 4 per cent is Muslim. The remainder either practise traditional beliefs or follow no religion. Kinyarwanda is the universal language of all Rwandans regardless of 'tribal' affiliation (US Department of State: 2006). Until Rwanda's independence from Belgium in 1962, the Tutsi had for centuries been the dominant element. But with the ascent to power of an ethnic Hutu party at independence, there was an intensification of a cycle of violence, directed primarily towards the Tutsi, that culminated in the genocide of 1994. The current population of Rwanda is estimated to be somewhat over 8.5 million. However, a further 2 million Hutu and Tutsi live in neighbouring states, around 400,000 of whom are resident in the DRC. As many as 1 million Hutu live in Tanzania, and tens of thousands of both Hutu and Tutsi reside on the Rwandan–Ugandan border.

The Tutsi first moved into what is now Rwanda in the 1300s, and gradually established their suzerainty over the Hutu and the longer established Twa. In 1890 the area became part of German East Africa. The Belgians occupied Rwanda in 1916, and in 1923, as part of Ruanda-Urundi, it became a UN trust territory under Belgian supervision. In addition, during the colonial carve-up of the late nineteenth century, the Belgian Congo was assigned land that had previously been ruled by the Rwandan monarchy. The result is that mineral-rich areas today fall to what is now the Democratic Republic of Congo leaving Rwanda almost wholly dependent upon agricultural production. Rwanda is still overly reliant upon agriculture, although there are some deposits of, among others, gold and tungsten.

The racism that gave rise to the 1994 genocide is as much as anything else a testimony to the effectiveness of Belgian, and to a lesser extent German, racist practices that succeeded in creating racial divisions in the popular consciousness, where in reality no such differences existed. In short, the Belgians took the view that, by virtue of the fact that they led a well-ordered and advanced society, the Tutsi had to have been of Caucasian origin. As 'proof' of the racial differences between Tutsi and Hutu, they emphasized physical dissimilarities between the two and conveniently ignored any similarities. For Hutu militants who came to accept the basic tenets of Spenserian racial theory, the Tutsi came to be viewed as alien immigrants who had enslaved the indigenous Hutu. It followed that, as the Tutsi were not prepared to leave of their own accord, in order for the Hutu to regain what had been lost, the Tutsi had to die.

Not only are the Hutu and Tutsi genetically linked, but the ascriptions of Tutsi and Hutu were not those of primary allegiance. Rather, every Tutsi and Hutu was a member of one of eighteen common clans. Depending upon socio-economic status or proximity to the (Tutsi) monarchy, an individual could be designated as Tutsi or Hutu. In other words, Rwanda was marked by a system that allowed for both intermarriage and social mobility between caste and clan. In effect, the Belgians introduced a system of apartheid in Rwanda that acted as an incubus of resentment that manifested itself in all its horror in the genocide of 1994.

In the 1950s, under pressure from the United States as much as anything else, Belgium began to prepare for eventual withdrawal and independence. However, the aforementioned Hutu resentment and Tutsi fears of such resentment did not augur well. In 1959, three years before independence, the Tutsi monarchy was overthrown by Hutu rebels. In the process an indeterminate number of Tutsi were killed, and anything up to 200,000 fled the country. A referendum in 1961 paved the way for independence in 1962 under a Hutu leadership that was convinced of its mission, by all means necessary, to redress past wrongs meted out by the Tutsi. Further massacres of Tutsi occurred in 1963, following an incursion by Tutsi rebels based in Burundi. In turn, the post-independence civilian government was overthrown in 1973 by Major General Juvenal Habyarimana, who ruled the country in various guises until his death in April 1994.

In 1990, in the face of continued anti-Tutsi discrimination in Rwanda, the rebel Tutsi Rwandan Patriotic Front (RPF) launched an offensive from its bases in southern Uganda. It was contained by the Rwandan army, and the rebels were confined to mountainous areas in the north of the country. In August 1993 the two sides reached an agreement in Arusha in neighbouring Tanzania. The warring parties, however, found it difficult to implement the agreement, and between July 1992 and April 1994 what in fact existed was a situation of 'neither war nor peace'. Then, in early April 1994, the presidents of Rwanda and Burundi were killed as their plane approached Kigali airport. A subsequent French report pointed the finger of blame at the RPF, an accusation that it strenuously denies. Regardless of where responsibility might lie, the incident seemed to act as a signal for the commencement of the genocide, which had been long and well prepared in all respects – from the acquisition of weapons to the intense hatred of Tutsis propagated by Hutu radio stations and prominent Hutu individuals.

Armed by Uganda, the RPF immediately went on another offensive, and as its forces pushed deeper into government-held territory the scale of the carnage became clear. The Rwandan capital, Kigali, fell on 4 July, and millions of Hutu, fearing revenge attacks, fled into Zaire (now the Democratic Republic of Congo) and other neighbouring countries. Between April and July, anything between 500,000 and 1 million Tutsi, together with Hutus who refused to condone or take part in the slaughter, were murdered by the Rwandan army and the Interahamwe militia. A figure of 800,000 is taken by most commentators as being the most likely death toll. Based on the 2001 census, the government cites a figure of 937,000 (Asiimwe 2004).

Undoubtedly, the main causes of the genocide in Rwanda are local, and its outbreak is clearly the responsibility of those who prepared and steered the killing and those who willingly committed it. Yet the tensions between Hutus and Tutsis, present before and throughout the post-independence period, cannot be fully understood without reference to a bigger picture. The colonial past and the mismanagement of independence – of Rwanda and the Great Lakes region more generally – contributed in no small amount to the eventual tragedy. Regional tensions between states, notably between Rwanda and Uganda, and the latter's support of the Tutsi RPF, were further factors, as was the failure of the UN to react to the warning signs that, not just with the benefit of hindsight, were so clearly there. Yet the end of the genocide in Rwanda unfortunately did not spell the end to a conflict in the area that is regional, and at times almost continental, in scale. As we shall see later on in a case study of the Democratic Republic of Congo, Rwanda's neighbour to the west, the flight of many Hutus there, including *genocidaires*, contributed significantly to the subsequent escalation of local and statewide conflict that was, in terms of pure numbers, even more costly than the Rwandan genocide.

2.3 The Philippines[4]

The Spanish established a colonial presence in the Philippines in 1565 which lasted until 1896, when independence was proclaimed following a national uprising supported by the United States. This was a fitting end to the entire period of Spanish rule, which was peppered with local revolts and attempts by European imperial rivals to wrest control of the territory. Unfortunately for the revolutionaries of 1896, US support of their insurgency was not an exercise in selfless support of an anti-colonial self-determination movement. Rather than achieving independence, the Philippines remained a territory administered by the US until 1946. Since then, the country has not been noted for either stability or clean government. Civil unrest and politically inspired violence have been integral to political life ever since the late 1960s, when Ferdinand Marcos and his wife Imelda established their authoritarian kleptocracy. The Marcos regime was overthrown in 1986 following a largely peaceful popular revolt, and Ferdinand Marcos died in exile. Imelda, herself exiled with her husband, has since returned to the country and remains politically active. Subsequent presidents have included two women (Corazon Aquino and the current incumbent, Gloria Macapagal-Arroyo), a former army general (Fidel Ramos) and a film star (Joseph Estrada, who was overthrown by yet another popular uprising in 2001, in the wake of accusations concerning ballot rigging and corruption).

Ethnic identity in the Philippines is for the most part fluid. Interestingly, the only official national or ethnic group is the Filipinos themselves. For the great majority of the population, ethnic identity is highly situational and of no great significance. Exceptions arise with regard both to the 30,000 aboriginal inhabitants scattered around the islands and to Muslims, whose religious identity sets them apart from other Filipinos despite the fact that both groups are in essence drawn from the same ethnic stock. The large majority of the population is descended from Austronesian migrants who arrived around 1,000 years ago. Today their descendants are divided into three primary ethnolingustic groups: the Bisaya, Tagalogs and Ilocanos. Over 170 languages are in use, including Chinese and Arabic, which is spoken by some Muslims on Mindanao. Tagalog and English are the official state languages.

With regard to religious affiliation, Filipinos are overwhelmingly Roman Catholic. Roman Catholic missionaries arrived with the Spanish colonists and gradually converted most of the inhabitants from either a series of traditional beliefs or Islam, which has had a presence in the Philippines since the fourteenth century. Today, around 81 per cent of the population is Roman Catholic, and a further 11 per cent subscribes to other Christian denominations. Approximately 5 per cent of the population is Muslim, and the remainder either follow traditional belief systems or are unaffiliated.

In general, Mindanao and other predominantly Muslim islands have been less penetrated by Western influences than any other part of the archipelago. The most visible sign of this difference is the persistence of Islam, which originally arrived in the Philippines from modern-day Malaysia. The Muslim Filipinos are also known collectively as Moros, derived from the Spanish *Moor*. Until the middle part of the twentieth century, low levels of industrialization, the absence of mass communications and ethnolingustic fragmentation hindered the growth of a unified political consciousness among the Muslim population. However, industrialization and modernization, coupled with inward migration, served to create a shared identity among many Muslim Filipinos, a factor that has contributed to the conflict that currently exists between Muslim rebels and their Christian co-nationals. Further factors include the unequal distribution of wealth, the consequent poverty that pervades Philippine society, and a feeling on the part of many Muslims that they are further disadvantaged by virtue of their religion. As is the case with so many other ethnic conflicts, the causes are to be found not in irreconcilable ethnic differences, but rather in discrimination and deprivation determined by ethnic difference. This is not only apparent in relation to the situation of the approximately 5 million Muslims in Mindanao compared to the rest of the Philippines but also holds true for the minority of Christians in Mindanao, predominantly indigenous islanders and recently arrived migrants, who resent the fact that their interests are being subordinated to the claims of the Muslim community.

Armed opposition to the national government first appeared in the shape of the Moro National Liberation Front (MNLF), which emerged in the early 1970s. In 1976 the MNLF signed a ceasefire with the government which broke down shortly thereafter and thereby established a pattern of warfare punctuated by ceasefires and peace agreements that persists to this day. Over 120,000 deaths have resulted as a direct consequence of the armed conflicts in Mindanao (ICG 2008). Estimates of the number of internally displaced people (IDPs) vary, and range from anything between 150,000 and 300,000. Civilians, rather than combatants, are the primary victims. Death squads operate, and some military units are beyond the control of their notional commanders (Amnesty International 2008), exacerbating the suffering of civilians caught between the fronts.

In 1996 the MNLF and the government reached a peace agreement that has by and large held. Under its terms, the Autonomous Region of Muslim Mindanao (ARMM) was established with its own political institutions and a legal system that is somewhat distinct from that in operation elsewhere in the country (ICG 2008). However, critics have argued that, as the autonomous region lacks financial capacity, its autonomy is largely notional (cf. contributions in Stankovich 2003). The MNLF's chairman and founder, Nur Misuari, became the ARMM's first governor, only to end up in jail in the spring of 2001 when he led a failed uprising against the government.

The 1996 peace agreement did not, however, end the fighting. The Moro Islamic Liberation Front (MILF), which emerged as an offshoot from the MNLF in 1971, did not lay down its arms. It is estimated to have a core base of around 12,500 fighters and draws most of its support from among the rural poor of Mindanao (Muslim 2003). It lays a greater emphasis upon religion than does the MNLF. Eventually, in the spring of 2001, the MILF signed a ceasefire with the government; this broke down in February 2003, but was renewed in July 2003. In March 2004 a further series of talks began between the MILF and the government. This time the ceasefire held until January 2005, with a breakthrough being achieved in April the same year concerning land rights for Muslims.

While the MNLF and MILF can be considered by and large rebel groups with demands that arise from various grievances of Muslim Filipinos in Mindanao, and can in principle be accommodated in a peace settlement, the same cannot be said for the Abu Sayyaf (Sword of God) group, another splinter group that emerged from within the ranks of the MNLF in 1991. It is the smallest and most militant of the rebel groups operating in Mindanao, with a core of only around 400 fighters, and is suspected of having links with Jemaah Islamiah (JI), a regional al-Qaeda offshoot active in Southeast Asia. Apart from its jihadist tendencies, Abu Sayyaf is known for its criminal enterprises, especially hostage-taking for ransom. It thus represents one clear example of the dangerous links between ethnic conflict, international terrorism and organized crime that weave together a multiplicity of actors with diverse motives, beyond local opportunities, and often greatly enhanced means to pursue their struggle. Benefiting as they do from the continuation of conflict rather than its settlement, such groups contribute to the protracted nature of many similar conflicts and illustrate clearly that the original causes of conflict are not necessarily the same as the causes that prevent its settlement. Their intransigence fuels the continuation of conflict, not least because it provides a convenient justification for some factions in the government who also seek the continuation of armed conflict until a victory on the battlefield can be achieved, no matter how unlikely this may be or what its costs. In Mindanao, as well as elsewhere, this is unfortunate, as it decreases the prospects of a sustainable settlement. Yet the outlook is nonetheless not too bleak. In the August 2005 elections, Zaldy Ampatuan became governor of the ARMM, his victory signalling two things. The first is the continuing importance of clan ties despite the existence of an overarching sense of Muslim identity. Ampatuan comes from an important clan that has close ties with Manila. Second, the fact that he has never been a member of a rebel group indicates that support for such groups is waning. However, as is indicated in chapter 7, localized violence is still a regular occurrence.

The conflict in Mindanao, like many of similar duration, offers important insights into the motives, means and opportunities of those choosing violence over accommodation. First, it provides evidence that there are no singular motives over time. What may have begun as a grievance-based struggle for greater rights of a religious minority began gradually to take on far greater complexity, and now presents a mix of yet unsatisfied political demands, greed-based criminal motivations and a jihadist agenda which sees Mindanao as simply another front in a global fundamentalist struggle. In the case of Mindanao, change of motivation brought change of opportunities and of means. The proceeds of organized crime contribute a significant amount of funding, in particular to Abu Sayyaf, which enables them to frame their activities into more of a political struggle and thus keep a conflict alive that in turn benefits their criminal agenda. The involvement of JI, on the other hand, brings with it a wealth of 'expertise' in guerrilla warfare gained by some of its cadres in Afghanistan, the possibility of drawing on a wider regional network of Islamist extremists, and a global propaganda machine linking JI's struggle in Mindanao to what once originated from demands for greater equality among a Muslim minority, thus imbuing it with a degree of legitimacy and at least limited popular support. Even without any prospect of 'success', the involvement of such actors, their links to regional and global networks of violence, and the opportunities that this offers for government repression of even legitimate protests has the potential to undermine sustainable solutions. In order to devise specific policy responses at all of these levels, it is therefore important to distinguish carefully between different local actors and their agendas (and their changing nature over time) and to understand the regional and global structures that enable them.

3 The quiet before the storm and after: understanding the causes of ethnic conflict in Macedonia

Our choice of the particular case of Macedonia was deliberate in that it helps us to illustrate the interaction of many different factors on, and across, our four levels of analysis. Moreover, the case of Macedonia is interesting because, contrary to many predictions, existing inter-ethnic tensions did not escalate into ethnic conflict for a decade; once violence did break out it was brief, and a settlement was quickly achieved. This does not mean that Macedonia is so specific a case that verifying the usefulness of our approach here is meaningless because it cannot be 'transferred' to other cases. First, as our framework is not a theory per se, and because we have already provided some evidence for its broader applicability as an analytical tool, the specificity of the Macedonian case is not an argument against its analysis. Second, and as we will demonstrate below, precisely because of its complexity it is a very useful example for our purposes: we can demonstrate the viability of our approach to establishing causal relationships between different factors in our levels-of-analysis model, and we can do so in a case that allows us to establish whether the model is useful for understanding the occurrence, resolution and absence of conflict.

3.1 Demographic and socio-economic background

The Republic of Macedonia has a population of just over 2 million people, with a land area of 26,000 square kilometres. One of the successor states of the Socialist Federative Republic of Yugoslavia, it borders Albania, Bulgaria, Serbia, Greece and Kosovo. As a distinct political-territorial entity, Macedonia was established only in mid-1944, and soon afterwards it joined the Socialist Federative Republic of Yugoslavia as one of six republics. Macedonians were at the same time recognized as one of the constituent nations of the new Yugoslavia. The republic itself, however, contained sizeable numbers of members of other ethnic groups. According to the 1953 census, of the more than 1.3 million Yugoslav citizens of the republic, 860,699 declared their ethnic background as Macedonian, 162,524 as Albanian, 203,938 as Turkish, 35,112 as Serb, 20,462 as Roma, and 8,668 as Vlach (see table 4.1).[5]

By the time of the 2002 census, these figures had changed dramatically. What was once the largest non-Macedonian ethnic community in the now independent state – Turks – had shrunk to some 40 per cent of its former size (77,959). This can be explained primarily by the Yugoslav–Turkish agreement in the 1950s concerning the transfer of ethnic Turks from Yugoslavia to Turkey. Albanians, on the other hand, more than tripled in absolute number (509,083 in 2002) and more than doubled their proportion in the total population of Macedonia to over 25 per cent, mostly because of a significantly higher birth rate and intra-Yugoslav migration (see figure 4.1).

This shifting balance in the population of Macedonia has also had a socio-economic impact. Ethnic Albanians, far less urbanized than Macedonians, suffered disproportionately from rural economic underdevelopment. This created a situation in which unemployment among ethnic Albanians generally grew – by 2001, less than 20 per cent of working-age Albanians were believed to be formally employed (ESI 2002) – and their representation among public-sector employees is less than half of their proportion in the population overall.[6]

The rural concentration of ethnic Albanians, combined with underdevelopment and underemployment in the public sector, also affected the educational opportunities for the ethnic minority. On the one hand, educational

Table 4.1 The ethnic demography of Macedonia, 1953–2002

	1953		1961		1971		1981		1991		1994		2002	
	Number	%	Number	%	Number	%	Number	%	Number	%	Number	%	Number	%
Macedonian	860,699	66.0	1,000,854	71.3	1,142,375	69.4	1,279,323	67.1	1,328,187	65.3	1,295,964	66.6	1,297,981	64.2
Albanian	162,524	12.6	183,108	13.1	279,871	17.1	377,208	19.8	441,987	21.8	441,104	22.7	509,083	25.2
Turkish	203,938	15.7	131,484	9.4	108,552	6.6	86,591	4.6	77,080	3.8	78,019	4.0	77,959	3.9
Roma	20,462	2.2	20,606	1.5	24,505	1.5	43,125	2.3	52,103	2.6	43,707	2.3	53,879	2.7
Serb	35,112	2.8	42,728	3.1	46,465	2.9	44,468	2.4	42,775	2.1	40,228	2.1	35,939	1.8
Vlach	8,668	0.7	8,046	0.6	7,190	0.5	6,384	0.4	7,764	0.4	8,601	0.5	9,695	0.5
TOTAL	1,304,514	100	1,406,003	[99]	1,647,308	[98]	1,909,136	[96.6]	2,033,964	[96.0]	1,945,932	[98.2]	2,022,547	[98.3]

Source: Ilievski (2007).

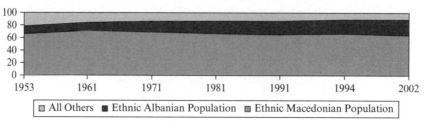

Source: *Ilievski (2007).*

Figure 4.1 *Relative proportion among the population of ethnic Albanians and Macedonians, 1953–2002*

facilities in rural communities were less well developed while, on the other, ethnic Albanians were less keen to finish secondary education, let alone obtain a university qualification, because they did not perceive any value in this, given their lack of opportunities to gain public or private sector employment. The lack of Albanian-language higher education facilities further limited the opportunities for ethnic Albanians to gain university degrees. Unsurprisingly, the lack of development, employment and education combined to inflame the situation and fed into a vicious circle in which the ethnic Albanian community in Macedonia perceived its increasingly desperate situation as the result of a deliberate policy of discrimination. Yet the lack of ethnic Albanian university graduates in Macedonia, in particular, and their consequent under-representation in public sector employment, can be blamed only in part on the short-sightedness of Macedonian government policy to refuse the establishment of an Albanian-language university. The closing of Prishtina University in Kosovo, which had served as a major centre for Albanian-language university education throughout the region, by the Milošević regime in the early 1990s was another significant contributory factor (Ilievski 2007).

The perception, on the part of ethnic Albanians, of being wronged by a system ultimately biased against them was further aggravated by the fact that the education system facilitates segregation between the two communities. The concentration of Albanians in rural areas creates, for many of them, an educational environment devoid of any contact with ethnic Macedonian students. Where mixed schools exist, classes are separated between the two communities, as they study in their respective native languages. Moreover, ethnic Albanians attend classes in which they are taught the Macedonian language only from third grade onwards, making it effectively a foreign language and limiting opportunities for them to become truly bilingual; Albanian-language tuition for Macedonian students remains a rare exception. Segregation between the two communities at this early age was further exacerbated by the instrumentalization of the education system for political purposes: students of both groups are frequently called upon by the political

elites of their community to boycott classes and protest against specific policies seen as discriminatory or unduly favouring the 'other side'.[7]

3.2 The political system in post-independence Macedonia: corrupt elite exchanges and grass-roots polarization and radicalization at the local and state levels

Macedonia gained its independence from Yugoslavia in 1991. However, since
it was one of the poorer republics of the federation and thus heavily dependent on subsidies from the centre, independence had not been the first preference of the country's political elites. Yet, by the time that the then Macedonian
president, Kiro Gligorov, presented a proposal for confederation, the process
of Yugoslav disintegration had progressed beyond the point of no return.
Secession was seen as preferable to being left in a Serb-dominated rump
Yugoslavia, and a referendum was called. Boycotted by ethnic Albanians, the
referendum saw some 95 per cent of the 72 per cent of participating voters,
including Macedonians living abroad, approve of independence. Contrary to
the developments in Slovenia, Croatia, and Bosnia and Herzegovina, no hostilities broke out between Serbia and Macedonia, and the Yugoslav People's
Army (JNA) had peacefully left the country by April 1992 – taking with it, however, every piece of equipment that it could. Therefore, from the very point
of its inception, the new Macedonian state was in a very precarious situation,
with ill-equipped and underfunded security forces.

Macedonia has two major Macedonian and two major ethnic Albanian parties fighting over the respective vote in their communities while governing
in coalitions, normally based on ideological proximity. The two dominant
ethnic Macedonian parties are the Macedonian Revolutionary Organization–
Democratic Party for Macedonian National Unity (VMRO–DPMNE) and the
Social-Democratic Union of Macedonia (SDSM), which in turn is in alliance
with the smaller Liberal-Democratic Party (LDP). The first is a right-of-centre
party without links to the former communist party, whereas the SDSM is
more left-of-centre and carries structural and personal legacies from the
communist past. It led the governing coalitions in Macedonia between 1991
and 1998, working jointly with the Albanian Party for Democratic Prosperity
(PDP), which had a similar left-wing orientation and traced its roots to partisan and socialist origins. In 1998, VMRO–DPMNE gained most seats in the parliamentary elections and entered into a coalition with the Democratic Party
of Albanians (DPA), which was born from a merger, in 1997, of the People's
Democratic Party (NDP) and the Party for Democratic Prosperity of Albanians
(PDPA). The NDP had been one of the two ethnic Albanian parties formed in
1990 (the other one being the dominant PDP), while the PDPA was founded
in 1994 after a radical faction, dissatisfied with the compromises the PDP had
made in government, was expelled from that party.

The 1998 elections are interesting in two ways. First, despite their policy differences and significant levels of personal enmity between party leaders, the two ethnic Albanian parties – PDP and DPA – cooperated in the elections and gained twenty-five seats, fourteen for the PDP and eleven for the DPA. Second, the government coalition that emerged between VMRO–DPMNE and the DPA, as well as the smaller Macedonian Democratic Alternative, seemed to 'unite' the polar opposites of the Macedonian political scene. VMRO–DPMNE and DPA had obviously nationalist, ethnocentric agendas aimed at promoting the interests of their own communities. Yet governing in a coalition suited both their aims. For VMRO–DPMNE, including an Albanian partner in the government meant that there would be less of a challenge from the Albanian community, a lesson learned from, and a 'tradition' continued in the vein of, seven years of SDSM/PDP government. Being a part of government allowed the DPA, on the other hand, to turn the tables on the PDP: much in the manner that the latter had used its position in the governing coalitions after 1991 to reward its supporters, the DPA managed to get ethnic Albanians appointed in highly visible and significant posts, thus being able to elevate its cadres to key offices (in the ministries of justice, labour and local self-government, as well as local police chiefs) and send signals to the ethnic Albanian community in Macedonia as a whole about how successfully it worked in the interests of its people. As a result, the PDP became increasingly marginalized within the Albanian community, leading almost to its complete paralysis by the late 1990s and the replacement of its leadership.

Throughout the 1990s, the political system in Macedonia thus found itself under significant stress from two sources domestically. First, the main political parties in each of the two dominant ethnic groups – Macedonians and Albanians – competed with their main intra-group rival for a limited number of votes. Among ethnic Albanians in particular, this state of affairs contributed to the growth of intense ethnocentric rhetoric, especially at election time. Each of the two parties tried to give itself the image of the more determined defender of their group's interests. Once in power, however, the reality of governing a deeply divided country with few resources, and often fewer political skills, meant that one-time radical activists became moderates. With no one else is this more obvious than with the DPA leader Arben Xhaferi, who soon after joining the VMRO–DPMNE government in 1998 declared that 'Albanians have made an agreement with Macedonia and do not want to destroy it. Democracy of consensus is a guarantee of stability and peace in Macedonia' (ICG 2000). Yet, in the same way in which the PDP had lost its credibility with a large section of the ethnic Albanian electorate by 1998–9, the DPA's more consensus-oriented approach eventually backfired when a majority of ethnic Albanians failed to see any real improvement in their own situation.

The second source of stress from which the Macedonian political system suffered was the increasing level of tension between its two main ethnic groups. It had always been present, even before the country's independence in 1991, as members of both groups harboured deep distrust of each other's aspirations. At the geopolitical level, Albanians feared that the real agenda of ethnic Macedonians was either the establishment of a Greater Macedonia or union with Bulgaria. Such suspicions were matched by concerns among ethnic Macedonians that a majority of their Albanian co-citizens sought the creation of a Greater Albania at the expense of Macedonia. At the everyday level, ethnic Albanians felt that they would never achieve real social, economic, cultural and political equality in the country, even though they made up 25 per cent, and potentially more, of its population. Macedonians, on the other hand, remained distrustful of ethnic Albanian politicians' declarations that apparently committed them to democracy in Macedonia while seeing them maintain links with Kosovo, and the KLA in particular, and being involved in organized crime. At the same time, both groups became disillusioned with the country's political class as a whole: Macedonians because they saw too many concessions being made to Albanians; Albanians because these concessions remained mostly on paper and did not translate into real-life improvements; and both because none of the governments after 1991 managed to turn the country's desperate economic situation around. The deep polarization of both communities at the grass-roots level and the increasing radicalization, especially of the large number of young unemployed ethnic Albanians, thus came to create a situation by the end of the 1990s in which the traditional elite consensus failed more and more to manage inter-ethnic tensions below the threshold of violence.

The relatively brief period of violence that ensued began in late 2000 and ended with the conclusion of the Ohrid Framework Agreement (OFA) in August 2001. The settlement provided in the OFA had become possible only after the (Albanian) PDP and DPA, who had earlier agreed to join a government of national unity, had adopted a common political platform with the National Liberation Army (NLA), an ethnic Albanian guerrilla group in Macedonia heavily linked to, and supported by, the KLA in neighbouring Kosovo. Moreover, achieving a political settlement facilitated a face-saving solution for both sides: Macedonians could claim a military victory following the withdrawal and subsequent disarmament of the NLA, while ethnic Albanians could point to the concessions they had achieved in the OFA. Yet all was not well. Diaspora Macedonians mobilized and forced a referendum on the planned redistricting of local government units. The referendum was defeated, but it demonstrated that there was significant resentment among Macedonians about the OFA. On the ethnic Albanian side, in June 2002 the NLA formed its own political party, the Democratic Union for Integration (DUI), and immediately became both the largest ethnic Albanian party in the September 2002 parliamentary elections and the third-largest party overall in parliament, with almost 12 per cent of the total votes cast. Subsequently, the DUI joined a coalition government with the SDSM and the small Liberal Democratic Party. Four years later it increased both its share in the vote (to 12.1 per cent) and its seats in parliament (to seventeen) in an electoral coalition with the PDP and the League of Bosniaks. The electoral campaign was marred by serious violence between parties of the same community, with DUI and DPA supporters clashing on several occasions – as did, on at least one occasion, the supporters of VMRO–DPMNE and SDSM. With the victorious party on the Macedonian side being VMRO–DPMNE, the DUI, although it had won the intra-Albanian contest, found itself outside government, while the DPA, who had gained only eleven seats, was invited into the governing coalition.

Perceiving its exclusion from the government coalition as a betrayal and a violation of a long-standing tradition that the largest Albanian party should form part of the government, the DUI/PDP coalition organized several protests and threatened to block any law in parliament that required concurrent majorities within both communities. Even though the PDP abandoned its coalition with the DUI and joined the government in May 2007, the DUI still commanded half of all ethnic Albanian seats in parliament. With forty-five policy areas requiring concurrent majorities before a law can be passed in parliament, the legislative process frequently came to a halt, and eventually early elections were called for June 2008. Intra-Albanian violence became even more the distinctive hallmark of the elections than had been the case in the 2006 campaign, forcing a rerun in 192 (out of just under 3,000) polling stations. The VMRO–DPMNE-led coalition won an absolute majority of sixty-three seats yet, weary of the legislative stalemate in the previous parliament, invited the DUI, which had won eighteen seats compared with the DPA's eleven, to join its coalition. The coalition agreement was formalized in July 2008, giving the government a total of eighty-one out of 120 seats in the Macedonian parliament. The PDP, once the dominant ethnic Albanian party, gained a mere 2.5 per cent of the ethnic Albanian vote and not a single seat in parliament. Soon after its defeat in the polls it announced its intention to merge with its erstwhile rival, the DPA. Yet, even so, the DUI remains the strongest ethnic Albanian party in Macedonia, commanding around 60 per cent of the total Albanian vote.

This outcome, both within the Albanian community and in terms of the likely stability of the new government in Skopje, bodes well for Macedonia's development. Provided political leaders take their responsibilities seriously and rise to the challenges of the mandate they were given by their electorate, Macedonia may eventually be able to overcome the consequences of more than a decade of internal and external threats to its statehood and identity.

3.3 The regional challenges to Macedonian statehood and identity: Albania, Bulgaria, Greece and Kosovo

The internal challenges to Macedonian statehood and identity – high levels of inter-ethnic tensions between the country's two main ethnic groups, a desperate economic situation, and low state capacity to deal with both – were matched by an equally difficult external environment in which Macedonia had to prove and defend its viability as an independent state.

Unlike the case in Slovenia, Croatia, and Bosnia and Herzegovina, the Serbian leadership had little interest in opening another front in the bloody disintegration of Yugoslavia in Macedonia. Despite occasional ramblings by hard-line nationalists that Macedonia had never really been anything but South Serbia (its name during the inter-war years of the first Yugoslavia), and the fact that the Serbian Orthodox Church to this day refuses to recognize the Macedonian Orthodox Church as a separate and independent entity, the very small number of ethnic Serbs in the country and the not limitless military capacity of Serbia ensured that Milošević's appetite to resist Macedonia's declaration of independence was relatively small.[8] While Macedonia was not challenged militarily in its independence, the external threats to its statehood and identity were nonetheless formidable and can be divided into two different types: on the one hand, Bulgaria and Greece challenged the very idea of the existence of a distinct Macedonian nation while, on the other, Albania and Kosovo proved a threat to the social, political and territorial integrity of the new state. All of these different threats and challenges fed into, and exacerbated, domestic shortcomings and tensions.

Historically, the 'Macedonian Question', as a question of national identity, is related to territorial disputes, primarily between Greece, Serbia and Bulgaria. The creation of a Bulgarian Orthodox Church and its recognition by the Ottoman Empire in 1870 required the territorial delimitation of this Church's authority. Apart from present-day Bulgaria, this territory also included the then Ottoman province of Macedonia, which, in turn, was perceived as a challenge to Serb and Greek national and territorial aspirations. Competition among these three aspiring nation-states culminated in the Balkan wars of 1912–13 and resulted in the territorial division of the Ottoman province of Macedonia, with the lion's share – Vardar Macedonia and Aegean Macedonia – going to Serbia and Greece, respectively, and only Pirin Macedonia remaining with Bulgaria.[9] Yet, as noted earlier, a Macedonian nation proper was 'established' and equipped with the symbols and status of statehood only in 1944 as part of the process that led to the creation of socialist Yugoslavia. While Macedonia was thus relatively secure as part of Yugoslavia, the breakup of the federation in 1991 reopened those dimensions of the Macedonian question that were related to Greek and Bulgarian claims.

Both countries' claims vis-à-vis Macedonia are distinct, yet together they pose a serious challenge to Macedonian identity and statehood, even though they never explicitly made any territorial claims.[10] Bulgaria, while among the first to recognize Macedonia as a newly independent state, 'refused to acknowledge the separateness of the Macedonian language from Bulgarian' and thus implicitly denied the existence of a Macedonian nation (Engström 2002: 6). Macedonia and Bulgaria are also at odds over the 'ownership' of St

Kliment Ohridski, a key figure in both nations' historical narrative and vari-
ably credited as the father of their respective languages and literatures. He
died in 916 in Ohrid – at the time part of the first Bulgarian Empire, today
part of Macedonia. The town of Ohrid, moreover, is claimed by both nations as
the cradle of their national cultures and churches. While these contradictory
narratives continue to exist side by side, the language dispute was eventually
resolved in 1999 as part of a larger package of agreements between the countries that also confirmed that neither had any territorial claims on the other.

The dispute between Greece and Macedonia, however, continues unabated.
Initially, Greece completely refused to accept that the name 'Macedonia'
could be applied 'to anything that was not Greek'. Greece further alleged that
the 1991 constitution of Macedonia made territorial claims to the Greek province of the same name, and rejected the use of the so-called Vergina sun as
part of the Macedonian flag, claiming it as an integral part of Greek cultural
heritage (ibid.). The name issue was temporarily resolved in 1993 when agreement was reached at the UN to admit Macedonia under the designation 'the
former Yugoslav Republic of Macedonia', and the two sides eventually agreed
in 1995 on a change to the Macedonian flag (removing the Vergina sun) and a
revision of the Macedonian constitution (removing alleged territorial claims
on Greece). While this dispute at times has reached farcical dimensions,[11] it
continues to this day. At present, and short of a permanent resolution to the
name dispute, Greece has vetoed an invitation for Macedonia to join NATO;
even though the country had officially been granted EU candidate status in
2005, official accession negotiations had not been opened by 31 July 2009.[12]
Alongside the double effects of the UN blockade on Yugoslavia in the early
1990s and the Greek blockade until 1993 and near-civil war in 2001, the
delays in joining NATO and the EU are clearly among the most serious threats
to stability and development in Macedonia.

The challenges to Macedonian statehood and identity from Albania and
Kosovo are of a different kind, yet they are no less severe, as they are
most directly linked to the inter-ethnic relations between Albanians and
Macedonians and thus had, and possibly still have, the greatest potential for
escalating tensions between the two groups into open violence. Albania faced
a whole host of serious challenges throughout the 1990s, when the country
embarked on a long and arduous transition from its isolationist communist
past to a more open, European and democratic future, culminating in the
country's collapse in 1997 following the implosion of a financial pyramid
scheme that wiped out the life-time savings of more than half of the Albanian
population. From the beginning Albania was keen on establishing good relations with Macedonia and emphasized that tensions between Macedonians
and ethnic Albanians needed to be resolved within the borders and constitutional framework of Macedonia. Occasionally, the Albanian governments
of Sali Berisha between 1991 and 1997 would issue statements of support for
their 'ethnic brethren' in Macedonia, but generally they abided by a policy

of non-interference, prioritizing state-to-state relations over the affinity link with ethnic Albanians in the northeastern neighbour (see Jenne 2007; Koinova 2008; Perry 1992; Reuter 1995; Thayer 1999). Nonetheless, a potential threat to Macedonia's identity as the nation-state of ethnic Macedonians lay even in the relatively low-key policy vis-à-vis Macedonia and its ethnic Albanian community, in which Albanians, and other ethnic groups, would be accorded certain minority rights but not treated as co-equal or constituent nations.

The lack of Albanian enthusiasm to become involved in the tensions in Macedonia throughout the 1990s has its reasons also in the preoccupation of Albanian foreign policy as a kin state with Kosovo, where the rhetoric was often sharper and where more significant support was lent to the independence movement. Most importantly, the collapse of public order in 1997 and the looting of army arsenals provided arms for the KLA, while Albanian army cadres acted as trainers and Albanian territory served as a safe haven for KLA guerrillas (Koinova 2008). It is primarily through this support of Kosovo that Albania posed a challenge (albeit indirect) to Macedonian statehood and identity. This, however, also underlines that the threat from Kosovo was far more severe and significant.

Clan and familial links between ethnic Albanians in Macedonia and Kosovo predate the foundation of Yugoslavia. Many ethnic Albanians took refuge in Macedonia during the 1980s when, following the death of Tito in 1980 and the escalation of ethnic Albanian demands for republican status in Yugoslavia, violence ensued in Kosovo. Throughout the 1990s, and in particular during NATO's bombing campaign against Serbia, ethnic Albanians in Macedonia once again offered shelter to their brethren and provided bases for the KLA. Moreover, party-political links between the DPA and one of the political parties to emerge from the KLA – Hashim Thaçi's Democratic Party of Kosovo – intensified and contributed to the climate of mistrust between the two communities in Macedonia (ICG 2000: 15). At the same time, ethnic Albanians from Macedonia were active as KLA guerrillas, while KLA splinter groups and the Liberation Army of Preševo, Medveðje and Bujanovac (UCPMB), operating in Albanian-populated areas of southern Serbia, had bases and training camps in western Macedonia. Already in the late 1990s there had been a number of attacks on police stations in Albanian-populated areas of Macedonia for which the KLA had taken responsibility (ICG 2001: 4). The idea of a Greater Kosovo, incorporating areas of southern Serbia and western Macedonia, had also been part of KLA rhetoric since that time. While the violence in the Macedonia–Kosovo border region brought the country to the brink of civil war in 2001,[13] it had actually been a regular presence in this region throughout the late 1990s, with isolated incidents dating back to 1992. Yet not all violent incidents can clearly be linked to the ethnic Albanian struggle for greater rights and participation. This area is rife with organized crime and simple smuggling dating back to the period of UN sanctions against the former Yugoslavia in the early 1990s (ibid.: 1). The proceeds from organized crime since then have often directly aided armed groups, making it possible for them to pay their soldiers and acquire weapons. As is common in such instances, the lines between criminality and political activity are blurred, and it is sometimes difficult to draw neat distinctions between politically motivated activists and freebooters.

Yet Kosovo mattered in another way, too, by setting a precedent for the utility of violence in the pursuit of political goals. In Kosovo, ethnic Albanians had unsuccessfully tried peacefully to improve their political status for almost two decades before, in the mid-1990s, the KLA began an organized campaign against the Milošević regime, which eventually succeeded in its aim of provoking the latter into a disproportionate response and engineering NATO involvement on the side of the KLA. While international actors did not go to similar lengths in the case of Macedonia (see below), they nonetheless acted as midwives for the OFA that introduced very substantial constitutional changes in Macedonia, among others increased decentralization and a reform of local government boundaries both to render districts ethnically more homogeneous and to create more areas with an ethnic Albanian majority. While this is a far cry from the federalization of the country once envisaged by Albanians in Macedonia, it constituted at the time a significant improvement of their status in a country in which they had long felt discriminated against.

3.4 International efforts to stabilize Macedonia: from preventive deployment to EU candidate status

Contrary to the regional-level challenges to Macedonian statehood and identity, the relevant factors at the international level were almost all consistently positive and aimed at Macedonia's stabilization in the face of the challenges the country encountered. The main players in this process were the UN, the NATO-led Kosovo Force (KFOR), the EU and the US. Other regional and international organizations, such as the OSCE, the Council of Europe and the World Bank, have also played a role in stabilizing Macedonia, but their impact on the development of the ethnic conflict was of a more indirect nature compared with the four actors that will be our focus in this section.[14]

As elsewhere in the Balkans, the United Nations was one of the earliest significant contributors to the international stabilization effort in Macedonia. Throughout the 1990s stabilization was seen mostly in terms of preventing a spillover of conflict from neighbouring crisis areas into Macedonia. Yet by the time a resolution was passed by the UN Security Council on 9 December 1992 mandating the extension of UNPROFOR to Macedonia,[15] the ground for de-escalation had already been prepared. The International Conference on the Former Yugoslavia's Working Group on Ethnic and National Minorities had defused much of the initial conflict potential by persuading ethnic Albanians to abandon their claims for territorial autonomy in exchange for Macedonian guarantees for improvements in Albanian-language education and media (see Ackermann 1996, 2000). The viability of this compromise was enhanced by the deployment of an OSCE Spillover Monitor Mission to Skopje in September 1992 and the subsequent deployment of UN peacekeepers from January 1993 onwards. This was the first UN mission ever to see a preventive deployment of peacekeepers, and, despite its relatively small number of only some 700 military personnel, it proved effective in monitoring the border between Macedonia and the Federal Republic of Yugoslavia (Serbia and Montenegro) and Albania. The UN mission was extended at regular intervals until 1999, when China used its veto in retaliation for Macedonia's recognition of Taiwan.

The withdrawal of UN peacekeepers came at a crucial time (1999), as the conflict in Kosovo escalated and NATO intervened with its bombing campaign. Since the withdrawal of UNPREDEP, the UN's role in the conflict in Macedonia has been limited to resolutions supporting the efforts of others to contain the ensuing violence and reach a consensual settlement.[16] Yet these others were, initially at least, less effective. NATO, mandated through Security Council Resolution 1244 (1999) to provide a security force for Kosovo, KFOR, deployed some 4,000 troops in Headquarters Rear in Skopje and took over the monitoring of the 130-mile long border between Kosovo and Macedonia. Only in March 2001 did NATO increase its activities and reinforce the border zone with some 300 British and Norwegian troops. It also provided a limited number of military advisors to the Macedonian government to help fight the NLA insurgency.[17]

NATO's real contribution to international stabilization efforts came in the implementation phase of the OFA. Already on 29 June 2001, six weeks before the signing of the agreement, NATO members approved the operational plan for Operation Essential Harvest, the collection of NLA weapons. Between 27 August and 26 September 2001 more than 3,300 weapons were collected, and on 27 September NLA leaders announced the complete disbandment of their forces. On the same day, and in order to avoid a security vacuum in Macedonia after the withdrawal of NATO troops, the NATO's North Atlantic Council activated Operation Amber Fox, thereby mandating the continued presence of some 1,000 NATO troops in Macedonia. It is important to note in this context that both NATO operations were at the explicit request of the Macedonian president, Boris Trajkovski, and thus did not require a formal UN mandate. However, the UN's support for these missions increased their broader legitimacy. Initially mandated for a period of only three months and tasked to provide security for the civilian OFA implementation monitors, Operation Amber Fox eventually concluded on 31 March 2003, by which time details of an EU successor mission had been finalized. That NATO has remained an important factor in the development of the situation in Macedonia became evident in the renewed controversy over the country's name in the context of NATO membership. The Greek veto at NATO's Bucharest summit on 1 April 2008 prevented an invitation of membership being extended to Macedonia and was the trigger for the Macedonian parliament's vote on 12 April to dissolve itself – a motion proposed by the DUI and supported by the VMRO–DPMNE, and with the domestic consequences detailed above.

The other major anchor of Macedonia's stability over the past decade has been the EU, which has been the country's most significant foreign donor of humanitarian and economic aid since the 1999 Kosovo conflict. On several occasions during the 2001 crisis, the EU expressed its support for the Macedonian government and urged the conflict parties to settle their differences peacefully. While at the time not yet in a position to launch its own military crisis management operation, the EU, through its foreign policy chief, Javier Solana, was instrumental in both negotiating the OFA and creating the conditions under which its implementation could succeed. Already in April 2001, when violence was still in full swing and fears of all-out civil war dominated the news headlines, the EU invited Macedonia to become the first country to conclude a Stabilization and Association Agreement in the framework of the Stability Pact for Southeastern Europe. This was symbolically and materially of high significance. It clearly signalled EU support for the government coalition, which by then had entered into negotiations with the SDSM and PDP to form a government of national unity,[18] and it made available a package of financial aid of almost $40 million. The EU also contributed to the actual negotiation of the OFA. When talks between the sides stalled in July 2001, it dispatched to the country its own envoy, François Léotard, who together with US diplomat James Pardew managed to unlock the talks and lead them to a successful conclusion a month later.

Subsequently, the EU has taken a greater role in providing security for Macedonia. Operation Concordia was the EU-led successor mission to NATO's operation Allied Harmony, mandated to ensure sufficient levels of security and stability in Macedonia to enable the continued implementation and operation of the 2001 OFA. Closely linked to the implementation of the OFA is the EU's Operation Proxima, a civilian police mission deployed to five locations across Macedonia to monitor, mentor and advise the country's police force and promote European policing standards. Both operations were concluded successfully – Concordia in December 2003, when a security presence was no longer deemed essential to monitor OFA implementation and operation, and Proxima in 2005. At the same time the EU Monitoring Mission, which has operated in the Western Balkans since 1991, retains a strong presence in Macedonia with a mission office and three team sites, in Kumanovo (near the border with southern Serbia), Tetovo and Struga (near the Albanian border). Since 2001 the EU has also had a special representative in Macedonia, who, since 2005, has been simultaneously head of the Commission delegation to the country. The establishment and maintenance of this office further underlines the EU's commitment to closer ties with Macedonia and the eventual promise of membership. Yet, as with NATO, the continuing name dispute between Macedonia and Greece poses a serious obstacle to the opening of formal accession negotiations.[19]

Despite the EU's continuing and increasing presence in, and commitment to, Macedonia, the United States remains the most influential player. Having recognized the country in early 1994 and established full diplomatic relations in 1995 after the Greek–Macedonian agreement on changes to the flag and constitution of Macedonia, the US has been a major donor, especially of military aid, ever since. In the context of the Ohrid Agreement, the US can be credited with dispatching two special envoys – Robert Frowick, who facilitated intra-Albanian talks that resulted in the joint PDP–DPA–NLA platform, and James Pardew, who, together with EU envoy François Léotard, in July 2001 presented a comprehensive framework agreement to the parties which formed the basis of the OFA concluded in August. In particular, Frowick's ability to forge a joint Albanian position was a major contribution to the eventual success in late July and early August 2001 of the negotiations in Ohrid. This was possible, in part, because of the significant weight held by the US among ethnic Albanians following the decisive intervention on their behalf in Kosovo in 1999. On the other hand, the US role in the actual negotiations in Skopje and later in Ohrid assured the Macedonian government that ethnic Albanians were unlikely to defect from the agreement, precisely because the US backed it and because they needed continued American support if they ever wanted to achieve an independent Kosovo. American influence in the country was further consolidated when the United States recognized Macedonia by its constitutional name in 2004, just prior to the referendum on the redistricting of municipalities. This move can also be credited with contributing to ensuring the defeat of the referendum, as it was seen by many Macedonians as an endorsement also of Macedonia's territorial integrity.

3.5 Motive, means and opportunity revisited: Macedonia, 1991–2008

Based on the empirical material presented so far in section 3 of this chapter, we can now apply our analytical framework more systematically and begin by establishing the relevant actors and structures at each of our four levels of analysis (see table 4.2).

At a domestic level, the ethnic conflict in Macedonia is characterized by two sets of relationships – the first between the two ethnic communities of Macedonians and ethnic Albanians and the second between rival factions of Albanian elites. These relationships are further shaped by the influence exercised by regional and global actors and structures. From this perspective we need to analyse primarily how the actions of ethnic Albanians and Macedonians, and especially of their respective elites, were enabled, or constrained, by various factors at each of these levels. In other words, we are not so much interested in explaining why, for example, Bulgaria took certain steps in relation to Macedonia at particular points in time, but rather what

Table 4.2 Macedonia through the prism of the levels-of-analysis approach[20]

	State structures and actors	Non-state structures and actors
Local (Albanian-populated areas, especially in western Macedonia)	• Political elites affiliated with ethnic Albanian political parties, esp. DPA, PDP, DUI • Local government authorities, incl. police and judicial officials • Decentralized structures of government • Impoverished rural economy	• Ethnic Albanian community • Macedonian community • Smugglers • Local branches of organized crime networks • Ethnic Albanian guerrilla groups, esp. NLA
State (Macedonia)	• Political elites of major national parties (VMRO–DPMNE, SDSM, DPA, PDP, DUI) • Government and presidency • Unitary, decentralized state structures • Slow-growing, post-socialist economy	• Ethnic Albanian community • Macedonian community • National branches of organized crime networks
Regional (Balkans)	• Albania • Bulgaria • Greece • Serbia • Sanctions regime	• Albanian communities in neighbouring countries • Albanian guerrilla groups in Kosovo and southern Serbia • Regional organized crime networks
Global	• UN[21] • NATO • EU • US • International law	• Macedonian diaspora

the impact of these was and how this impact helps us understand actions taken by the conflict parties.

As far as the motivations of ethnic Albanians go, the empirical material presented in the case study suggests a number of different motives that determined a greater or lesser appetite for the use of violence. Two of them clearly stand out. First, the desperate economic situation in which predominantly rural ethnic Albanians found themselves throughout the 1990s and which have persisted through to the early twenty-first century. Even though Macedonia as a whole suffers from the destruction of former Yugoslav economic structures and the subsidies these entailed, ethnic Albanians are disproportionately affected, not least also because of their lower rates of educational attainment, lower degree of urbanization and higher birth rates. The second motive is a certain degree of political disenfranchisement felt by ethnic Albanians at large: the highly centralized, unitary structure of the Macedonian state left little space for local self-government before 2001; ethnic Albanian political parties, to the degree that they shared power at the centre, delivered little, if anything, of their political platforms that would have contributed to measurable improvements in the living conditions of ordinary ethnic Albanians; and rivalries between these parties affected negatively both their ability to deliver and the image that they had in the broader ethnic Albanian population.

Several consequences can be attributed to this. First, many ethnic Albanians were able to survive only in the grey and black economies, especially through simple smuggling and through participation in larger-scale organized criminal activities. Second, their demands, articulated but rarely delivered on by their political elites, ranged from improved development to greater rights, but eventually centred on two issues: an improvement in Albanian-language education provision at all levels, including higher education, and a greater degree of political participation through both power sharing and self-governance. It took a decade after Macedonian independence, however, until the levels of frustration with their situation had grown to such an extent that existing political structures were seen as completely inadequate to achieve either of these aims. Moreover, by the turn of the century ethnic Albanian belligerence in the region as a whole had grown significantly – and been successful. Ethnic Albanians in Macedonia had supported the KLA and their ethnic brethren in Kosovo in their violent confrontation with the Milošević regime, learned valuable political and military lessons, and now also had access to arms, equipment and expertise. Readily available young, unemployed and frustrated ethnic Albanians provided the pool from which the NLA could draw its recruits; smuggling networks in Kosovo and southern Serbia facilitated the availability of arms and expertise; and a generally weak Macedonian state capacity, combined with an initially lacklustre international response, did little to curtail the build-up of the NLA guerrilla force. Broadly discredited ethnic Albanian political parties had lost their ability to contain the groundswell of discontent and the strong support that the guerrillas received locally. Where it had been possible, up to the late 1990s, to manage grass-roots frustrations through a system of clientelism distributing spoils among key local activists, this no longer worked as soon as there was a more activist 'counter-elite' willing and capable of using violence in pursuit of ethnic Albanian demands that had been left unsatisfied for a decade and more. Yet as soon as the NLA 'counter-elite' established itself as a political party, after achieving significant concessions on key Albanian demands in the OFA, violence aimed at the Macedonian state gave way to the traditional game of politics, bringing into sharp relief once more intra-Albanian rivalries that soon escalated into sporadic violence, especially around election time.

As much as it takes two to tango, ethnic conflict can hardly ever be attributed to the actions of one party alone. Why, then, did the Macedonian state, and especially the two dominant Macedonian parties that alternated in the exercise of power following the country's independence in 1991, not do more to avoid the violent escalation of Macedonian–Albanian relations in 2001? The core issues to consider here are state capacity, the electoral dynamics of the Macedonian political system, and the external challenges to Macedonian statehood and identity. First of all, Macedonia's general economic situation, affected badly by the sanctions against the former Yugoslavia and the land blockade by Greece in the context of the name and flag dispute between the two countries in the early 1990s, put extreme limits on the state's ability to invest significantly in its own development, attract foreign investment, and respond effectively to the demanding nature of a transition from a socialist to a liberal economy. This limited its capacity to address some core demands of its ethnic Albanian population – to invest in education and local development. In addition to these 'objective' limitations, one must consider that in a situation of general poverty, with around one-third of the population unemployed throughout the 1990s, concessions to minority demands are hardly popular, being often seen as taking away the few resources from those who are entitled to them – i.e., the titular nation. This translates both into tense inter-ethnic relations (as a result of competition over scarce resources) and into an intra-community political competition over which political party is better placed to defend the nation's interests. The kind of ethnic outbidding that followed saw the VMRO–DPMNE generally adopt more nationalist positions than the SDSM. While in government, both parties accepted the need to share power with their ethnic Albanian counterparts, thus forming an elite cartel that facilitated the kind of corrupt exchanges that discredited the political system more and more, and thus increased pressure on the Macedonian political parties to adopt a tough line in the face of ethnic Albanian demands. As a consequence, power sharing at the centre amounted to little more than a symbolic gesture that had material benefits for the ethnic Albanian elites participating in government but did not translate into real benefits for their constituents.

Limited state capacity also existed in relation to security forces. The withdrawal of the JNA in early 1992 left Macedonia with little usable military equipment or expertise, and the country's economic situation did not allow much investment in the security sector. The police forces were generally found wanting, were often corrupt, and were unprepared to deal with the NLA attacks from 2000 onwards. Military observers and advisors, provided to the Macedonian government through NATO's Partnership for Peace, were unable to shift the balance decisively in favour of the Macedonian government, whose options in responding to the NLA threat were thus further constrained. This, together with international pressure, incentives and mediation, prevented an escalation into full-scale civil war and brought about a government of national unity that, more or less willingly, entered into negotiations with the NLA before major loss of life occurred.

While the formation of a national unity government in May 2001 increased the room for manoeuvre of the Macedonian political parties, and while international pressure, incentives and mediation helped the two sides reach an acceptable compromise, this is not enough to explain in full why the Macedonian side felt it was able to accept that far-reaching a set of changes to the constitution, and the policy consequences that this brought with it, and why the Macedonian public did not take the opportunity offered by the diaspora-inspired referendum to reject the settlement package of the OFA. In the early 1990s, when it would have taken far less politically to accommodate ethnic Albanians than had to be conceded in 2001, Macedonia faced three very serious challenges to its statehood and identity – from Albania, Bulgaria and Greece and, to a lesser extent, from Serbia. Ten years on, Macedonian statehood and identity had been more or less consolidated. Albania had made it clear that, while it was concerned about the well-being of ethnic Albanians in Macedonia, it did consider this first and foremost a domestic Macedonian affair. Bulgaria and Macedonia had, in 1999, found a formula that made it possible for them to enjoy good neighbourly relations without undermining each other's identity as distinct nations. Even though the dispute with Greece was far from over, an interim solution had been accepted by both sides that allowed Macedonia to become a full member of the international community and, most importantly, enter into economic, political, and security arrangements with European and transatlantic institutions. Before these challenges had been addressed, Macedonian political elites found it impossible to make any significant concessions to ethnic Albanians in the newly independent state, especially if these concessions were of a nature that would further question the viability of the state or its identity.

The Kosovo crisis of 1999, and its aftermath, also posed a significant threat to the project of a Macedonian state, especially at a time when frustration among ethnic Albanians inside Macedonia grew and when military expertise and equipment became more readily available. International intervention on behalf of the Kosovo Albanians did not initially put Macedonian minds at rest either, yet, as the same international actors subsequently sided firmly with the Macedonian government – insisting that the country's territorial integrity and sovereignty were inviolable – helped to bring the ethnic Albanian factions together and to the negotiation table, and mediated and endorsed the OFA, this was seen as sufficient insurance against later Albanian defections and renewed escalation of the conflict. The role of factors at the international level, while particularly prominent during and after the 2001 violent escalation, must not be underestimated with regard to the 1990s. Undoubtedly, the preventive deployment of UN peacekeepers, early mediation to dissuade ethnic Albanians from escalating their demands, and the facilitation of a crucial Greek–Macedonian compromise contributed to

Macedonia's stabilization in the years after independence and prevented an otherwise highly likely spillover of violence. The withdrawal of UNPREDEP occurred at a time when the conflict in Kosovo escalated, when links between radicalized Albanians throughout the former Yugoslavia intensified, and when the attention of the international community, especially of the US, shifted decidedly to regime change in Serbia as a top priority. It is hardly a coincidence, then, that some among Macedonia's ethnic Albanians perceived far better opportunities to pursue their aims with violence and had the means available to do so.

This account of the situation in Macedonia from 1991 to 2008 has relied on a single framework of analysis, assessing how factors at four levels of analysis – from the local to the global – affect the motives, means and opportunities of key domestic actors in an ethnic conflict. While we have shown why violent escalation occurred in 2000–1, but neither before nor since, we have implicitly relied on a number of individual theories of ethnic conflict. Economic explanations hold partly true: there was a readily available pool of recruits, diaspora support was forthcoming, and conflict-specific capital was in rich supply. Yet these factors alone do not fully explain the events of 2000–1: there were also real grievances among ethnic Albanians that had built up over a decade, had been left unaddressed, and had contributed to deep disaffection with the political system and high levels of mistrust between the two communities. The security dilemma approach also helps us make sense of the events: Macedonians, when confronted with a military insurgency for the first time since independence, and with the example of Kosovo in fresh memory, could not but try to meet force with force until external security guarantees began to be provided, and ethnic Albanians could not accept disarmament before they could be sure that the deal they had negotiated would stick. Comparing the situation in 2000–1 with that of the preceding decade, we find that the absence of most of these factors explains the lack of conflict as much as it does for the years after the Ohrid Framework Agreement. In particular, the ability of both sides to refrain from an arms race and from threatening the use of violence has meant that neither perceives a security dilemma, a situation that is further aided by the presence of a range of international actors and the country's stronger ties with the European Union. In the 1990s, an arms race that could have led to a security dilemma was prevented by an effective international peacekeeping presence, the limited economic capacity of the Macedonian state, and an elite compromise that kept aggressive rhetoric in check. Economic 'opportunities' for conflict were equally more limited and grievances less pronounced, in particular because political elites managed to exercise sufficient control over their communities through a system of clientelism and in the absence of a viable 'counter-elite' that could have undermined such corrupt elite exchanges. A final point that it is worth making here is that both the lack of conflict in the 1990s and its swift containment in 2000–1 were significantly helped by the fact that there are no deeply traumatic events in the history of the two communities that would have led either one of them to believe that its very existence was under acute threat.

4 Conclusion

The cases studies we have examined here are all in some ways as different from one another as they are similar. They are similar in that we cannot give a proper account of the causes and consequences of such conflicts without considering actors and structures at all levels of analysis – from the local to the international. They are different in the sense that actors and structures at these levels matter, and interact, in different ways in the conflicts we have discussed. Poverty and the lack of fully functional social and political structures facilitate the goals of ethnic entrepreneurs who seek to accumulate political capital by essentializing ethnic difference, as in Rwanda, and they provide a degree of legitimacy for criminal entrepreneurs, as in Georgia and Mindanao. Similarly, history matters in justifying one's own actions: it becomes acceptable to use violence first if history 'proves' the malign intent of others and a secure future cannot be predicted confidently in the face of collapsing or non-existent state structures, as all our cases vividly demonstrate. Links across borders can be enabling for some actors and add to the threats perceived by others, as illustrated by the case of Macedonia. Yet, Macedonia also shows very clearly that recognizing such a pathway to escalation can be an important tool to stop a downward spiral to violence.

Part II

Responses to Ethnic Conflict

5

The Prevention, Management and Settlement of Ethnic Conflicts

1 Introduction

Conflict regulation, in our view, comprises three elements – prevention, management and settlement. This distinction, and the very terminology we use, may seem arbitrary, and we do not claim to offer the definitive resolution to a long-standing debate in the literature on responses to ethnic conflict. We are using prevention, management and settlement as concepts to aid in the understanding of different policies pursued by the parties to an ethnic conflict and by third parties involved in it. This becomes immediately clear when we consider the following three definitions.

Conflict prevention refers to a set of policies adopted at an early stage in a conflict, before violent escalation or after a ceasefire/settlement has been negotiated to prevent the resumption of violence. Conflict prevention aims at channelling conflict into non-violent behaviour by providing incentives for peaceful accommodation and/or raising the costs of violent escalation for conflict parties. Normally, a distinction can be made between short-term crisis management (averting an imminent escalation in violence) and long-term structural prevention (eliminating the root causes of conflict). While conflict prevention thus has a place in the life cycle of an ethnic conflict before its violent escalation and after its settlement, conflict management and conflict settlement can be defined more clearly in terms of a 'single moment' at which they occur. We thus define *conflict management* as the attempt to contain, limit or direct the effects of an ongoing ethnic conflict. In contrast, *conflict settlement* aims at establishing an institutional framework in which the opposing interests of different ethnic groups can be accommodated to such an extent that incentives for cooperation and the non-violent pursuit of conflicts of interest through compromise outweigh any benefits that might be expected from violent confrontation. Thus, conflict management is a strategy that is chosen in one of two situations – when the settlement is either impossible or undesirable for one of the parties involved. Furthermore, conflict management is not always a benign attempt to contain an ethnic conflict and limit its negative consequences; it can also be a strategy of manipulation that seeks the continuation of a conflict for reasons beyond the conflict itself, such as the preservation of power and/or economic gain. Conflict management, thus, describes the wide range of policies adopted by actors instead of negotiations, or after failed negotiations or implementations, whereas conflict settlement implies negotiated, accepted and implemented institutional structures.[1] In this sense, conflict settlement and conflict prevention, if successful, have fairly similar outcomes.

Having made these conceptual distinctions, we need to acknowledge that, in practice, conflict prevention, management and settlement often occur in parallel, and in some cases the same policy can even be seen as prevention from one perspective and as management from another. For example, in the Balkans during the break-up of Yugoslavia, the UN, and later NATO, deployed a border monitoring mission to Macedonia in order to *contain* the violent conflict that took place in other parts of Yugoslavia and to *prevent* it from escalating the tensions that already existed in this country into full-blown violence. Prevention, moreover, is a difficult idea anyway, as it always has to rely on counterfactuals: was something really prevented or did it simply not happen because its likelihood was exaggerated from the start? In addition, was one particular preventive policy responsible for its not happening? These questions may be relatively easy to answer in the case of Macedonia, where violence did eventually break out in 2001 in the aftermath of NATO's intervention in Kosovo, which had brought, temporarily, several hundred thousand refugees from Kosovo to Macedonia, set an important precedent for minorities and, in the case of Macedonia, provided equipment and know-how on how to fight a guerrilla war. In other words, had the border monitoring mission been able to control the flow of refugees better, and stepped in when weapons were smuggled across the border and when Macedonian and Kosovo Albanian guerrillas crossed the border in both directions between safe havens and operations, violent escalation might have been avoided. As it did not, NATO and the EU were left to manage and resolve the resulting conflict by swiftly containing it through pressure on all sides and by both strengthening their border mission and pressing the parties, including the (ethnically Albanian) National Liberation Army (NLA), to sign up to the Ohrid Framework Agreement, the aim of which was to provide the institutions where the competing claims of Macedonians and ethnic Albanians could be resolved. The answer is less clear with reference to Burundi in the early 1990s. While it could be argued that genocide similar to that in Rwanda was prevented, around 150,000 people died in inter-ethnic violence. With short intense periods of violence having been a common feature in Rwanda since independence in 1962 and the ascent to power of parties representing the majority Hutu, the question is not only whether conflict prevention is a constantly moving target (from preventing violence to preventing genocide) but whether, whereas it had never been the case before, genocide was indeed on the cards in 1993.[2]

In the following we explore three further sets of conceptual issues that are relevant for our understanding of conflict regulation. First we demonstrate the relevance of our levels-of-analysis approach for the theory and practice of conflict regulation. Second, we offer a broad overview of different options for conflict settlement – a menu, as it were, of different mechanisms that apply in specific situations of conflict – and subsequently discuss, with particular reference to conflict settlement, the nature and dynamics of its three distinct phases of negotiation, implementation and operation. Third, we examine the different policy instruments available to the international community, and the different individual and collective actors within it, towards achieving outcomes that can provide sustainable settlements to ethnic conflicts. In conclusion, we return to our levels-of-analysis approach and consider how success and failure of international conflict regulation can be explained.

2 Mapping the situation

The various case studies on which we have so far drawn to illustrate our arguments demonstrate clearly that most of today's ethnic conflicts are complex situations determined by multiple factors that shape the agendas of the individual parties and provide opportunities and constraints for their realization. Since one of our basic premises is that ethnic conflicts can, in principle, be settled by establishing institutions that will allow the parties to have their grievances addressed effectively, we need to put ourselves in a position, first of all, in which we can gain clarity about three sets of issues before we proceed to make any attempt to prescribe the right 'mix' of institutions for a particular conflict situation. Thus we need to determine (1) the concerns and demands of the conflict parties, (2) the relevant actors at local, state, regional and global levels and what the balance of power is between them, and (3) the factors that shape their opportunity structures and motivations.

2.1 Fault lines of ethnic conflict: ethnicity and territory

As we have seen in chapter 2, ethnicity is an important resource around which conflict groups can crystallize. The more central it is to the identity of the groups, the more every aspect of the conflict will be seen through the prism of ethnicity. 'Ethnic difference per se is not necessarily the cause of conflict in communities with a diverse ethnic composition. However, when and where conflict does occur . . . a common denominator in the period leading up to outright conflict and during conflict is the polarising of identity' (UNPO 2006). So let us be clear that ethnic conflicts are not in fact conflicts about ethnicity, but rather conflicts between ethnic groups (or between them and the states in which they live) that compete with each other over the resources that they consider essential in order to establish or preserve conditions that are conducive to the preservation, expression and development of their individual and group identities. Thus ethnic groups are likely to have concerns about the conditions in which they live that normally fall into one or more of the following categories: security, political participation, cultural identity, and economic opportunities that determine the political agenda they might

Table 5.1 Nature and addressees of ethnic claims

Nature of the claim	Addressee of the claim	Example
Self-determination Internal	Host state	Gagauz in Moldova, German-speakers in South Tyrol
External		Abkhaz in Georgia, Southerners in Sudan
Linguistic, religious and/or cultural rights	Host state/host nation	Roma across Central and Eastern Europe, Moros in the Philippines, Tatars in the Crimea
Access to resources/ equality of opportunity	Host state/host nation	Arabs in Israel, western movements in Darfur, Sudan
Material and/or political aid/support	Kin state	Armenians in Nagorno-Karabakh
	Kin nation/other kin group	Ethnic Hungarians in Romania and Slovakia
	International actors	Kosovo Albanians, Kurds in Iraq

pursue – secession (and possible unification with another state), autonomy, power sharing, more extensive cultural rights, etc. These political demands reflect both the historical continuities enshrined in group identities and the contemporary opportunities (or lack thereof) that groups perceive. As table 5.1 indicates, the resulting claims are generally related to one or more of four closely intertwined areas: self-determination; linguistic, religious and cultural rights; access to resources/equality of opportunity; and/or material and political aid in support of these other three claims. Ethnic minorities make these claims vis-à-vis their host state or their host nation, and/or, where applicable, their kin state or kin nation. In the absence of a kin state willing or able to support an external minority, kin groups in countries other than the kin state or other external actors (international organizations, individual states) may be sought out and lobbied to assume this patron role.

Alongside ethnicity, the other core component of many an ethnic conflict is territory. For states, territory possesses certain values in and of itself. These include natural resources, such as water, diamonds, precious minerals, oil or gas. They extend to the goods and services produced by the population living in this territory and the tax revenue generated from them, and they can comprise military or strategic advantages resulting from natural boundaries, access to the open sea, and control over transport routes and waterways. Throughout European history, many wars have been fought over territory, territories have changed hands as a result of wars, and as a consequence new wars have arisen.

Table 5.2 Nature and level of territorial claims

Nature of the territorial claim	Level of the territorial claim	Example
Irredentist/secessionist	Kin state vs. host state and group vs. host state	Northern Ireland pre-1998, Nagorno-Karabakh
Irredentist/non-secessionist/autonomist	Kin state vs. host state and group vs. host state	Alsace in inter-war period
Non-irredentist/secessionist	Minority vs. host state	Albanians in Kosovo, Southerners in Sudan
Non-irredentist/non-secessionist/autonomist	Minority vs. host state	Gagauz in Moldova, Moros in Philippines

Territory is very often a crucial component of the identity of ethnic groups, i.e., it is crucially linked to ethnicity. Territory is then conceptualized more appropriately as place, bearing significance in relation to the group's history, collective memories and 'character'. The deep emotional attachment to territory that ethnic groups can develop and maintain often leads to intense conflict. Nevertheless, for ethnic groups territory is, or can become, a valuable commodity as well, because it provides resources and a potential power base in their bid to defend or challenge the status quo. Territory, or rather control thereof, thus becomes crucially linked to ethnicity, as it may be one of the conditions whose presence or absence determine whether a group and its members feel that they are in a position in which they can fully express, preserve and develop their identity. In the case of groups with a kin or patron state, a relationship is also established between that state and the host state of the ethnic group, which shapes, and is in turn shaped by, the relationship held with the group by each of the states. In many cases, this state–state relationship is not so much determined by the concepts of 'ethnicity' and 'nation', but rather founded on the notion of 'territory', precisely because of the value territory has for states.

Territory thereby becomes a phenomenon of inter-state relations as well as of inter-ethnic relations and gives rise to three different kinds of claim: secession (if the group wants to establish its sovereign independence from the host state); irredenta (if a neighbouring/kin state seeks to 'acquire' the group and the territory on which it lives); and autonomy (when the group seeks a greater measure of self-governance within its host state). As illustrated in table 5.2, territorial claims by groups and states are not always compatible, and this is one of the most important drivers for ethnic conflict.

In their attempts to preserve, express and develop their distinct identities, ethnic groups perceive threats and opportunities. The more deeply felt are these perceptions, the more they will be linked to the very survival of the group and the more intense will be the conflict that they can potentially

a lot of this is about minority groups striving for recognition
but in Rwanda it was the majority...

84 ▨▨▨▨ *Responses to Ethnic Conflict* ▨▨▨▨▨▨▨▨▨▨▨▨▨▨▨▨

generate. This links the issue of ethnicity to the notion of political power. The connection between ethnicity and power has important political consequences in that any ethnic group that is conscious of its uniqueness, and wishes to preserve it, is involved in a struggle for political power. It seeks either to retain a measure of political power it already possesses, or it strives to acquire the amount of power that it deems necessary in order to preserve its identity as a distinct ethnic group – that is, to defeat the threats and seize the opportunities it faces. This desire to gain political power for an ethnic group is expressed in the concept of (ethno-)nationalism: according to Smith (1991: 20), 'an ideological movement aiming to attain or maintain autonomy, unity and identity for a social group which is deemed to constitute a nation'.

Often, incompatible nationalist doctrines are at the centre of the relationship between minority and host state. It is within this context that opportunity and threat have various yet concretely identifiable meanings. They may be either positively or negatively related to the preservation, expression and development of a group's ethnic identity and to the ability of the host state to preserve the integrity of the territorial or civic nation. For a minority, opportunities will manifest themselves, for example, through different regimes of self-government. Such rights may be realized in local, regional or federal frameworks within the host state. Alternatively, opportunities may also arise in the separation from the host state, leading either to independent statehood or, where applicable, to unification with the kin state. Threats generally occur when state institutions deny an ethnic group access to the resources that are essential for the preservation, expression and development of a group's identity – access to linguistic, educational or religious facilities as well as to positions of power in the institutions of the state. Threats can also become manifest in policies of unwanted assimilation, in discrimination and in deprivation. Put another way, ethnicity in itself does not cause conflict, but becomes a factor when groups seek domination by excluding 'others' defined in ethnic terms (INCORE 2006). At their most extreme, such domination attempts take the form of 'ethnic cleansing' and genocide.

It is in these most extreme cases that the relationship between minority and host *state* coincides with that between minority and host *nation* – that is, the titular or dominant ethnic group has monopolized all institutions of the state. So ethnicity becomes a point of contestation when dominant ethnic groups hold power to the exclusion of others, and in so doing assume an essential superiority over the remainder of society (INCORE 2006). Although recent European history has provided a number of examples of this kind, this is, nevertheless, not the rule. Yet, even in its less extreme forms, the relationship between minority and host nation is often characterized by inter-ethnic tension, resulting from the politicization and radicalization of different ethnic identities and claims for the establishment of conditions conducive to their preservation, expression and development. Responses to such claims are then perceived as threats and/or opportunities.

This is why we hold that ethnic conflict is best described as a form of conflict in which at least one of the parties involved interprets the conflict, its causes and potential settlements along an existing or perceived discriminating ethnic divide and pursues policies related to one or more of the ethnic and territorial claims outlined above. Participants in such conflicts may seek either to counter or to realize such claims. Thus ethnic conflict can occur either as group–state conflict, i.e., between an ethnic minority and the institutions of its host state, or as inter-ethnic conflict, i.e., between an ethnic minority and its host nation (or parts thereof). The two may, but need not, occur in parallel or coincide. In addition, as ethnic conflicts are rooted in the perception of threats and the policies formulated to counter them, they may also give rise to other forms of conflict within a country – for example, as a result of an actual or perceived 'over-accommodation' of the interests of an ethnic minority, which (sections of) the host nation may regard as being detrimental to their own interests. This is very often, but not necessarily, the case where accommodation of minority interests is pursued territorially, and the territory also contains a significant portion of members of the host nation. The simultaneous occurrence of inter-ethnic and group–state conflict is another potential reason for conflict between host state and host nation. As inter-ethnic conflict threatens the social integrity of the host state, actions of the host nation may be perceived as one source of this threat and be countered by the host state. This, in turn, can be perceived by the host nation, or at least by some sections within it, as being denied an opportunity to defend, or establish, conditions conducive to the preservation, expression and development of its own ethnic identity.[3] Table 5.3 gives

Table 5.3 Perceived threats as sources of ethnic conflict in the host state

		Threats perceived by	
	Group	Host state	Host nation
Group		Territorial integrity Societal integrity	Competition for resources deemed essential for the preservation, expression and development of ethnic identity
Host state	Unwanted assimilation Discrimination Deprivation Ethnic cleansing Genocide		'Over-accommodation' of minority interests
Host-Nation	Competition for resources deemed essential for the preservation, expression and development of ethnic identity[4]	Societal integrity	

(row label: Threats allegedly originating from)

an overview of the different types of threat (perceptions) that can become sources of ethnic conflict.

A somewhat different pattern of relationships emerges in cases where a minority has a kin state. Here, the relationship between the two is based on common ethnicity and a territorially divided ethnic nation, and is therefore normally not one of ethnic conflict, but rather one of patronage. Patronage results from one of two aspects, and often from a combination of both – national sentiment and national interest. Popular sentiment concerning the fate of members of the nation living in another state and the desire to unite the national territory and bring together in it all the members of the ethnic nation finds its expression in irredentist or pan-nationalism (Smith 1991: 83). Yet, as national sentiment is not always expressed in irredentist nationalism, so is the relationship between minority and kin state not always about secession and subsequent unification with the kin state. Informed by domestic and foreign national interests, territorial unification may not be considered desirable for either kin state or minority, or it may not be possible given geopolitical or regional interest and opportunity structures.[5] Alternatively then, the relationship between minority and kin state can be one of 'repatriation', as with the Federal Republic of Germany and ethnic German minorities in Central and Eastern Europe in the post-1950 and, especially, post-1989 period. Or it can be one of facilitating the establishment of conditions in the host state conducive to the preservation, expression and development of the ethnic identity of the kin groups in this state. With varying degrees of success, the numerous bilateral treaties concluded between the states of Central and Eastern Europe after 1989 testify to this.[6]

A conflictual relationship between minority and kin state is then likely to develop when their respective political agendas are mutually incompatible. This can be the case if the irredentist nationalism of the kin state is not reciprocated by the minority, or of sections within it, for which the cases of the Sudetenland (in Czechoslovakia) and Alsace (in France) during (parts of) the inter-war period are good examples. Vice versa, a conflict-prone relationship develops if the 'secessionism' of the kin group is not welcomed by the kin state, or when some of its manifestations are perceived as a threat to the kin state's security and relationship with the host state. There are two classic examples of this phenomenon. The first is South Tyrol, whose secessionism throughout most of the inter-war period was 'inconvenient' for both Austria and Nazi Germany. The second is Northern Ireland. In this instance, despite a formal constitutional commitment to 'irredentism' that existed in the form of Articles 2 and 3 of the Irish constitution until the end of 1999, violent Republicanism in the wake of partition in 1920 and the subsequent civil war was perceived as a threat to the Republic of Ireland. Yet these two cases also show that, given a responsive and responsible host state, a non-irredentist kin state can have a moderating effect on the policies pursued by its ethnic kin group abroad.

2.2 The conflict settlement menu and its demographic determinants

Once a conflict between ethnic groups, or between one group and the state, has emerged over competing claims to power, resources and status, the design of the macro-level institutions meant to enable the contestants to resolve their dispute by non-violent means depends, in significant part, on the demography of any given situation. The criteria according to which such a categorization can be undertaken, thus, include the size of communities (both in absolute terms and relative to the overall population of the state in which they live), their settlement patterns (compact, with or without exclaves; or dispersed, with or without local concentrations), the size of the territory they occupy (again in absolute and relative terms), whether this territory is ethnically more homogeneous or more heterogeneous, and whether they straddle existing international boundaries. These criteria are key factors in establishing the need for, and feasibility of, various institutional arrangements to ensure that their demands can be addressed adequately and appropriately.[7]

The importance of establishing such basic indicators of a particular situation must not be underestimated. Accurate data both on demographic indicators and on the demands that communities derive from them is crucial when thinking about possible institutional designs to ensure that violent conflict can be prevented or settled. A basic range of features of such institutional designs to manage the relationships between states and communities in a non-violent way can be outlined as including territorial and non-territorial forms of self-governance, local and central-level power sharing, cross-border institutions and para-diplomacy, and human and minority rights provisions. These can occur individually and in various combinations.

For illustrative purposes, consider the following cases. Chechens live in a largely homogeneous region in the northern Caucasus in south Russia. In 2004 it was estimated that the population of the area was somewhat over 1 million, of whom around 98 per cent were thought to be ethnic Chechens. In 1989, the last year for which we have reliable data, the total population was estimated to be in the region of 1,400,000, of whom 23 per cent were ethnic Russians. These figures illustrate a forgotten fact about the Chechen conflict, namely that the decline of ethnic Russians resident in the republic has been greater than that of their Chechen counterparts. The rebel demands range from the construction of an Islamic caliphate in the northern Caucasus, to independence or self-governance. Short of Russia agreeing to the region's secession, substantive autonomy for Chechnya and local arrangements to ensure fair treatment of non-Chechens (for example, through local power sharing, minority protection, local cultural autonomy and public participation rights) would be elements of a reasonable settlement, and are not unlike the agreement achieved after the first Chechen war. A relatively homogeneous region such as the French island of Corsica, on the other hand, where the relevant group in question does not straddle existing boundaries either, normally requires substantive autonomy only. As the Agreement on Northern Ireland (in both its original 1998 and revised 2006 versions) exemplifies, heterogeneous regions in which at least one of the groups concerned straddles international boundaries requires a broader range of institutions: substantive autonomy, regional power sharing and other local mechanisms to manage inter-community relationships, as well as cross-border institutions and para-diplomatic competences. The very homogeneous, and in demographic terms small, region of the Swedish-populated Åland Islands that are part of Finland has survived very comfortably for almost a century under a regime of substantive territorial autonomy and cross-border institutions.

With the partial exception of the Åland Islands, none of the cases just mentioned has seen a straightforward path to settlement. The Northern Ireland Agreement was preceded by thirty years of conflict, costing over 3,000 lives. Attempts to endow Corsica with adequate levels of self-governance have repeatedly faced stiff resistance in a country whose very foundations are built upon the assumption of the one and indivisible republic as the home for the one and indivisible French people speaking the national language of French. The best that can be said for Chechnya after years of war with terrible atrocities committed is that it is now experiencing a period of relative calm and stability, predicated, to a large extent, on the presence of Russian security forces and the alliance, quite possibly of mutual convenience, forged between the Russians and the powerful Kadyrov clan and their allies. Beyond these few European cases, the view that ethnic conflicts are often intractable is empirically further substantiated when one looks at the apparently unending conflicts that have plagued places as diverse as Sri Lanka, northeast India, the Great Lakes region of Africa, Sudan and the Middle East. The conflicts in these areas have cost millions of lives, displaced even greater numbers of people, wrecked entire national economies for decades, and seem to be 'solution-proof', notwithstanding the occasional glimmer of hope in the form of a short-lived peace deal.

Yet not all ethnic conflicts are that violent and destructive – Quebec and Belgium provide two cases in point – and there has been no serious violence in the Crimea, Romania, Slovakia and the Baltic states, despite the occasionally highly charged atmosphere between these countries' majority and minority populations. Nor do all ethnic conflicts permanently evade solutions: Northern Ireland has already been mentioned as an obvious case, but there are other examples as well. South Tyrol in Italy is often cited as one of the most successful instances of accommodating the claims of minority groups through autonomy and power sharing institutions. Constitutional arrangements in Bougainville, Mindanao and Gagauzia, for example, may not be perfect, but they have provided an institutional setting in which ethnic groups can pursue their self-determination claims by political, non-violent means.

3 The phases of conflict settlement: negotiation, implementation and operation

We conceive of conflict settlement as a three-stage process, comprising a negotiation phase, an implementation phase and an operation phase. Within this framework, the negotiation phase is the one which is the most significant for shaping the institutional design of the agreement, and thus the nature of the political process during both the implementation and operation phases. Moreover, today most settlement agreements are at the same time very complex post-conflict reconstruction plans, involving economic, social, cultural and other issues alongside constitutional design (see O'Leary 2005a; Paris and Sisk 2008; and Roeder and Rothchild 2005). Implementation refers to the process of putting in place the institutions and procedures agreed during negotiations. As this can often be a prolonged process, especially where agreements are complex and are applied to post-war situations (e.g., in Bosnia and Herzegovina) or require substantial legislative and administrative changes to existing structures (e.g., in Macedonia), implementation and operation often run in parallel for a considerable period of time. This means that the implementation of an entire settlement agreement is often far from complete when the former conflict parties have to operate at least part of the institutions established in the agreement.[8] Uneven or incomplete implementation may affect the operation of a conflict settlement agreement: for example, constitutions are normally designed as whole packages and require, for their proper functioning, the existence and operation of all their institutions. If either the agreement as a whole or some of its institutions do not perform well, there is a danger of its unravelling or of renewed negotiations being necessary (e.g., in Northern Ireland in the post-1998 period). While we accept that the adoption of conflict settlement agreements is a process requiring a certain measure of flexibility, including optional or mandatory reviews over time, we also want to stress that there needs to be a certain degree of institutional stability and predictability to create an environment in which all parties feel sufficiently secure to revisit the original agreement. This is unlikely to be the case if the implementation phase is flawed and the early stages of the operation of an agreement cast doubt on its overall viability, be it because some signatories defect or because institutions designed with parties' physical security in mind only do not 'fit' the broader complexities of life in a post-conflict society.[9]

As we will consider, in the next chapter, the role of international organizations in ethnic conflict regulation, we add at this stage several further preliminary observations on the basis of our conceptualization above, using the examples of the European Union and the United Nations consider the case of the EU. As an international actor in its own right, it was a latecomer in the Western Balkans in the sense that it had at best limited influence during negotiations of agreements that were subsequently seen through to full implementation and operation. At the same time, however, the EU has been, and continues to be, a major player in the implementation and operation of agreements into whose institutional structure it has had little or no impact during the negotiation phase. This is problematic in the sense that it thus becomes the main sponsor of the implementation and operation of conflict settlement agreements with whose content it may not necessarily agree and whose structure it may subsequently wish to change. But one also needs to bear in mind that the EU, through its constituent states and their membership in other international organizations such as the UN, the OSCE, and the Peace Implementation Council for Bosnia and Herzegovina, does exercise some degree of influence even in the negotiation phase, if only by way of supporting/endorsing the outcomes of the relevant processes leading to a negotiated conflict settlement. Thus, for example, Wolfgang Ischinger, a senior German diplomat, was closely involved in the negotiations that led to the Dayton Accords for Bosnia and Herzegovina in 1995 and represented the EU in the last-minute efforts of the so-called troika, also involving Russia and the US, to bring about a negotiated settlement between Kosovo Albanians and Serbia in the run-up to the final status decision on Kosovo in 2007–8. Further afield, senior EU diplomats were also heavily involved in the drafting of the Annan Plan for Cyprus, developing, in particular, the economic provisions of the UN-sponsored settlement proposal to bring about an end to more than three decades of partition on this Mediterranean island. A similar pattern of cooperation between the UN and the African Union (AU), another regional organization, has emerged over the Darfur crisis in Sudan. Several rounds of negotiations between the western, i.e., Darfur-based, rebel movements and the government in Khartoum were jointly presided over by UN and AU officials. Their success has been limited not only by the attitude of the Sudanese government but also by the fact that the various rebel groups lack any kind of coherent political programme, and appear in some cases to be motivated simply by an ill-defined and unfulfilled sense of entitlement.[10]

4 The policy instruments of international conflict regulation: diplomatic, economic and military interventions

The anecdotal evidence offered so far in this chapter highlights that the international community, and individual and collective actors within it, uses a variety of tools in the process of conflict regulation. Before we come back to the question of these different tools, and their utility in the three different phases of conflict regulation, it is worth pointing out that there has been a clear trend of late, associated primarily with the end of the Cold War,[11] towards ever more international efforts to resolve ethnic conflicts. This is clearly evident from two sets of figures. While during the Cold War period the UN normally had no more than a few truce supervision or observation operations at any given time, the total number of ongoing UN peace operations in late 2008 stood at sixteen, nine of which were deployed in cases of ethnic conflict.[12] The EU, similarly, has massively increased its engagement in international conflict management. Barely noticeable as a global political player throughout the 1990s (except for its failures in the Balkans), the organization has conducted a total of twenty-two operations since 2003. Of these, nineteen missions were deployed in countries experiencing ethnic conflict, and ten of them were ongoing in 2008.[13]

There is no suggestion here that all of these missions are even similar in terms of their objectives, personnel commitment, costs, length or success. Nor do we imply that they are the only tools at the disposal of, or deployed by, international actors in their efforts to prevent, manage and settle ethnic conflict. Yet, because of the comparative scale of the ongoing commitments, it is worthwhile discussing them in a little more depth before looking at other tools of international conflict regulation. During the Cold War, the predominant type of operation conducted is commonly referred to as traditional peacekeeping or observation – after the conflict parties agree a cease-fire, observers are deployed to monitor the situation and/or provide a buffer zone between them (Diehl 2008: 44). Two of the UN's oldest missions – those in Kashmir (UNMOGIP) and Cyprus (UNFICYP), dating back to 1949 and 1964 respectively – fall into this category. This type of operation continues to be of importance in the post-Cold War period, but increasingly international or regional missions are more complex. These so-called peace-building, peace support or stability operations have much broader objectives, reflecting a growing acceptance of the need for a comprehensive approach to post-conflict reconstruction. For example, a number of EU missions are aimed at security sector reform (especially capacity-building in relation to police forces and border guards, such as in Bosnia and Herzegovina, Macedonia and Georgia) and/or the development of the culture and institutions of the rule of law (Kosovo, Georgia). The UN mission to East Timor was perhaps the most ambitious of these new-type operations, as it aimed to build a new state, enabling East Timor's transition from a territory occupied by Indonesia to a fully fledged member of the international community of sovereign states. Moreover, even in cases of international intervention that retain traditional peacekeeping elements, other tasks have been added. Humanitarian operations, especially in the aid of refugees and IDPs, election organization and observation, and institutional capacity-building, are now almost standard components of peace-building missions, as evidenced by the EU mission in Bosnia and Herzegovina and the AU mission in Darfur.

Most of the missions referred to above fall four-square into the area of conflict management and settlement as defined at the beginning of this chapter. There are, however, also some that are more preventive in nature, i.e., are deployed prior to the outbreak of violence. The UN's preventive deployment mission to Macedonia, and its successors, is the prime example here not only of such missions in general but also of their success. Taking a slightly broader view of prevention, however, extending the notion to include also actions taken during the violent and post-violent phases of a conflict to prevent further violence (see Ackermann 2003; Kronenberger and Wouters 2004), is analytically useful as it allows us to assess any external action taken to prevent the eruption, escalation, diffusion or intensification of violent conflict in its proper context. From this perspective, then, the deployment of peacekeepers in Bosnia and Herzegovina from 1992 onwards did little either to prevent the escalation of the ethnic conflict there or to resolve it, while their presence post-Dayton was clearly an effective measure to prevent renewed violence, (so far) without contributing to an actual resolution of the conflict. The same holds true for the UN mission to Cyprus, while the one in Kashmir on three occasions failed to prevent military hostilities between India and Pakistan.

The deployment of missions to conflict zones is not the only tool that the international community has at its disposal to achieve desirable outcomes in the process of its engagement in conflict prevention, management and settlement efforts. A range of other options are available, and their use is far more frequent and involves a much broader set of actors. Multiple tools and actors invite different classifications of external interventions, but this is not the place to discuss the merits of different ways of approaching the issue of how to distinguish between different types of intervention.[14] Rather, we simply list a set of common types of diplomatic, economic and military forms of intervention and illustrate what they involve in the context of ethnic conflict.

4.1 Diplomatic interventions

Diplomatic interventions normally precede other forms of intervention and aim at either averting violent escalation of a conflict or establishing conditions conducive to de-escalation. The failure of diplomatic efforts to change the behaviour of parties on the ground often leads either to more coercive measures being applied to both parties or to selective coercion and/or support for individual parties.

Fact-finding missions offer the international community an opportunity to gain first-hand knowledge of a particular situation and to raise broader awareness of an impending crisis. For example, the UN dispatched a fact-finding mission to Abkhazia, Georgia, in the early 1990s prior to establishing its own permanent operation there, while the OSCE deployed such a mission to Kosovo in a last-ditch effort to avoid a military intervention against Serbia.

Mediation can follow fact-finding in an effort to intensify prevention efforts, but can also be applied as a tool to aid de-escalation once conflict parties on the ground have decided that they cannot resolve their dispute through

violence. A joint effort by the EU and NATO in Macedonia in .
ple of successful mediation, while the Rambouillet negotiat
in 1999 failed. In some cases, mediation succeeds in achievin
agreement between the parties, while the agreement itself
breaks down. The AU-mediated Arusha Accords for Rwanda a
most tragic illustrations of this.

Confidence-building measures often accompany other forms of
economic and/or military intervention. They are designed to enable parties to
begin rebuilding trust and often involve a variety of different actors, including political elites, the private sector and civil society groups. Above all, they
aim to make the actions and intentions of different parties more transparent
in order to reduce fear and increase a sense of security, for example through
regular meetings and day-to-day coordination of activities, such as in the case
of the Joint Control Commission established after the 1992 Sochi Agreement
on South Ossetia or the UN-facilitated Coordinating Council established in
Abkhazia in 1997. They can also involve civil society initiatives, such as the so-
called Standing Technical Working Groups established after 1999 in Kosovo
by the NGO European Centre for Minority Issues, to enable Albanians, Serbs
and members of other communities to deal with both very pragmatic issues
(such as healthcare and economic development) and highly sensitive issues
(such as education and refugee return).[15]

International judicial measures are a relatively recent addition to the set of
instruments available to the international community when it comes to
dealing with ethnic conflicts. These can either involve prosecution for crimes
committed during a conflict after a settlement has been achieved, such as in
the cases of Yugoslavia and Rwanda, or be used as a tool of intervention in an
ongoing conflict, such as the indictment in 2008 of the Sudanese president,
Omar al-Bashir, by the International Criminal Court. International judicial
measures serve two purposes: they are meant to be punitive for crimes already
committed and to have a deterrent effect as regards future conflicts.

4.2 Economic interventions

Economic interventions, with the exception of humanitarian aid, can be used
to induce behaviour by parties deemed to be in concordance with international efforts to prevent, manage or settle a particular conflict and to sanction
behaviour that runs counter to such efforts.

Humanitarian aid frequently accompanies other measures taken by the
international community. It is applied without any conditions attached
and aimed at relieving civilian suffering by providing food, shelter and a
minimum of healthcare. While often initiated as an emergency response to
an escalating crisis, such as the November 2008 UN relief operation in the
eastern DRC, humanitarian assistance can, in some cases, continue for decades, as in the case of UNRWA, the United Nations Relief and Works Agency

for Palestine Refugees in the Near East, which has been active since 1 May 1950 and remains the principal aid organization for currently 4.6 million Palestinian refugees. Another potential problem with humanitarian aid and assistance is the potential for abuse. Operation Lifeline Sudan, launched by the UN in cooperation with more than thirty NGOs in April 1989, was meant to provide food aid to civilians suffering from the violence between north and south, but it essentially introduced a commodity into a civil war that created an income opportunity for the warring parties, who seized food convoys and sold on their bounty or extorted protection fees to guarantee safe passage.

Technical assistance covers a broad range of measures that can be partisan or non-partisan in nature, from the delivery of arms and deployment of military advisors to one of the parties (a frequent feature of superpower intervention during the Cold War), to pre-negotiation capacity-building for one or both parties (a more common practice today, often delivered through NGOs), to post-conflict economic assistance (as, for example, through donor conferences).

Embargoes and sanctions aim to deprive one or both conflict parties of the means to fight and to coerce them to comply with international demands. They are a frequent first step in increasing international involvement once diplomatic efforts have failed. Their impact and utility, however, are controversial. The arms embargo on the former Yugoslavia during the 1992–5 wars arguably benefited the Serbs most, as they controlled the assets of the Yugoslav People's Army, while the targeted (or so-called smart) sanctions against Milošević later in the decade contributed more clearly to his downfall by denying him the resources necessary to maintain his clientelist regime. Another problem with embargoes and sanctions is that of enforcement (which is difficult to ensure at the best of times). For example, once Russia stopped enforcing the CIS embargo against Abkhazia in the late 1990s, Georgian efforts to coerce the leadership of this separatist region to engage in meaningful negotiations had lost all leverage. Related to the problem of enforcement is the inevitable smuggling and corruption that sanctions create, often consolidating operations of criminal networks across borders (and ethnic boundaries) and entrenching them within society by giving them a degree of legitimacy as 'essential service providers' – as has been the case across the Western Balkans since the early 1990s.

4.3 Military interventions

The category of military interventions covers a broad spectrum of international efforts, from the deployment of traditional peacekeeping forces to oversee ceasefires and separate warring factions, to military components of international post-conflict reconstruction operations, to the use of force on the territory of a state which has not consented to such an intervention.

Peacekeeping was, for most of the Cold War period, the predominant measure taken by the international community (i.e., the UN) to manage ethnic conflicts. Their track record is mixed at best. The UN operation in Cyprus (UNFICYP) was unable in the early days after its launch in 1964 to prevent violence between Greek and Turkish Cypriots and was helpless in the face of the attempted Greek coup in 1974 against the elected Cypriot president, Archbishop Makarios, and the subsequent ethnic cleansing on the island following a Turkish invasion. Since then, however, it has overseen a relatively high degree of stability. This ambiguous success, however, is dwarfed by the monumental failure of the UN operation in Rwanda (UNAMIR) to prevent the 1994 genocide against the Tutsis. UN peacekeepers in the former Yugoslavia struggled equally to keep a non-existent peace in Bosnia and Herzegovina until the summer of 1995, when a more robust (US/NATO-driven) approach of using the full scope of the mandate provided by the UN Security Council, including airstrikes against Serb forces, contributed to bringing the Serbs to the negotiation table in Dayton. This, however, was only after the massacre at Srebrenica, in which Serb forces killed several thousand Bosniak (Muslim) men, virtually under the eyes of a Dutch peacekeeping battalion.

Peace support or stability operations have by and large replaced traditional peacekeeping operations. These are more complex operations in terms of their mandate, extending far beyond ceasefire observation and the separation of combatant forces on the ground. While there is a recognition that security is a *conditio sine qua non* for sustainable peace in the aftermath of ethnic conflict, there is equally a realization now that mere peacekeeping does little to settle an actual conflict – at best it contains violence, at worst it gives conflict parties an opportunity to rearm and regroup before the next round of violence. Peace support operations are thus meant to create conditions in which other efforts can succeed. Take the example of the UN mission in Kosovo (UNMIK), for example. Established after NATO's intervention in 1999, it brought together a multitude of actors to perform a wide range of different tasks deemed necessary to rebuild Kosovo economically, socially and politically and contribute to settling the underlying conflict. Under the leadership of the UN, NATO was to provide security, the OSCE was charged with building democratic institutions, and the EU was given the task of economic reconstruction. While far from a resounding success, UNMIK embodies the very complex nature of contemporary peace support operations and illustrates their potential for success and failure shaped equally by organizational factors and conditions on the ground.[16]

The use of force by the international community without the consent of the state on whose territory the intervention takes place remains the exception among military interventions. Yet what is often referred to as humanitarian intervention or humanitarian military intervention remains highly controversial, despite its infrequency. Moreover, while by the end of the 1990s a consensus seemed to emerge around the recognition of the 'responsibility to protect' populations from systematic and gross violations of their human rights, this consensus has more or less evaporated again in the aftermath of the US-led intervention in Iraq.[17] While the moral case for the use of force in protecting civilians from violence has, arguably, not diminished since NATO's intervention in the Kosovo conflict in 1999,[18] the international environment that facilitated its *ex post facto* legalization in UN Security Council Resolution 1244 of 1999 simply no longer exists. This is not to argue that we will not see future unauthorized military interventions by third parties in ethnic conflicts. Rather, the point is that these are going to be determined even more by what intervening states consider their strategic interests. To be sure, these played a role in the NATO intervention in Kosovo, too, but their absence in the case of Darfur explains to some extent the lack of any serious commitment on the part of the international community to intervene actively in what is today's greatest humanitarian emergency.

5 Explaining success and failure of international conflict regulation

This increasing involvement of regional and international organizations in conflict settlement, on the one hand, clearly justifies our inclusion of international-level factors in the analysis of ethnic conflicts and conflict regulation. Even if their involvement is by no means a guarantee for achieving sustainable settlements, those settlements that have had even a small measure of success, if only in the form of conclusive negotiations, have all involved such organizations: from Burundi to Dayton, from East Timor to Northern Ireland, from Gagauzia to Aceh. Yet there are as many, if not more, cases in which regional and international organizations have been unable to succeed in achieving and sustaining successful settlements. Before we turn to the issue of how we can apply our analytical model to the explanation of both the failures and successes of regional and international organizations, we want briefly to explore their role in the two post-negotiation stages. Again, let's look at the example of the EU. The important role played by the Union in the Western Balkans has significant bearing on the influence – direct or indirect – that it can exercise on the implementation and operation of conflict settlement agreements in the region.[19] Association with and potential future membership of the EU are both significant attractions to the conflict-torn countries of the former Yugoslavia and give the Union additional leverage to ensure that conflict settlements, once negotiated, are implemented and operated to its liking. This strategy has been successful as far as Croatia is concerned, but markedly less so with regard to Serbia, where a negotiated settlement over Kosovo is absent and a majority of EU member states have recognized Kosovo's independence. Other regional and international organizations have fewer such carrots available to them, and the EU itself, of course, is geographically limited in the application of this approach. Having said that, there is a greater tendency among individual donor countries and international organizations such as the World Bank and the International Monetary Fund to make their assistance conditional on recipient countries' compliance with certain requirements, including those related to the implementation of conflict settlement agreements, or otherwise face cuts in aid and development assistance or sanctions.[20] Finally, regional and international organizations have used both force and the threat of force to compel local conflict parties to achieve a settlement, thereby often shifting the balance of power between them. Just consider the UN and NATO interventions in Bosnia and Herzegovina and Kosovo respectively, the Australian-led intervention in the Solomon Islands, and the US- and UK-enforced no-fly zone over the Kurdistan region of Iraq, which helped the region establish itself politically and economically as a distinct entity within Iraq with significant autonomy from the centre, a situation that had become so entrenched that it was formally recognized in the 2005 constitution.

While in the next chapter we will offer a more systematic assessment of these and other kinds of international intervention, let us return at this stage to the question of how far our levels-of-analysis model can help explain the success and failure of international conflict regulation. One predominant feature of much of the relevant literature is the inductive approach taken by many authors, starting from their specific case/s towards more general lessons (see, for example, Caplan 2005a, 2005b; King and Mason 2006). This is not a criticism of the doubtless quality of the analysis and scholarship offered, but it provides an opportunity to problematize the issue of a conceptual framework in which the outcomes of international interventions, and of the state-building missions that frequently follow, can be investigated.

The need for and nature of such a conceptual framework can be well illustrated by the growing role of the European Union in this area of international politics. Scholarly investigation of the part played by the EU in international conflict regulation is, so far, a relatively underdeveloped area of academic inquiry.[21] However, significant work has been done on both the internal policy processes related to the development of the Common Foreign and Security Policy (CFSP) and the European Security and Defence Policy (ESDP) and the application of these policies to specific countries and regions,[22] also including a growing body of literature on the EU's European Neighbourhood Policy (ENP).[23]

While the different literatures on international organizations, on international intervention and on conflict regulation in the case of the EU remain to date relatively unconnected,[24] existing scholarship, to the extent that it is focused on the role of the Union, offers comparative insights in relation to other international and regional organizations[25] or examines conflict management as part of other, broader EU policies, most recently and most significantly enlargement.[26]

A conceptual framework that can provide the analytical tools for the study

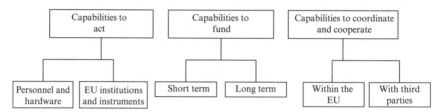

Figure 5.1 *Necessary capabilities for regional and international organizations engaged in ethnic conflict regulation*

of the EU, and by extension of other regional and international organizations, needs to incorporate an analysis of factors within the Union, or at least predominantly related to its capabilities, and of factors that are exogenous yet determine the nature and dynamics of the particular conflict situation the EU confronts. We have already offered a systematic discussion of these exogenous factors in chapter 2, and thus concentrate in the following on the internal dimension of such an analysis. Relevant factors here relate to three sets of capabilities that the Union must possess in order to succeed in conflict management: those to act, to fund, and to cooperate and coordinate (see figure 5.1).

Capabilities to act include political will, the availability of personnel and hardware, as well as of appropriate institutions and policy instruments. The ability to fund various conflict management operations in the short and the long term relate to questions of the overall availability of funds, and also to the speed with which funding can be provided. Finally, coordination and cooperation capabilities within the EU have two dimensions: a horizontal one (coordination among different policy areas) and a vertical one (between the EU as a supranational organization with its own institutional structures and the EU member states). At the external level, coordination and cooperation relate to the EU's ability to work with other regional and international organizations (e.g., NATO, the UN, the OSCE, etc.) and with individual third-party states (e.g., Russia, the US, Switzerland).

Consequently, when it comes to the study of international ethnic conflict regulation, we need to expand our levels-of-analysis approach and conduct a more elaborate investigation into one specific dimension – namely the nature of the relevant actor engaged in the conflict regulation effort. To be sure, this is a refinement, rather than a revision, of our general approach, and one that is necessitated by the specific direction of an inquiry into the causes of success and failure of international conflict regulation. There is, of course, a theoretical implication that goes with this explicit additional focus on conflict regulation actors, in that we hypothesize that success and failure are determined in two dimensions: the capabilities of these actors and the situation that they face on the ground.[27] As we will demonstrate in the following chapters in this part of our volume, neither of these is sufficient in itself to guarantee success, but they are both necessary conditions. This also means that we will make an argument against the widespread tendency to attribute blame for failed efforts to prevent or settle ethnic conflicts to regional and international organizations alone.[28]

6

International Intervention

1 Introduction

As outlined in chapter 5, external actors have a variety of options to intervene in ethnic conflicts, ranging from cooperative measures aimed at inducing the parties to reach a negotiated settlement to the use of military force. While we need to be careful not to lose sight of the fact that not every intervention per se is aimed at ending conflict (or at least containing it), our focus in this part of the book is on conflict settlement. Hence, we are particularly interested in the dynamics and outcomes of those interventions that have the specific purpose of ending (or containing) conflict. This, however, is not to say either that they will achieve such outcomes in every case or that there are no unintended consequences of such interventions that may produce opposite outcomes to those intended.

In the next part of this chapter, we give a general overview of the track record of international interventions in ethnic conflict, illustrated by three brief case studies: Burma, the DRC and Sudan. This is meant to contextualize our more theoretical observations in chapter 5 and illustrate the breadth of different interventions and interveners, their dynamics and outcomes. By its very nature, this will be a selective account that by no means claims any degree of comprehensiveness. Rather, we explore in more detail the 'workings' of international intervention in one specific case that has long exercised students of ethnic conflict and those dealing with it in governments, think tanks and regional and international organizations: Kosovo. Applying our levels-of-analysis approach to international efforts since the 1990s to settle the conflict, we examine the role that different factors played at the local, state, regional and global levels in three specific, sequential outcomes: military intervention in 1999, UN administration between 1999 and 2008, and a unilateral declaration of independence by the parliament of Kosovo, followed by selective, predominantly Western, recognition on 17 February 2008.

2 The track record of international interventions

We shall commence this overview by providing a rationale for the inclusion of the three cases that we focus upon in this section – Burma, the Democratic

Republic of Congo (DRC) and Sudan. These have been chosen for a number of reasons. First, together with our more detailed assessment of Kosovo, they illustrate the fact that ethnically related conflicts are a global phenomenon. Second, they exemplify that such conflicts involve a multiplicity of actors, and thereby show the efficacy of our levels-of-analysis approach. Third, they demonstrate in different ways how international actors become involved in efforts to bring about conflict settlement and alleviate suffering. Fourth, each case provides evidence of how the internal dynamics of conflicts interact with a number of other factors in such a way that in each case a distinct solution, or maybe no solution at all, comes about.

2.1 Burma

Burma is a multi-ethnic society. Ethnic Burmans constitute a large major-ity of its citizens, and as such dominate the professions, the economy and, crucially, the army. Among Burma's many minorities, the most prominent are the Karen, Mon, Shan and Wa, who together with other minorities have been in a state of intermittent rebellion ever since independence from Britain in 1948 (Fink 2001: 14ff.). Since 1962, Burma has been ruled by the military, which, despite promoting occasional changes to both the governing nomen-clature and the country itself, has had but one paramount objective: to minimize as far as possible the political, cultural and social influences of the outside world, and in particular of the 'West'. In terms of its economic poli-cies, autarky has been a primary aim. Politically this has been complemented by an ill-defined commitment to a uniquely Burmese form of socialism.

In part, the politics of ethnicity comes into play as a consequence of the British colonial legacy. British rule tended to favour the political periphery, populated largely by non-Burman peoples, at the expense of the Burman centre. Burman nationalism was therefore geared towards not only achieving the restoration of independence but also reintegrating the periphery firmly within the ambit of a Burman-led state. Soon after independence in 1948, ten-sions quickly became apparent between centre and periphery and, as stated previously, violent conflict broke out almost at the point of independence. By the early 1980s a combination of economic problems, caused as much as any-thing else by gross mismanagement, and a deteriorating political situation led to the fabric of the state coming under severe strain. In 1988 the famous pro-democracy uprising occurred, which in turn catapulted Daw San Suu Kyi onto the world stage, and led in 1990 to a general election which the generals lost to the opposition National League for Democracy (NLD).

The reaction of the generals was simply to ignore the vote and to carry on governing. Importantly, they embarked upon a strategy that resulted in their crushing all opposition. First, they engaged in a limited opening to the outside world, in particular to China, India and Russia. These choices were deliberate: all three have proven to be valuable trading partners. In addition, all three are ruled by governments which do not advocate regime change or reform in countries that in no way threaten their strategic interests. Second, the military was keen to ensure that NLD activists and ordinary Burmans did not make common cause with the myriad rebel armies that operated in the Burmese hinterland. In a complicated series of moves from the early 1990s onwards, a large majority of rebel groups were neutralized. The Burmese military used its superior firepower and resource base in combination with peace initiatives, which in effect very often resulted in former rebel groups laying down their arms and acknowledging the rule of the Burmese state. In return the former rebels were left alone, and legitimized their previous sometimes dubious economic activities. Today, any remaining rebel armies are divided and demoralized and do not constitute a serious threat to the Burmese authorities.

What, then, of the wider world and its response to this ongoing crisis? Burma's neighbours host hundreds of thousands of refugees, primarily from the ethnic minority peoples, and the large majority of those who remain in Burma live in penury. Burma does not constitute a military threat to its neighbours, who have dealt with the military regime in various ways. However, the spillover effects of the country's internal strife do affect the region. In addition, Burma is strategically located between Southeast Asia's two biggest powers: China and India. Both Thailand and India seem to have approached Burma with somewhat contradictory policies. At times they have supported the pro-democracy movement, at times the ethnic minority armies, and at times the regime. China, on the other hand, currently wholeheartedly endorses the Burmese junta, as the Burmese regime sells off more and more oil, gas and hydropower concessions. This stance represents a complete turnaround from China's Cold War position, when it supported the Communist Party of Burma (CPB).

The Association of Southeast Asian Nations (ASEAN) admitted Burma as a member in 1997. Under the principle of 'constructive engagement', ASEAN seemed confident it could change some of its latest member's more repressive and embarrassing policies. However, its attempts at influencing the regime have proved futile. Even its more serious warnings of possible expulsion from the organization have seemingly had not the slightest effect (Zaw 2003: 44).

The United Nations has experienced a similarly fraught relationship with the Burmese junta. The various envoys and rapporteurs employed by the UN to engage Burma have encountered many obstacles. For instance, the UN Secretary General's Special Envoy to Burma, Razali Ismael, resigned in January 2006, having been unable to enter the country since 2004. As of the time of writing, he has yet to be replaced. The UN special rapporteur on human rights in Burma, Paulo Sérgio Pinheiro, has faced similar restrictions (Human Rights Watch 2007). The UN's General Assembly and the Human Rights Commission have together produced close to thirty resolutions, all expressing grave concerns over the systematic human rights abuses in Burma, but the regime has chosen to ignore them all. Neither did the junta relent in any meaningful form in the wake of mass anti-government demonstrations in September 2008, or indeed when natural disaster struck in the south of the country in May 2008. Although, in both instances, UN representatives were eventually granted an audience with senior military figures, it was clear that for the junta this was largely a window-dressing exercise.

Since the 1988 uprising, the US has adopted an increasingly critical stance towards Burma. The US approach includes the severance of military and economic assistance, refusal to nominate an American ambassador, banning of all American investments in, and imports from, the country, and freezing the assets of, and denying visas to, high-ranking officials. In addition, the US government has consistently lobbied for the regime to respect the 1990 elections and release Daw San Suu Kyi, and has been active in the Security Council, where it has pushed for resolutions critical of the government in Burma (Steinberg 2004). As of the summer of 2009, there is no immediate prospect of either the NLD or the remnants of, for example, the Karen National Union (KNU) being able to engineer change. The junta's reaction to offers of foreign, especially Western, aid in the wake of the cyclone that killed approximately 100,000 people in May 2008 was that of a government wary of the outside world and disdainful of its own people in equal measure.

Burma, thus, represents a case that has, so far, proven intervention-resistant despite the severity of the conflict in the country, the length it has lasted – the Karen conflict started in the late 1940s – and the impact it has had on its neighbours. This is partly a result of the regime's self-isolation and limited contact with, and dependence on, the outside world, which at the same time minimizes the leverage of regional and global actors in effecting a change in its stance, for example to accept international mediation. In addition, ASEAN, as the principal regional organization in the area, while at least rhetorically committed to improving the situation in Burma, has a very strict policy of non-interference into its member states' 'internal affairs', which in itself is not surprising considering the degree to which other ASEAN members are affected by ethnic conflicts and have resisted any external involvement. Thailand, India and China – the immediate neighbours – have also not helped the situation. Thailand and India have frequently switched loyalties between the pro-democracy movement, armed ethnic groups and the regime, thus both sending contradictory messages to the parties and limiting even further any potential for sustainable impact. China, today, must be seen as the major protector of the regime in Burma: domestically it enables the junta to keep a minimal functioning economy by offering a market for exports, while regionally and internationally its political clout has so far prevented any more serious and concerted international action.

2.2 The Democratic Republic of the Congo

In a continent scarred by tragedy, the appalling history of the country now known as the Democratic Republic of the Congo (DRC) is in a league of its own. The DRC is the third largest country in Africa and is extraordinarily rich in resources. There are large reserves of, among others, uranium, copper, diamonds, coltan, magnesium, silver, tin, oil and timber. Lust for these resources has often been a source of misery for the indigenous population. It is estimated that over 3 million people have died as a result of the violence that has engulfed the DRC for more than a decade now, a similar magnitude of civilians remain internally displaced, and a further 400,000 have sought refuge in neighbouring countries – and increasingly also in North America and Europe. As befits its size and the arbitrary nature of its borders, over 200 different ethnic groups are estimated to reside within the DRC. Unsurprisingly there is no lingua franca. French is the official language, but at everyday level a variety of languages are widely spoken.

If we turn now to the DRC's historical legacy and in particular its colonial experience, we find that Europeans first established a permanent presence in the area in the 1870s. Keen to present Belgium as a potential great power, King Leopold II secured this vast territory in 1885 at the Conference of Berlin. The area was then renamed the Congo Free State as the private domain of the Belgian monarch. Leopold's rule was characterized by the ruthless exploitation of raw materials and widespread human rights violations that had mass murder and amputation as their hallmarks. It is estimated that anything up to half of the estimated population of 15 million died as a direct consequence of Leopold's policies. In 1908, following immense international pressure, the Free State was transferred to Belgium as a colonial possession.

The extent to which the Belgian state redressed the wrongs visited upon the indigenous population is a matter of debate. Education was introduced for Africans and a health service also came into existence. The overall economic infrastructure was also improved. Despite these reforms, the indigenous population possessed absolutely no political power and little social status. From the mid-1950s, pressure both at home and abroad began to be exerted upon Belgium to grant independence. Eventually the Belgians agreed to a hurried programme of decolonization and elections were held that paved the way for the formal procedure and independence. The former Belgian Congo became the independent Congo-Leopoldville in 1960, and in May of that year the Congolese National Movement (MNC), led by Patrice Lumumba, duly won the inaugural elections. Lumumba became prime minister, with Joseph Kasavubu of the rival Bakongo Alliance (ABAKO) becoming president.

The almost complete absence of a state infrastructure, the lack of any overarching sense of Congolese national identity, and the presence of foreign actors with competing agendas combined to produce a situation that by September 1960 resulted in Congo-Leopoldville being plunged into a series of wars that have still not ended. Matters were complicated by the actions of Joseph Mobutu, then the army's chief of staff, who quickly sought to boost his own personal standing by channelling Belgian and US money to disaffected soldiers with the aim of sparking a mutiny among the armed forces. For its part, the US viewed Lumumba as a communist who needed to be overthrown. The Belgians were more concerned with maintaining their grip on the production of raw materials, particularly Katangan copper and diamonds. Amid a situation of general chaos, with the national government split into various competing factions, Katangan forces assassinated Lumumba in January 1961.

A period of intense civil war followed, which involved regular Belgian forces and, in Katanga, assorted European mercenaries. By 1965 Mobutu had emerged as the dominant figure and declared himself president. Although fighting subsided, the far east of the country was never fully brought under the control of the government in Leopoldville (later renamed Kinshasa), and Katanga (renamed Shaba by the victorious Mobutu) in particular remained prone to periodic revolts. Mobutu's reign was marked by the systematic disregard of the needs of wider society. Like King Leopold, Mobutu and his allies regarded the state as their own personal property. In 1971, as part of a wider 'Africanization' campaign, the Mobutu kleptocracy changed the country's name to Zaire. Until the collapse of the Soviet bloc, Mobutu was able to operate with impunity. However, with the Soviet Union dead and buried by the end of 1991, so his usefulness to the US waned. The result was a reduction in aid and growing domestic and international pressure for reform.

Reform did eventually come. However, when it did, despite the best efforts of an increasingly vocal domestic opposition, it came from without and catapulted the country into a cycle of violence that became known as 'Africa's world war'. As previously mentioned, Mobutu never succeeded in establishing full control over the east of the country. Among the desultory band of (former) rebels who resided in the border areas between Zaire, Uganda, Rwanda and Burundi was one Laurent Kabila, an old comrade of Lumumba.

With the defeat of the Hutu *interahamwe* in Rwanda by Ugandan-backed Rwandan Tutsi forces, a new political order was beginning to emerge in the Great Lakes region. Uganda's Yoweri Museveni and Rwanda's Paul Kagame saw themselves as representatives of a new type of African leader who sought to combine elements of Western liberal democratic practices with their traditional African counterparts. What was decisive in their choice of sponsoring Laurent Kabila was their disdain for Mobutu and, more immediately, the presence of thousands of *interahamwe* in eastern Zaire.

Faced with this security threat, Uganda and Rwanda chose Kabila to be their man in Kinshasa. In September 1996, ethnic Tutsis rose in revolt against the Mobutu regime. Rwanda, in alliance with Uganda, began supplying Tutsi rebels with arms and ammunition and entered into joint actions against *interahamwe* remnants still active in eastern Congo. Then, in May 1997, Kabila loyalists backed by regular units from the Ugandan and Rwandan armies invaded Zaire. The Mobutu regime collapsed and the old dictator fled into exile in Switzerland, where he later died. The newly renamed DRC did not, however, enter a period of peace or stability. In August 1998, his former allies turned against Kabila and launched another rebellion.

In this phase of the struggle, Uganda and Rwanda acted as joint sponsors to the Congolese Rally for Democracy (RDC). Growing tensions between the RDC's sponsors and within the RDC itself resulted in its splintering into several warring factions, the largest of which restyled itself the RDC-Goma. To try and map the shifting alliances is beyond the scope of this chapter, but the essential point is the remarkable savagery with which all sides pursued this particular phase of the conflict.

Kabila loyalists hung on long enough to allow successful intervention by a coalition of Zimbabwean, Angolan, Namibian, Chadian and Sudanese forces. Once more space does not allow for detailed analysis as to why this incoherent coalition came into being. In general, we can say that those fighting against the (former) Rwandan–Ugandan alliance were wary of seeing Kagame and Museveni emerging as regional strongmen. They were also worried about any reconfiguration of state borders and, in the case of Angola, seized the opportunity to finish off domestic opponents who used the DRC as a base and conduit for supplies. However, the main prize for all was raw materials.

By the summer of 1999, around 3 million people had died and the international media had brought the conflict to a worldwide audience. As a consequence, international pressure mounted and eventually forced various rebel factions, the government in Kinshasa and all foreign governments to sign the Lusaka Accord, which, although it failed in the short term, did at least begin to create a peace dynamic in the country (S. Smith 2005). It provided for a partial withdrawal of foreign forces, but, in the east, Rwanda and Uganda retained an armed presence, which was complicated both by the fact that the two were now at odds with one another and by the violence of rival tribal-based militias.

The situation began to stabilize only following the assassination of Laurent Kabila in January 2001. In 2002, his son and heir, Joseph Kabila, signed a peace accord in Pretoria, South Africa, that paved the way for more effective UN intervention and the eventual withdrawal of Rwandan and Ugandan forces. The role of South Africa has been particularly important in the entire peace process, and in integrating the DRC within an expanded Southern African Development community (SADC).

Since 1999, the United Nations Organization Mission in the Democratic Republic of the Congo (MONUC) has maintained peacekeepers in the country (S. Smith 2005). They are based largely in the east of the country, where they have at times been engaged in heavy fighting with local militias. Over the years since their initial deployment, the UN Security Council strengthened both their mandate and their numbers on the ground, with the total military personnel close to 17,000 by the end of 2008. The increased peacekeeping presence and its more robust mandate greatly reduced the effectiveness of various militia groups in eastern Congo, without completely depriving them of the means and opportunities to wreak havoc on the civilian population.

This, however, is not just a reflection of the limited effectiveness of the UN's mission in the DRC. One of the most tragic characteristics of the war in Congo has been the dramatic growth of militia movements with a propensity for extreme violence. Forces have emerged that engaged in actions that have no clear military objective other than to kill and to acquire natural resources and the labour necessary to exploit them. The various militias of eastern Congo, whose agenda is essentially local and personalist, are the most prominent among this type. As if that were not enough, Rwandan Hutu *interahamwe* units remain active in eastern Congo, and neighbouring Rwanda continues to take an 'active' interest in the conflict as well.

Nonetheless, a regionally and internationally mediated peace agreement for the DRC has been in place for some time now. The Pretoria Agreement of 2002 brought about a marked reduction in violence in the civil war that had drawn eight of the DRC's neighbouring states into the fighting on the sides of different parties to the conflict. The agreement also established a transitional parliament (this ceased to function with the inauguration of the new directly elected National Assembly in 2006) and also provided for the creation of an electoral cycle that finally got underway in 2006. In the presidential election, Joseph Kabila emerged as the winner, but in the elections to the National Assembly the same year no party won a majority in the 500-seat parliament. The elections were contested by a mix of civilian political parties and militia-cum-political parties. In the latter, in particular, personal and ethnic loyalties dominate coherent ideological strategy. In the end, Joseph Kabila's People's Party for Reconstruction and Democracy (PPRD), which itself was a coalition of several different groups, emerged as the strongest faction, with 111 seats.

Since then the UN has sought to complement MONUC with civilian-led programmes. In early 2006 it presented the DRC Humanitarian Action Plan (HAP), which called for governments, donor agencies and NGOs to contribute $700 million in aid to the DRC. It was argued that not only did the country need and deserve such aid but that, in order for aid to be channelled more effectively, a new approach was necessary. In addition to the United Nations, numerous states and NGOs have attempted to promote stability and bring structural development in tandem with everyday succour to the benighted wider population (ICRC 2009). Belgium, Sweden and Canada have been particularly prominent as donors of aid. The DRC has also benefited from the International Monetary Fund's poverty reduction and debt reduction strategies, although the scope and rationale for this programme remains controversial, as with much of the IMF's work.

Although fighting diminished throughout 2006–7, unrest was still apparent. In the east, Ituri, North and South Kivu, and Bunia remained as flashpoints, as did parts of Katanga in the south. In September 2008 the DRC once again captured the attention of the world's media when large scale fighting erupted in North Kivu between the forces of the rebel general Laurent Nkunda (himself an ethnic Tutsi) and the Congolese army in alliance with local militias. Nkunda claims, as does the Rwandan government, that the DRC government has reneged on pledges to disarm the *interahamwe*, and that Kinshasa has in fact allied itself with that organization. The fighting sparked a mass flight of the civilian population from the area, leading to yet another refugee crisis involving some 250,000 people. Immense African and international pressure on all states in the Great Lakes region to end the conflict in the DRC offered the opportunity to form a new alliance between the DRC government, Rwanda and Congolese Tutsis, but Nkunda and around 2,000 of his men failed to support this new consensus concerning a joint effort to take on Hutu rebels in the eastern DRC, many of whom had been perpetrators in, and fled after, the Rwandan genocide. He thus lost the support of his Rwandan backers, who apprehended him in January 2009. While violence still continues in early 2009, there seems to be a greater degree of regional resolve to bring it to an end.

2.3 Sudan

The Republic of Sudan gained independence from the United Kingdom in January 1956. Sudan sits on substantial oil reserves, the exploitation of which has been crucial to fanning the conflict in Darfur in the west of the country, and could yet hamper the peace that currently exists between north and south, despite a ruling by the Permanent Court of Arbitration on boundaries that had remained disputed after the 2005 Comprehensive Peace Agreement.[1] Sudan's population is estimated to be about 37 million, of whom approximately 6 million live in southern Sudan. The two main cultures are the Arab/Nubian and non-Arab black Africans. These two broadly defined groups are further divided in terms of ethnicity and clan allegiances, and neither possesses a unified lingua franca. Sudan supplies us with a prime example of where the application of the term 'nation-state' at the point of independence carried no real meaning. As a result the Sudanese have periodically contested, and continue to contest, the nature of their relationship.

Religion is the primary cleavage in Sudanese society. The north and the centre of the country are largely Muslim, while the south is primarily Christian or animist. Ethnicity is a fault line that alternately cuts across or reinforces the religious division. The population of the south is overwhelmingly black African, and this fact in turn has helped to solidify difference. The war in Darfur is being fought ostensibly between black Africans and Arab Muslims, with various rebel groups claiming discrimination at the hands of their Arab co-citizens.

A cursory glance at the newspapers would leave the casual reader with the impression that the conflicts that have bedevilled Sudan ever since independence in 1956 have at their root irreconcilable ethnic and religious differences. Yet such a simplistic assessment would mask a more complex but, nevertheless, readily comprehensible story that has occurred in the midst of chronic institutional instability, economic underdevelopment, mismanagement and corruption on the part of political elites, and a deteriorating physical infrastructure. Through this persistent socio-economic malaise, alliances among predominantly Muslim Arab Northerners' and Christian and Animist Southerners are pitted against one another in the competition for resources.

The wars that have plagued the country are, as much as anything else, about competing visions of what kind of a state Sudan should be and who indeed is a Sudanese. At another level, and this is particularly the case in Darfur, the struggle for resources enhances and confirms ethnic identity. The 'Northerners' who support and form the backbone of the pro-government Janjaweed (Men on Horseback) militias often are Arabs by virtue of the fact that they are herders who have assimilated Arab culture and have come into conflict with pastoralist black African farmers over increasingly scarce resources.

If we now turn to the conflict between the north and the south we find that, by May 1983, the Sudan People's Liberation Army (SPLA), led by Colonel John Garang, had emerged as the major guerrilla force. The SPLA represented those in the south who found the constitutional rearrangements of 1983 unacceptable and insisted that Shari'a law must not be applied to the non-Muslim inhabitants of south Sudan. What followed was an eighteen-year civil war that claimed an indeterminate number of lives. A further 4.5 million are estimated to have either fled the country or become internally displaced persons (IDPs).

The war was one without fixed fronts, and, as today in Darfur, there are claims that the government singled out certain groups, such as the Dinka, for particularly harsh treatment. As is common in such cases, both sides were adept at manipulating clan loyalties and tensions. By the early 2000s, following years of inconclusive fighting, the climate for peace had improved. On the one hand, it had become clear to Khartoum that the chances of defeating the SPLA militarily were slight, while the SPLA had realized that the possibility of linking up with other rebel groups and disaffected civilian opponents of the government in order to overthrow the Khartoum authorities was similarly slim. Both sides, therefore, had an incentive to reach some kind of compromise. Further, with the example of al-Qaeda and Afghanistan firmly in mind, the authorities in Khartoum were nervous of America becoming militarily involved in the war. The result was the Comprehensive Peace Agreement of January 2005, signed in Naivasha, Kenya. Put briefly, under the terms of the agreement the SPLA obtained power sharing at the national level, resource- and revenue-sharing, public sector jobs and autonomy, with the promise of a referendum on independence within six years.

A factor that had raised the stakes in the war in the south was the discovery of oil in three regions to which both the SPLA and Khartoum lay claim. The routing of oil pipelines and the exact demarcation of the internal border between the south and the remainder of the country meant that final status negotiations dragged on longer than originally anticipated. Self-evidently, oil is a valuable commodity, the income from which can help to regenerate producer economies. For this reason alone, the July 2009 ruling of the Permanent Court of Arbitration is significant: it is the best chance for these oil-producing regions not to become a bone of contention when in 2011 the south votes on, and most likely gains, independence.

The charismatic John Garang died in a helicopter crash in July 2005, only a few weeks after having been sworn in as vice-president of Sudan. His successor and long-term deputy, Salva Kiir, has so far proven to be more adept at maintaining the momentum towards peace than was at first feared. Apart from inheriting Garang's post of vice-president, Kiir is currently president of South Sudan, and as such has a considerable power base upon which to build.

In recent years it has, however, been another conflict that has imprinted itself upon the collective consciousness of many inside and outside Sudan: Darfur. The tragedy of Darfur is instructive of the power of celebrity and the media, for it was only with the greater engagement of both that in 2003 the wider world came to hear about a conflict that in fact began in 1987. The background to the conflict is one of drought, famine and consequent pressure upon scarce resources. Further, it is alleged that ever since the late 1980s the government has sided with 'Arabs' and against black Africans, although the truth is more opaque (ICRC 2005).

In February 2003, just as Khartoum and the SPLA were edging towards compromise, full-scale war broke out in the impoverished western region of Darfur. Just why the smouldering Darfur conflict erupted when it did is a matter of conjecture, if not outright dispute. The various rebel factions claim that the upsurge in fighting was a natural response to ever-increasing discrimination against black Africans by Arabs. By way of alternative explanations, some observers point to the success of both the Kosovo Liberation Army (KLA) and the SPLA in involving 'the international community' in their respective conflicts as a means of obtaining favourable settlements (Belloni 2006). Indeed, in Darfur it is common to see demands for UN or American intervention on the part of IDPs and refugees who have been displaced by the fighting. A third explanation is that, under the terms of the Naivasha Accords, the SPLA secured its objective of obtaining a slice of Sudan's oil revenue and posts in the public sector for its supporters. It is argued that the SPLA's success at forcing the government to negotiate favourable terms in these matters may have acted as spur for the rebels in Darfur to raise the stakes. It was also in the spring of 2003 that various governments, in particular that of the United States, in concert with a variety of NGOs, accused the Sudanese government of pursuing a policy of genocide in Darfur, based on credible estimates of some 250,000 people killed and several million displaced. Since then, Sudan's president, Omar al-Bashir, has been indicted by the International Criminal Court on five counts of crimes against humanity (murder, extermination, forcible transfer, torture and rape) and on two counts of war crimes (intentionally directing attacks against a civilian population and pillaging).

Following two years of mounting pressure, in May 2005 inconclusive peace negotiations held in Nigeria dashed hopes of a breakthrough in the conflict. The Sudanese government attempted to reach a settlement with three rival rebel groups, none of whom speaks for the black African population of Darfur as a whole. The situation was complicated by the vague nature of rebel demands and their lack of a structured political programme. The two main rebel movements involved were the Justice and Equality Movement (JEM) and the Sudan Liberation Army (SLA). Since then, the number of rebel groups has proliferated, and some have been known to switch sides and engage in banditry.

In the event, only one faction of the SLA reached agreement with the government. It was rejected by the JEM, which up until 2004 had in fact been aligned with the former speaker of the parliament and prominent Islamist Hassan al-Tarabi and his supporters in Khartoum. Khartoum agreed to take steps to disarm the Janjaweed and integrate (former) rebels in the national army. However, it appears that at the bottom of the refusal of two rebel groups to sign was their belief that the deal secured by the SPLA should have served as a model for Darfur.

In contrast to Darfur, we do have another example, alongside that of the south, where peace has recently been achieved. In the late 1990s armed conflict began between the indigenous people of the east and Khartoum. The Sudanese government regularly accused the Eritrean government of backing the rebels. Fortunately, in July 2006 this conflict was brought to an end. Following negotiations in Eritrea itself, the Eastern Front and a series of smaller groups with which it is allied accepted a deal under the terms of which Khartoum agreed to address long-standing grievances with regard to discrimination and revenue-sharing. What facilitated the success of this agreement was the prior settlement between Sudan and Eritrea of outstanding bilateral issues.

Sudan is an authoritarian state dominated by an executive presidency. The current government is formed of a coalition of the National Congress Party (NCP) and its former enemies the Sudan People's Liberation Movement (SPLM), the political arm of the SPLA. Shari'a Law applies in the northern part of the country, although it is not uniformly applied to non-Muslims, particularly since the peace agreement of 2005 (Human Rights Watch 2006).

Sudan has difficult relations with a number of its neighbours, especially Chad. In the past it has also become embroiled in disputes with Kenya, Eritrea and Uganda. The position of Sudan's government with regard to the quasi-Christian mystical sect the Lord's Resistance Army (LRA), which has been waging war against the Ugandan government since the early 1980s, shows how Realpolitik is never far away in such situations. For some years, up until the conclusion of the Naivasha Accords, the Khartoum government allowed the LRA to use those parts of southern Sudan controlled by its forces as a rear base from which it launched attacks into Uganda (GSO 2008).

Sudan's current dispute with Chad is particularly dangerous. Given that some of the 200,000 Sudanese refugees in Chad are also rebel fighters, the spillover of the conflict was as inevitable as it was tragic. In early 2005 Chad became embroiled in the Darfur conflict. In April 2005, and February 2008, rebel forces and their Sudanese allies actually reached the Chadian capital of N'djamena before they were defeated by troops loyal to President Idriss Deby, who, in turn, could count on the support of France. In May 2008 Darfur rebels backed by Chad reached the outskirts of the Sudanese capital.

The role of the African Union (AU) in the Darfur conflict has been significant both for what it did and for what it did not achieve. The Africa Mission in Sudan (AMIS) was established by the AU in April 2004, following the signing of a ceasefire agreement between the Sudanese government and two rebel groups in Darfur. The AU force has been bitterly criticized on the grounds that it is understaffed, inadequately trained and not nearly proactive enough. Eventually, in 2007, Khartoum agreed to the establishment of a joint AU–UN force in Darfur, which has been equally ineffective in bringing hostilities to an end. Both the government and the rebels are better motivated than the peacekeepers, and they are not short of arms. A plethora of UN resolutions bears testimony to the concern that this organization feels about the situation in Darfur, even though many of its draft resolutions were either blocked or watered down by China, which has strong economic and political links with Sudan. Thus backed by China, Sudan has long resisted any serious UN or AU intervention in Darfur, including humanitarian efforts.

Sudan perpetually stands at the cusp of disintegration. As with the DRC, it is difficult to talk of the existence of either nation or state according to common European definitions. Clashes between the SPLA and government forces still occur. While the conflict in Darfur is not (yet) one of secession, it remains confused and confusing, with the JEM in particular making common ground with 'Arab' opponents of the Khartoum regime, who in turn actively seek help from Chad. The clear and present danger here is that such local conflicts, as in the DRC, easily precipitate a wider regional conflagration, embroiling Sudan and several of its neighbours. With the relative powerlessness and ineffectiveness so far of international mediation efforts in Darfur, Sudan remains at great risk of continuing and intensifying violence, especially with a view to the 2011 independence referendum in the south. Only a concerted and unanimous international and regional effort may be able to persuade all the conflict parties to reverse course and prevent a total collapse into all-out violence.

3 Success and failure of international intervention: the case of Kosovo

The conflict in Kosovo is an ethnic conflict with strong territorial and cross-border/international dimensions. The conflict and its various (interim) settlements have had implications far beyond Kosovo: for Serbia, for the region of the Western Balkans, and for the international system.

3.1 Background

Driven by concerns about the human rights situation in Kosovo and the implications of a further escalation in the latent conflict there, from 1990 onwards a number of international governmental organizations began to adopt various strategies of intervention, starting with the European Parliament's first resolution on Kosovo.[2] The intervention strategies adopted before NATO's air campaign ranged from declarations of concern and the funding of NGO initiatives to CSCE/OSCE monitoring missions and concrete proposals on how best to address the crisis. The organizations involved were, on the global level, the United Nations and the International Conference on the Former Yugoslavia (and its successor organizations), on the transatlantic level, NATO, the CSCE/OSCE and the Contact Group on Bosnia and Herzegovina, and, on the European level, the EU, the WEU, the European Parliament and the Parliamentary Assembly of the Council of Europe. Apart from this, there have been a number of bilateral and regional initiatives, such as the Kinkel–Védrine Initiative of November 1997 and the Turkey-inspired initiative to create a multinational Balkan rapid intervention force drawn from the armed forces of Albania, Bulgaria, Macedonia and Romania (DCWEU 1998). Individually, the governments of Russia, the United States and, to a lesser degree, Germany, Italy and Greece have played a part in the international community's response to the evolving and subsequently escalating conflict in Kosovo.

The difficulties the international community experienced in formulating and implementing a consistent and effective policy approach towards the conflict in Kosovo were several and had their sources within Kosovo, in Serbia (and, while they existed, the Federal Republic of Yugoslavia and the State Union of Serbia and Montenegro, respectively), in the wider Balkans region, and within the complex framework of relations between the main actors in the international arena. Together these factors, from the outset, limited the range of possible policies, resulting in international governmental actors

Table 6.1 Factors influencing the development of the Kosovo conflict

Situation in Kosovo	Situation in Serbia	Regional context	International context

• Inter-ethnic situation:
 	
  • socio-demographic structure
 	
  • level and nature of inter-group conflict and alliances
 	
  • nature of cleavages
 	
  • power and numerical balance
 	
• Intra-ethnic situation:
 	
  • dominant policy agenda
 	
  • strength of leadership
 	
  • existence of factions
 	
  • availability of resources
	• Political and economic importance of the conflict and the territory of Kosovo
	
	• Policy agendas of major parties in relation to the conflict
	
	• Availability and commitment of resources
	
	• Perceived impact of the conflict on potential or actual other conflicts
		• Impact of the conflict:
		
		  • stability of democratic institutions and ethnic balances
		
		  • spillover potential
		
		  • refugee movement
		
		• Impact on the conflict:
		
		  • policy agendas of major players in relation to the conflict
		
		  • regional interest structures
		
		  • cross-border ethnic alliances
			• Geopolitical significance of the territory
			
			• Interest structures and alliances
			
			• Availability and commitment of resources by international organizations

failing, individually and collectively, to prevent and subsequently settle the conflict via a negotiated solution.

Within our four-level framework of analysis, we need to consider the situation on the ground in Kosovo, in Serbia, in the region of the Western Balkans, and in the broader international context. In particular, we need to examine the following specific factors outlined in table 6.1.

3.2 *The constraints of conflict containment*

As previously mentioned, from 1990 onwards various policy initiatives by the international community had sought to prevent the violent escalation of the conflict in Kosovo, which intensified from February 1998, in the wake of years of rising inter-ethnic tension. Thereafter, the major objective of the international community was to prevent a spillover of the conflict into neighbouring countries, while simultaneously calming the situation in Kosovo and searching for an acceptable settlement. These efforts were frustrated by a variety of factors, which we will discuss in turn.

3.2a The inter-ethnic situation in Kosovo Relationships between Albanians, Serbs and members of other ethnic groups in Kosovo have rarely been harmonious. Culturally, the territory is significant for Serbs and Albanians alike, playing an important role in identity-shaping collective myths. With the creation of socialist Yugoslavia after the Second World War, hopes for the consolidation of a Greater Albania, created under Italian occupation, vanished into thin air. Several constitutional reforms between 1946 and 1974 increased the autonomy of Kosovo but failed to address the inter-ethnic unease. After 1974 the Serb population found itself increasingly pressurized by the Albanian majority in the province. The March 1981 riots in Prishtina were something of a watershed. Despite their mundane origins in a student protest at the quality of the food at the University of Prishtina, they quickly assumed a nationalist hue. Their violent suppression by Yugoslav security forces and the indeterminate number of deaths that resulted served to stimulate nascent Albanian nationalism. Albanian activists pressed ever harder for the republican status of Kosovo, which according to the Yugoslav constitution brought with it a conditional right to secession. Tensions between Serbs and Albanians in Kosovo and between the ethnic Albanian minority and the central government in Belgrade, along with the rise of nationalism among all ethnic groups in Yugoslavia, culminated in the abolition of Kosovo's autonomy in 1989. Policies of segregation pursued by Serbs in Kosovo and Belgrade resulted in the creation of two parallel societies – Serb and Albanian. Albanians, after being forced out of the public sector, set up their own institutions and, after a 'secret' referendum and parliamentary and presidential elections in 1991 and 1992, proclaimed the Republic of Kosovo.

The Yugoslav wars of secession diverted international attention from Kosovo but increased tensions in the region itself. Serbs and Albanians became increasingly radicalized, their fears and demands also being fuelled from political actors outside Kosovo, such as the Serbian government in Belgrade and the Albanian diaspora in Western Europe and the United States. A last (theoretical) chance of addressing the situation in Kosovo came with the Dayton Peace Accords in 1995. When Kosovo was mentioned only in passing in the agreement, Albanians realized that their thus far mostly peaceful struggle for independence had failed, while the government in Belgrade felt it had been given *carte blanche* by the international community in relation to Kosovo, despite the so-called Christmas warning issued in 1992 by US President G. H. Bush, which had threatened US armed action should Serbia use force in Kosovo. Consequently, inter-ethnic relations deteriorated further.

3.2b The intra-ethnic situation in Kosovo The two major problems which the international community had to confront with respect to the ethnic Albanian population in Kosovo were their demands for an independent state and the fact that otherwise no unified political platform among ethnic Albanians existed, and that all attempts to create one were frustrated by personal and political rivalries.

Until the mid-1990s, Ibrahim Rugova was the unchallenged leader of the ethnic Albanians' peaceful resistance to Serbia, and there seemed to be a widespread determination among the existing political parties of Kosovo Albanians not to let party-political differences come in the way of a joint political agenda. Initially, this aspired to a restoration of the *status quo ante* plus – i.e., the return to the 1974 constitutional regulations with a simultaneous upgrading of Kosovo to a republic and of ethnic Albanians to one of the constituent peoples of the Yugoslav state. Subsequently, however, continued Serbian repression made Rugova and his party demand independence. Two unofficial presidential and parliamentary elections administered by the Kosovo Albanians confirmed his claim to the presidency of the self-proclaimed Republic of Kosovo. While Rugova thus possessed a certain degree of democratic legitimacy, even though the elections were organized under very difficult conditions, he had hardly any substantive power. This became apparent at an internal level by the rejection of his authority by the emergent KLA. Externally, in his relations with Serbia and the Federal Republic of Yugoslavia (FRY), Rugova was not able to secure any substantial concessions from the Yugoslav president, Slobodan Milošević, apart from a March 1998 agreement to reopen Albanian language schools. Another severe blow to his strategy of non-violent resistance and of engaging the international community for the cause of an independent Kosovo was dealt by the European Union's official recognition of the FRY in 1996, before any resolution of the already obvious conflict in Kosovo. However, to some extent, blame also rested with Rugova himself. Insisting on the necessity and possibility of achieving Kosovo's independence from Serbia, he raised the hopes of ethnic Albanians even at a time when the international community had long made it clear that it did not support any unilateral change of borders.

At the time, Rugova's Democratic League of Kosovo (LDK) faced four main political rivals – the Independent Union of Albanian Students, which in 1997 was the first political organization to defy Rugova openly; Adem Demaçi's Parliamentary Party of Kosovo (PDK), which for some time also represented the KLA; the Social Democratic Party of Kosovo, which joined the former two in the boycotts of the March 1998 Kosovo elections; and the Albanian Democratic Movement, which was formed at the end of June 1998 by recruiting its members and leadership partly from dissatisfied former Rugova allies. The major, and eventually successful, challenge to Rugova's leadership came from the KLA, which became increasingly popular among Kosovo's Albanian population and was well funded both by the Albanian diaspora in Western Europe and the United States and by 'proceeds' from drugs and weapons trafficking.[3]

The major problem that arose from this constellation was that, even if a (temporary) settlement could have been negotiated in 1998, the structure of talks between Rugova's exclusive negotiating team and Serbian/FRY officials would have been unlikely to muster sufficient support among ethnic Albanians (and the various political groups that claimed to represent them) in order to implement successfully any agreement that fell short of independence, at least in the short term. This was particularly true for the KLA, which, through its then political representative, Adem Demaçi, made it clear on several occasions that only the realization of full independence, or at least the international community's clear support for this goal, would lead to a permanent end to its struggle. This stance increased the KLA's popularity further, and the international community had to accept the role of the organization and include it in its efforts to address the crisis in Kosovo.

To prevent Kosovo's independence at all costs was the foremost objective of a large majority of the ethnic Serb population in the province. In this effort, they had the overall backing of the Serbian government in Belgrade and the protection of the Serbian security forces. However, despite this active endorsement by the central government, ethnic Serbs in Kosovo were not in a particularly easy position. Their share of the population had shrunk from just under one-third in 1961 to less than one-tenth in the 1990s. This decrease had partly to do with emigration, motivated by the much lower standard of living in Kosovo compared to any other part of Yugoslavia during the years before the break-up of the state. In addition, the Serbian perception of the post-1974 period in Kosovo had been shaped by the experience of the 'national key' – a system that ensured proportional representation of ethnic groups in the public sector, which, as Yugoslavia had a more or less completely nationalized economy, included almost all sectors of the job market as well. Consequently, Serbs saw themselves (and indeed they were) at a disadvantage in Kosovo in a variety of ways, especially in comparison to their pre-1974 position, and chose to emigrate in significant numbers.[4] From the mid-1980s onwards, ethnic Serbs in Kosovo began to organize themselves in order to lobby the central government in Belgrade. In January 1986, prominent Belgrade intellectuals sent a petition to Serbian and Yugoslav authorities claiming an anti-Serb genocide was underway in Kosovo and demanding decisive constitutional and other steps be taken to reverse the fate of the Slav population in the province.[5] Towards the end of that year the Kosovo Committee of Serbs and Montenegrins was formed and sent petition after petition to Belgrade urging tough measures to ensure the 'survival of Serbdom' in Kosovo. After initially criticizing the government for not destroying the Kosovo Albanian shadow state in the mid-1990s, the Serb Resistance Movement (SPO) sponsored the so-called Serb–Serb talks and took a more conciliatory approach from 1997–8 onwards, recognizing the need for an inclusive settlement that would accommodate equally ethnic Albanian and ethnic Serb interests. Supported by the Serbian Orthodox Church in Kosovo, Momcilo Trajkovic, the party's president, repeatedly called for inclusive talks among all parties involved and criticized both President Milošević and the KLA for their uncompromising positions (Moffett 1998). The party recognized that the main obstacle to a solution of the conflict was the lack of a democratic political process in Serbia, but its efforts to remedy this situation and promote dialogue between Serbs and Albanians were not very successful, mostly because of the lack of mistrust that had grown between these two groups over a prolonged period of latent conflict.

In addition, it must be noted that the Serb population of Kosovo was far from homogeneous, and this affected political developments quite strongly. Several thousand Serbs who had been forced out of Croatia were resettled in Kosovo, many of them against their will. When, in addition to the traditionally depressed economic conditions in the area, the security situation worsened, resulting in some 2,000 registered Serb and Montenegrin refugees from Kosovo by mid-July 1998 (Yugoslav Helsinki Committee 1998), this section of the Serb population in Kosovo became particularly radicalized, providing an electoral stronghold for the Serbian Radical Party and its leader, Vojislav Šešelj.

It is also important to realize that, despite the fact that some of its sections were genuinely committed to the peaceful and democratic resolution of the conflict, the Serbian Orthodox Church had a vested interest in a settlement within the existing boundaries of Yugoslavia. In a 1998 interview, one church official referred to the fact that the independence of Kosovo 'could lead to a large-scale exodus of the Serbian population from the province. If this happened, it is a question whether our church and monastic communities could remain here' (Father Sava 1998). Given the central importance of Kosovo to the Serbian Orthodox Church, the latter clearly could not be seen as impartial in its mediation efforts.

The increased KLA targeting of Serbs and the continued instrumentalization of Kosovo in Serbian and Yugoslav politics diminished the chances of success for moderate forces among Serbs in Kosovo. Serb self-armament, 'retaliation' and cooperation with the security forces, in turn, contributed to the hardening of positions on the Albanian side, thus diminishing the already slim chances of an inter-ethnic accord as part of an agreement on the future of Kosovo.

We should pause at this point to acknowledge the fact that, although Albanians and Serbs are the two numerically strongest and politically predominant ethnic groups in Kosovo, they are not alone. According to estimates before the escalation of the conflict, Albanians accounted for 82.2 per cent of the total Kosovo population and Serbs for 10 per cent. Other ethnic groups included Bosniak Muslims (2.9 per cent), Roma (2.3 per cent), Montenegrins (1 per cent), Turks (0.6 per cent) and Croats (0.4 per cent).

Characteristic of all these other minority groups was the fact that they were politically poorly organized, internally split and unwilling to cooperate with other minorities. Among other things, this had its reasons in the assimilatory pressure put on other Muslim minorities by the Albanian community and the relative satisfaction smaller minorities felt with the rights granted to them by the Serbian authorities. This lack of cooperation among ethnic groups in Kosovo – and that included ethnic Albanians – and their failure to adopt a common stance and joint political platform vis-à-vis the Serbian authorities on the crucial issue of minority rights enabled the Serbian government to conduct a selective minority policy, encouraging the artificial division among and within ethnic groups and distinguishing between loyal and disloyal minorities, treating each of them accordingly.

However, for two reasons the presence of other ethnic minorities in Kosovo, or Serbian instrumentalization of this fact, must not be overestimated in their impact on the development of the conflict. First, numerically and politically these other minorities were rather insignificant when compared to ethnic Albanians and ethnic Serbs. Second, no kin state (Turkey, Bosnia and Herzegovina, Croatia) was willing to commit the level of resources necessary to intervene decisively with the government in Belgrade over the minority rights situation in Kosovo.

3.2c The situation in Serbia   The importance of Kosovo for Serbia or, more precisely, for the Serbian and Yugoslav governments is primarily political. Former Yugoslav President Milošević came to power in the region in 1986–7 on a platform of Serbian nationalism focusing on Kosovo, and from 1998 his grip on power became ever more dependent on his ability to instrumentalize the Kosovo crisis. Throughout the period before NATO's intervention – that is, when a political rather than military solution still seemed possible – Milošević succeeded in rallying Serbian nationalist support behind him. By incorporating the Serbian Radical Party (SRS) and the Serbian Renewal Movement (SPO) in his government, he managed to make two possible major critics share the responsibility for domestic and international consequences of government policy in Kosovo (ICG 1998a). Against this background of the growing influence of extreme nationalists, Milošević was also able to present himself as an indispensable guarantor of stability to the international community because of his influence in the region and because of undesirable alternatives after his departure. More importantly, he managed internally to prevent a democratization of the political process in Serbia and the FRY both by keeping some 1 million Albanian voters away from the polls and by keeping inner Serbian and inner Yugoslav democratic opposition parties in a state of antagonistic division (USIP 1998). Ironically, the electoral boycott of ethnic Albanians enabled the Socialist Party of Serbia (SPS) to increase its representation in parliament, as the seats not contested by Albanians went to the SPS.

Within the parameters of Yugoslav territorial integrity, Milošević publicly portrayed himself as someone committed to a peaceful settlement of the conflict. On 28 September 1998, the National Assembly of the Republic of

Serbia approved a number of resolutions concerning the Kosovo conflict, in which its members emphasized the need for a speedy resolution of the ensuing humanitarian crisis. The conciliatory stance adopted by the parliament followed the adoption five days earlier of Resolution 1199 (1998) by the UN Security Council. Although these resolutions contained important commitments in relation to the humanitarian dimension of the crisis, they did not imply a fundamental change in the Serbian political approach to its resolution. With Milošević gaining politically on several fronts from the ongoing conflict in Kosovo, initiatives aimed at a permanent settlement were unlikely to succeed without stronger international pressure. Without it, the odds were that Milošević would pursue a policy of moderate de-escalation (to avoid the risk of international intervention) and continuing tension in Kosovo (to maintain the conflict at a low-intensity and manageable level).

Apart from the political dimensions to the conflict, Kosovo was important for Serbia/the FRY in economic terms. Internally, its coal mines and power stations, important to the Yugoslav industrial and private energy market, and the cost of the ongoing conflict made the future of Kosovo an economic concern. Externally, the economic significance arose from the crucial role the conflict and its settlement were assigned in the Dayton Accord for the lifting of economic sanctions against the FRY.

3.2d Beyond Kosovo: the regional context of the conflict   Historically, the Balkans has been a region of great instability for over a century. The demise of the Ottoman and Habsburg empires and the withdrawal of Russia from the region for most of the inter-war period left behind a power vacuum that was filled only insufficiently by the new states that emerged from the ruins. The territorial arrangements adopted after the First and Second Balkan Wars and after the First and Second World Wars did not resolve many of the historical border and nationality disputes. These disputes, merely suppressed by the realities of the Cold War, came to the forefront of international politics once more after 1989.

One of the central problems was the so-called Albanian question, i.e., the presence of large Albanian minorities in Macedonia, Montenegro, Greece and Kosovo and some smaller areas of southern Serbia. In the 1990s, the worsening situation in Kosovo had its most direct impact on Albania, Macedonia and Montenegro, where domestic developments and responses to the crisis had consequences in turn for Kosovo.

In Albania, communism began to crumble at the beginning of the 1990s. Multi-party elections in 1992 and 1996 resulted in Sali Berisha's Democratic Party (PD) winning overwhelming victories. As early as 1990 this party had reintroduced the issue of Kosovo in the emerging democratic political process in Albania. In 1992 the Kosovo Albanian shadow state was recognised de facto by a decision of the Albanian parliament asking the Democratic Party government of the day to recognize the Republic of Kosovo. Although the government did not act upon this resolution (Schmidt 2000: 37), it still remodelled the concept of Albanian citizenship along *jus sanguinis* lines to include all ethnic Albanians regardless of their country of residence (ICG 1998b). Official support for Kosovo's independence from the Albanian government, however, did not extend far beyond verbal declarations, and even these stopped in 1994, after the government recognized the existing borders with the FRY in the wake of the escalating war in the neighbouring country. In early 1997 Albanian society was at the brink of collapse and only narrowly escaped civil war when pyramid investment schemes collapsed, taking with them the savings of a majority of the anyway poor Albanian population. The situation was blamed largely on the government in office, which was defeated in early elections that same year.

The incoming socialist government of Albania, preoccupied with the country's internal problems of a collapsed economy and increasing crime rates, tried not to get involved too deeply in the ongoing Kosovo conflict and, above all, not to lose critical Western support in the rebuilding of Albanian's economy and society. Facing an increasing influx of refugees, it pursued a policy of de-escalation and of recognition of the existing borders of the FRY, favouring a solution within Yugoslavia giving Kosovo equal status with Serbia and Montenegro. At a summit of the leaders of seven Balkan countries in November 1997, the new Albanian prime minister, Fatos Nano, and the Yugoslav president, Slobodan Milošević, had a private meeting at which they discussed the Kosovo issue. While the meeting did not result in a breakthrough regarding the constitutional position of Kosovo, it did at least indicate that the new Albanian government would continue to respect existing borders, rather than inflame the then latent violent conflict by making irredentist claims (RFE/RL 1997). On the other hand, this seemingly prudent approach taken by the new Albanian government did not coincidentally fall together with the radicalization of the political spectrum in Kosovo and the increasing influence of forces determined to realize the goal of independence by all means possible, including the use of violence. Statements by government officials in Tirana accusing the KLA of terrorism and rejecting the idea of an independent Kosovo were not popular among any of the ethnic Albanian political factions in Kosovo. During the summer of 1998, Albania's policy towards Kosovo changed from one of neglect and condemnation of 'KLA terrorism' to a more sober analysis of the situation, weighing carefully domestic and foreign interests. While public opinion seemed almost entirely in favour of showing solidarity with ethnic Albanians in Kosovo (Sunley 1998), the degree to which this should include more active involvement differed greatly. Through family ties, the influx of refugees and the operation of KLA support and supply networks, Albanians in the north of the country were already more deeply involved in the conflict than their fellow citizens in the south. The lack of government control over the northern region and the existence there of organized crime, drug trafficking and weapons smuggling networks run by Kosovo Albanians (UN Economic and Social Council 1996; US Department of Justice 1996), as well as cross-border pursuit by the Serbian security forces, increased the danger of a spillover of the conflict, in which Albania as a whole did not have any interest. Yet it was not entirely clear how far the government supported the KLA and cooperated in this with diaspora groups, especially in Switzerland and Germany, to all of which it had at least some ideological affiliations (Baze n.d.; Schmidt 2000: 37).

In assessing Albania's role in the Kosovo conflict, the country's political and economic dependence on other international actors needs to be taken into consideration as well. Relationships with Greece, Italy and Macedonia were very complex and in one way or another related to the Kosovo conflict. Greece, a country traditionally relatively close to Serbia, has its own Albanian minority, even if officially the Greek government is reluctant to admit to its existence. Italy, which is a member of the Contact Group, has, since 1990, had to accommodate a large number of Albanian refugees, both from Albania proper and from Kosovo. While bilateral relations with Macedonia have improved in recent years, the issue of the Albanian minority there remains sensitive, in particular because of close ties between northern Albanians, ethnic Albanians in Macedonia and their kin in Kosovo.

Albania's internal weakness in the mid- to late 1990s, and in particular its almost complete lack of an effective defence force, increased the country's dependence on Western military support. The Partnership for Peace agreement between NATO and Albania provided the Albanian government with some assistance in handling the evolving crisis in Kosovo. However, even if NATO or the UN had been planning a border control mission in Albania similar to the one in Macedonia, the lack of infrastructure in Albania would have seriously delayed any such operation, probably beyond the point of its usefulness in conflict prevention policy (ICG 1998b). The inability to protect effectively its northern borders, together with the ongoing feud among Albania's political parties and the response to it from the ethnic Albanian parties in Kosovo, once more increased the potential of a spillover of the conflict into Albania.

Similar to Albania, Macedonia was among the countries most affected by the Kosovo conflict, but at the same time it also had a significant impact on the development of the conflict and its future solution. Although Macedonia's secession from Yugoslavia was peaceful, the country has experienced serious ethnic tensions, especially before the signing of the Ohrid Agreement in 2001 (see chapter 4).

At the time, Albanians in Macedonia were politically split between two important ethnic Albanian parties, whose demands, however, are not fundamentally different. An unofficial referendum organized in 1992 showed that, at a turnout of 90 per cent of the ethnic Albanian electorate in Macedonia, roughly three-quarters supported the idea of their own political and territorial autonomous structures (ICG 1998c). On this basis, ethnic Albanian parties argued for changes in Macedonia's constitution to elevate the ethnic Albanian population to the status of a constituent people of Macedonia, for improvements of the Albanian language situation, for the establishment of an Albanian university, and for the inclusion of ethnic Albanians in the administration (Georgieff 1998).

In addition to this internal dimension, the relationship between Macedonia and Albania is complex and has undergone a variety of changes throughout Macedonia's post-independence period. Between 1992 and 1997, during the presidency of Sali Berisha and two successive Democratic Party governments in Albania, official relations between Macedonia and Albania were strained by Albania's actions directed against Macedonia's accession to the OSCE. Even though the post-1997 socialist government in Tirana pursued a more conciliatory policy vis-à-vis Macedonia, it also made it clear to its counterpart in Skopje that it would not turn a blind eye on the fate of its ethnic kin group in Macedonia (Moore 1997).

With a Macedonian army hardly in existence, the country depended heavily on United Nations support for ensuring its territorial integrity and patrolling and monitoring its borders with Serbia and Albania. An UNPREDEP force had been in place since 1992, its mandate being extended by the Security Council on a biannual basis. Yet, with only 1,050 personnel, the force was hardly more than a symbolic gesture, confirming the commitment of the international community to ensure Macedonian territorial integrity.

With an unresolved border dispute with Serbia, Greece's refusal to recognize Macedonia's name, and Bulgaria's failure to acknowledge the existence of a Macedonian language and nation until 1999, the tensions between ethnic Macedonians and ethnic Albanians in Macedonia made up only one among a number of issues threatening political stability in the country. However, as elsewhere, it could have been perceived as a purely internal matter easy to instrumentalize in election campaigns. Thus among the implications that the international community had to consider were not merely a spillover of the conflict from Kosovo but also a self-intensifying conflict in Macedonia, with the potential to contribute to the ongoing destabilization of the region. This would have been particularly likely if a settlement had been implemented for Kosovo that granted the ethnic Albanian community there either far-reaching autonomy or, even though this was unlikely in 1998, independence. From a Macedonian point of view, this would have set an unwelcome example for its own latent ethnic conflict with its Albanian minority. The further frustration of ethnic Albanian demands in Macedonia, therefore, could have led to a similar violent conflict emerging there. Equally dangerous would have been a development in which ethnic Albanians in both areas would have joined forces. Existing clan ties between Kosovo and western Macedonia were already being used for the smuggling of weapons, the provision of support bases and funds, and the recruitment of militarily experienced fighters for the KLA (ICG 1998c).

The impact of and on Montenegro had to be considered primarily from a Yugoslav perspective. In 1998, at the time when Milošević was able to rally nationalist support in Serbia, he did not manage to secure a victory for his candidate for the Montenegrin presidency, Momir Bulatović. The fear that pursuing a confrontational course vis-à-vis Montenegro and its president-elect, Milo Djukanović, could trigger the secession of Montenegro, and thus the end of the FRY, led Milošević to acknowledge Djukanović's victory. Although the Montenegrin president had to concede earlier than planned parliamentary elections, Milošević could not capitalize on this as, in the ensuing general election, Bulatović's Socialist People's Party won only twenty-nine out of seventy-eight seats in the Montenegrin parliament, being defeated into second place by a three-party coalition of Djukanović supporters which won an absolute majority.

By September 1998 Montenegro had accommodated around 40,000 refugees from Kosovo. Its resources to attend even to their most basic needs being stretched to the limits, the Montenegrin government decided to seal off the border with Kosovo and to turn away any further refugees. However, these economic difficulties, as important as they might have been, were not the only problems the Montenegrin authorities faced at the time. Existing clan ties between ethnic Albanians from Kosovo and Montenegro, in combination with the amount of destruction of private and public infrastructure in Kosovo, made it likely that at least some of the refugees would remain permanently in Montenegro, adversely affecting carefully consolidated ethnic balances in the republic. Moreover, the sheer number of refugees in Montenegro and their provisional accommodation relatively close to the border was likely to draw Montenegro directly into the conflict once KLA fighters established bases there. It was against this background that in autumn 1998 Montenegro expelled some 3,000 partly armed ethnic Albanian refugees from Kosovo to Albania. Within this context, the inner Montenegrin and inner Yugoslav power struggles could have become more intense again, resulting in a serious Montenegrin–Serbian dispute and adding to the instability of the whole region.

Beyond these three, there are a number of other Balkan countries whose position in the conflict deserves careful consideration. Bulgaria's relations with Macedonia have already been mentioned. The possible involvement of Turkey could have become an actuality through a treaty on mutual defence and cooperation that links the country with Albania. Greece, on the other hand, had been traditionally close to Serbia. The treatment of Albania's Greek minority and of migrant Albanian workers in Greece, as well as border demarcation disputes between Albania and Greece, had been the source of tension between the two countries for decades. Moreover, Greek–Turkish relations over Cyprus and territorial disputes in the Aegean Sea had been constant worries in the region for a long time before the Kosovo conflict and had brought the two countries on several occasions to the brink of war. In a sense, the regional context for international conflict regulation could hardly have been less favourable.

3.2e The international context: the United Nations, NATO and Russia   Another major problem that inhibited the international community's ability to devise and implement effective conflict prevention, management and resolution policies resulted from the fact that there was no unified approach to the Kosovo crisis. Not only was there a multitude of individual and collective players on the scene, with different mandates and capabilities, but there was also the problem of different allegiances, degrees of influence on the adversaries, and strategic interests. The rift between the Western powers and Russia in the Contact Group was the most obvious example of this. Since the idea of a potential NATO military intervention to restore peace in Kosovo had been proposed, Russia had consistently opposed it and constantly reiterated its conviction that there could be no military solution to the conflict. Russia's refusal to support a NATO strike in Kosovo in the UN Security Council was also accompanied by the implicit threat that such a move would be to the detriment of other strategic Western interests, as it would alienate Russia from NATO and other Western-dominated international organizations. On the other hand, Russia also feared that it was losing even more influence on the developments in the Balkans and therefore sought to remain involved in the international mediation efforts in Kosovo.

Russia's policy towards the conflict included both the refusal to recognize the KLA as a partner in negotiations over a settlement and a Russian engagement to broker a peaceful solution. After a meeting between President Milošević and President Yeltsin on 16 June 1998, the former agreed to begin talks with ethnic Albanians led by Ibrahim Rugova, whom the Russians saw as the only legitimate representative of Kosovo Albanians, and to allow a diplomatic observer mission unrestricted access to Kosovo. At this meeting, Russia took up the Serbian perspective by making it clear that a withdrawal of Serbian security forces without a curbing of KLA activities in the province would lead to a mass exodus of the Slav population and was therefore unacceptable to Serbia. Russia also cooperated closely with the United States and other Contact Group members in the diplomatic observer mission. In a joint statement in September 1998, presidents Yeltsin and Clinton demanded an end to violence, the withdrawal of Serbian forces to their permanent locations, the immediate commencement of negotiations, the granting to refugees of the possibility of returning to their homes, and increased international monitoring of the situation in Kosovo. Russia also participated in the NATO Partnership for Peace exercise in Albania in August 1998 and supported an extension of the UNPREDEP mandate in Macedonia. However, while Russia's involvement in international efforts to resolve the Kosovo crisis may have increased the international community's leverage over Serbia/the FRY, it also made it more difficult to find consensus because of the increased diversity of interest structures.

Further difficulties arose for NATO from the pending admission of three new members – Hungary, Poland and the Czech Republic. Hungary, in particular, had its own specific national interests in the conflict because of the large Hungarian minority in the northern Serbian province of Vojvodina, constituting around 20 per cent of the local population. During 1998, Hungary intervened several times on behalf of its kin group, ensuring, among other things, that ethnic Hungarians were not drafted for military service in Kosovo. In addition, public opinion in most NATO member countries was severely divided over the threat and use of force, and even the alliance's political leaders were far from united over this issue.

In September and October 1998, as the situation on the ground in Kosovo deteriorated, NATO leaders made it clear that a military strike had not been completely ruled out (US Department of Defense 1998). The willingness to deploy up to 50,000 troops for the enforcing of a negotiated ceasefire had been indicated, and a three-stage engagement programme had been made public to express a clear warning to President Milošević. Stage one of this programme – the underpinning of neighbouring countries – was already under way in summer 1998, with NATO Partnership for Peace agreements and exercises in Albania and Macedonia. Stage two was described as a phased escalation programme to punish further offensive actions, and stage three was described as full commitment of troops (ibid.). With the deteriorating refugee situation and no sign of an end to the violence in the conflict, international impatience grew. A letter sent by the UN Secretary General to President Milošević, although it stopped short of threatening military action, demanded immediate steps to end the violence and destruction in Kosovo, and could, in its directness, have been taken as an indication that the international community was edging towards action. Eventually, the UN Security Council passed another resolution on 23 September 1998. Reaffirming its commitment to support a peaceful resolution of the Kosovo problem by means of an enhanced status for the province within the existing borders of the FRY, it also stated that the situation in Kosovo was a threat to peace and security in the region and would therefore require the action of the international community according to Chapter VII of the UN Charter. In the resolution, the Security Council demanded that the warring parties put an end to violence and engage in a constructive dialogue. More specifically, the authorities of the FRY were asked, among other things, to stop all actions against the civilian population in Kosovo; to allow international monitoring, the return of refugees and humanitarian assistance; and to commit to a timetable for negotiations and confidence-building. Kosovo Albanians were requested to pursue their political goals exclusively by peaceful means, and their leadership was urged to condemn all terrorist acts. Most significantly, however, the Security Council reserved for itself the right 'to consider further action and additional measures to maintain or restore peace and stability in the region' in case either party, or both, should not comply with the demands of the two resolutions (UN Security Council 1998b). This was a much tougher stance than that adopted in the previous resolution on Kosovo, where the Security Council merely emphasized 'that failure to make constructive progress towards the peaceful resolution of the situation in Kosovo will lead to the consideration of additional measures' (UN Security Council 1998a). Eventually, NATO's obvious determination to act even without UN approval and despite Russian objections was the essential catalyst to force Serbia to back down for the time being and agree to withdraw its troops from Kosovo.

3.3 Settling for an interim arrangement

The complexity of a situation involving such a variety of local, regional and global actors with distinct interest structures, competing goals and different motivations for their involvement made it a foremost challenge for the international community to initiate an inclusive, meaningful negotiation process that would have been likely to result in a settlement. The difficulties with this approach were twofold. First, it had to be made clear to all parties involved that, in the absence of easy solutions, a readiness to compromise and a willingness to settle for less than their maximum demands was the essential prerequisite for any stable long-term solution, not only to the Kosovo conflict, but also to some of the region's other political problems. Second, it was necessary to bring the representatives of Kosovo Albanians and the Serbian/ Yugoslav government together. With the Rambouillet talks, an environment for such a negotiation process was created. Yet, like any other conflict, an ethnic conflict requires for its settlement the presence of a number of conditions, which in their totality create a situation of 'ripeness'. In the specific context of the Kosovo conflict, these conditions existed on each of the four levels of our analysis (see table 6.2).

On a general level, it is important to note that, individually, these conditions were necessary to make the settlement of the Kosovo conflict possible, yet only in their entirety would they have been sufficient to do so. Their joint presence indicates that a conflict is ripe for a settlement – that is, that a window of opportunity exists for decision-makers to achieve a settlement. The simultaneous presence of these conditions does not say anything about whether this opportunity will be taken, what kind of settlement will be agreed, or whether an adopted settlement will be stable; it merely points to the fact that the strategies of the conflict parties towards the conflict are no longer incompatible. Once this has been recognized – and there is no guarantee that every such opportunity will be recognized – the overall success of the settlement process depends upon the flexibility, determination and skill of those involved to design an institutional framework that fits the variety of contextual circumstances of their particular situation so as to provide for opportunities to resolve differences by peaceful and democratic means.

Table 6.2 'Ripeness' conditions for the settlement of the Kosovo conflict

Situation in Kosovo	Situation in Serbia	Regional context	International context

• Inter-ethnic situation:
 	
  • ability and preparedness of political elites to compromise on central issues
 	
• Intra-ethnic situation:
 	
  • strong leadership with a broad popular mandate to end the conflict
 	
  • marginalization of extremist elements
	• Strong leadership with a broad popular mandate to end the conflict
	
	• Limited chance of outflanking by anti-settlement parties
	
	• Greater political benefits from settlement compared to continuation of conflict
		• Limited chance of domestic instrumentalization of the conflict	• Joint and flexible policy with sufficient room for manoeuvre and leverage on each of the parties
			
			• Availability and commitment of resources to facilitate negotiation and implementation/operation of settlement

The previous analysis of the various contextual factors has already signalled the severe difficulties encountered by the international community in the search for a political rather than a military solution to the Kosovo conflict. We will now examine what factors accounted for the failure of the Rambouillet negotiations and the follow-on conference in Paris. With regard to the inter-ethnic situation in Kosovo, by the time the negotiations in Rambouillet began, the conflict was very much one between the central government in Belgrade and the KLA and ethnic Albanian population in Kosovo. Although the Serbian security forces used local Serbs as auxiliary forces, the conflict was primarily not an ethnic one between two local populations. All other ethnic groups in the area had been sidelined a long time ago and suffered the consequences of the conflict, rather than being active players in it. As a token gesture, the Serbian delegation in Rambouillet initially included representatives from other ethnic groups in Kosovo (to emphasize that the Albanian delegation did not represent Kosovo as a whole), but the more the Serbian delegation engaged with sincerity in the negotiations, the more these became replaced by specialists (Petritsch et al. 1999; Weller 1999). This meant that the influence of the situation in Serbia as well as the political constellations within the Albanian population in Kosovo became more significant for the course of the negotiations.

Before the negotiations began, the main point of contact for the international community had been Kosovo's secretly elected government and president. Since the escalation of the conflict in February 1998, their influence on the ground in Kosovo had dwindled in favour of that of the KLA and a broad coalition of political parties opposed to President Rugova. This turn of events, combined with international pressure, resulted in a Kosovo delegation in Rambouillet that consisted in equal parts of these three groupings, with the KLA playing a dominant role – reflected in one of the latter's members being elected head of the tripartite presidency of the negotiation team (Weller 1999: 179). This made the position of the international community more difficult, as the KLA's commitment eventually to achieve independent statehood for Kosovo clashed with the international determination, at the time, to preserve existing borders and to find a solution within them. The compromise found in Rambouillet that brought the KLA on board was one of far-reaching self-government for ethnic Albanians in Kosovo, with a mechanism for a final settlement (considering, among other things, the will of the people) to be adopted after further international discussions. While, more than anything else, this reflected the changed situation in Kosovo, international pressure as well as some concessions to the Kosovo negotiation team ensured that the delegation as a whole eventually consented to sign the interim agreement.

Whereas the international community thus possessed at least some leverage over the Kosovo delegation, this was not the case with the Serbian delegation. There were several reasons for this. Even though President Milošević had retained, if not increased, his political strength, there were very few incentives for him to utilize this strength to secure a successful outcome of the negotiations. Taking an accommodative stance in Rambouillet and Paris and negotiating within the parameters set by the international community could easily have cost him and his party their dominant position in Yugoslav and Serbian politics. Further political radicalization in Serbia and a shift of power to the extreme nationalists in the Serbian Radical Party would, together with the perceived weakness of the institution of the Yugoslav president, almost certainly have led to renewed pressure for independence from Montenegro, and thus to the likely end of the FRY – which is, of course, precisely what happened in June 2006. Similarly, it was quite obvious that Milošević was playing for time to prepare a final assault on Kosovo, including massive troop deployments and forced population displacements in the border zones with Macedonia and Albania (Petritsch et al. 1999: 325, 344). This would have enabled Milošević to claim a national victory. He realized that acceptance of the Rambouillet Agreement, with its mechanism for a final settlement after three years, would, in all likelihood, lead to the secession of Kosovo. In addition, he made his own judgement of the ability and willingness of NATO to act unilaterally against the will of Russia and for long enough to bring Serbia, which would rely on Russian support, to its knees (Marko 1999: 274–5). In the same vein, Milošević was apparently calculating that consensus within NATO would break apart over civilian casualties and that there would be no majority to engage in a ground war.

Compared to the problems generated from the situation in Serbia, the regional context was far less troublesome. Obviously, the international community could not encourage developments in Kosovo that would pose an immediate threat to the precarious stability of the Balkans. From this perspective, the outlining of the non-negotiable principles of a framework within which Serbs and Albanians had to find a mutually acceptable interim settlement was as much a result of taking the positions of the conflict parties on board as it was a sign of international awareness of the wider implications of the Kosovo conflict (Weller 1999: 177f.). The two most difficult challenges faced by the international community were the refugee problem and the situation in Bosnia and Herzegovina. Data collected by the UNHCR indicated as early as September 1998 that the Serbian military campaign and policy of ethnic cleansing had led to more than a quarter of a million Kosovo Albanians being internally displaced or seeking refuge in Albania, Macedonia, Montenegro and Serbia. This number had increased to over 300,000 by the beginning of March 1999, before the start of the NATO air campaign. The greatest number of those uprooted, about 250,000, were internally displaced in Kosovo, many of them trying to survive in the open. Another 55,000 had been displaced within Montenegro and Serbia, and about 10,000 people fled to Albania and to Macedonia. In connection with the policy of Serbs to destroy systematically the homes of ethnic Albanians, the international community saw it as its primary objective not only to put a stop to ethnic cleansing but also to establish conditions that would allow the displaced to return to their towns and villages as quickly as possible. Given the experience of ethnic Albanians with Serbia over the past decade, this meant in reality the deployment of an armed peacekeeping force under NATO control to instil in those who had been forced to flee from their homes enough confidence to return.

The Bosnian dimension, on the other hand, was again much more closely related to the situation in Serbia. Milošević had been instrumental in reaching the Dayton Accords, and it was not inconceivable that he could use the growing dissatisfaction and radicalization among the population in the Republika Srpska to increase his leverage over the international community. In addition, the implementation process of the Dayton Agreement tied up considerable international resources and, for a significant period before the beginning of the Rambouillet negotiations, seemed to take priority in international strategic considerations. This, however, changed rapidly with the deterioration of the humanitarian situation in Kosovo. Ironically, it could be argued that the focus on Bosnia and Herzegovina brought home to the international community its own tragic failure to prevent war crimes on a scale not seen in Europe since the Second World War, and facilitated the determination to prevent the same in Kosovo by taking decisive actions early enough.

Beyond a general commitment to humanitarian goals, consensus within the international community was thin. The Contact Group had agreed to seek a temporary settlement without territorial revisions, but had to concede to the Kosovo Albanians that some mechanism would be put in place after three years of operating an expected interim agreement that would also reflect the wish of the population in Kosovo (Weller 1999: 197). The fact that such a mechanism was to be found at another international conference served the interests of Russia in particular, as it assured the country's continued influence in the Balkans. It also allowed the Western members of the Contact Group to reconcile, at the time, the fundamental differences between Serbs and Albanians on the status of Kosovo. The major problem that remained for the international community, however, was the issue of the threat, and actual use, of force to obtain the consent of Serbia on the Rambouillet Agreement. While Russia was in principle opposed to such actions, consensus within NATO was for humanitarian intervention, yet the strength with which each alliance member backed this option differed. In the end, Serbia's refusal to sign must also be seen in the light of the open international disagreement about what to do in the event of a failure of the negotiations.

In conclusion, it can be argued that conditions of ripeness were not fulfilled at two levels – within Serbia and within the international community. The overall interpretation by Serbia of the conflict made it seem more beneficial for the Serbian and Yugoslav leadership to seek its continuation, rather than to settle for an accommodation along the lines proposed in Rambouillet. It is important to realize that the Serbian delegation until the last minute of the reconvened conference tried to renegotiate the entire agreement in its favour (Weller 1999: 186–8; Petritsch et al. 1999: 333, 337), and that their refusal to sign was not a matter of the 'mysterious' Appendix B on the deployment of the NATO-led implementation force. However, it must also be noted that the increasingly obvious rift between members of the Contact Group strengthened the Serbian/Yugoslav perspective on the costs and benefits of agreeing (or not) to the proposed settlement.

At the same time, the international community overestimated its leverage over the Serbian delegation in Rambouillet/Paris and over President Milošević in Belgrade. The Serbian delegation in Rambouillet was not susceptible to an offer by the European Union to lift all sanctions and allow the FRY to be reintegrated into European and international structures within two years in exchange for a greater preparedness to compromise at the negotiation table (Petritsch et al. 1999: 298). Likewise, increasingly credible threats of the use of force left Milošević and his negotiators unimpressed.

On the other hand, an extension of the negotiations in Rambouillet/Paris may have changed things in the short term. Yet further concessions to the Serbian delegation would then have been necessary, effectively meaning a renegotiation of the agreement to which the Albanian delegation had already given its consent. Given the Serbian demands in the final stages of the Paris follow-up talks, such a reopening of the negotiations was not in the international community's interest, nor was there much of a chance of the Kosovo Albanians making any concessions of the magnitude demanded by the Serbian delegation. Even if Milošević had agreed to a proposal made (unilaterally) by the Russian chief negotiator, Boris Majorski, to reopen talks on all aspects of the Rambouillet Agreement (Petritsch et al. 1999: 349), and if some time could have been bought through this, it is doubtful whether it would have made any difference in the long term, as a fundamental change of the situation in Serbia/the FRY or in the interest structure of its leadership was unlikely to occur.

The stated determination of NATO to act, even without prior and explicit authorization by the UN Security Council to intervene militarily, combined with the lack of agreement at Rambouillet and an assessment by NATO strategists that military intervention would be both successful and not provoke a military confrontation with Russia, thus created the conditions in which NATO's air campaign was initiated and succeeded in removing all Serb forces from Kosovo.

Subsequently, UN Security Council Resolution 1244 (1999) established the United Nations Mission in Kosovo (UNMIK), which was to provide the roof for a multi-functional peacekeeping operation in which the UN closely cooperated with the OSCE, NATO and the EU. While the resolution explicitly mentions that the Federal Republic of Yugoslavia's territorial integrity remains intact, it established UNMIK as a transitional authority to run Kosovo. Moreover, it also makes specific reference to the Rambouillet (non-)agreement, accepted by Kosovo Albanians and rejected by the FRY, and provides that a final status for Kosovo, considering the wishes of its population, should be achieved within three years.

3.4 The failure to reach a negotiated settlement: Kosovo's unilateral declaration of independence

Fast forward to 2007: after eight years of UN administration, with a mixed track record of success at best, local pressure in Kosovo and a growing frustration with the lack of any tangible progress in relations between Serbia and Kosovo led the UN to initiate final status negotiations. It appointed a special representative, the former Finnish president, Martti Ahtisaari, to facilitate negotiations between Kosovo and Serbia (the FRY having been transformed in 2003 into the State Union of Serbia and Montenegro, which was dissolved in 2006) and mediate between them. The so-called Ahtisaari Plan, presented in 2007, proposed Kosovo's independence conditional upon both extensive minority rights within Kosovo and a preclusion of any further boundary changes as a consequence of its independent statehood (e.g., unification with Albania or the break-up of Macedonia, with its large ethnic Albanian minority). This plan was rejected by Serbia, and no compromise solution was achieved after a period of further negotiations insisted upon by the EU. Thus, by the end of December 2007, the UN Secretary General had to report to the Security Council that his efforts to achieve agreement between the two parties on the final status of Kosovo had failed. Two months later, on 17 February 2008, Kosovo unilaterally declared its independence, which was promptly recognized by the US and a number of EU member states, among others, and equally rapidly denounced by Serbia and Russia. This may not be an unexpected outcome to those who are familiar with the conflict, yet it still requires an explanation.

The situation in Kosovo had changed in a number of dramatic ways over the preceding eight plus years. NATO's intervention was accompanied by the mass expulsion and flight of around 800,000 ethnic Albanians, who either became internally displaced, hiding out in the mountainous areas of Kosovo, or sought refuge in neighbouring countries, chiefly in Albania and Macedonia, with a smaller number in Montenegro. Of those leaving their homes, many also became temporary refugees in Western Europe. NATO's victory and the withdrawal of Serb forces from Kosovo, however, led to a process best described as reverse ethnic cleansing. Now local Serbs found themselves at the receiving end of revenge attacks from Kosovo Albanians. A high level of inter-communal tensions persisted after this immediate post-war period, occasionally escalating into serious violence – such as in March 2004, when nineteen Serbs were killed and some 3,000 driven from their homes after the (still unexplained) death of two Albanian youths. As a consequence of all this, there was not only a significant decrease in the Serb population in Kosovo – from an estimated 10 to 12 per cent just before the beginning of the NATO intervention to around 5 per cent by 2008 – but also a retreat of Serbs to the northern Mitrovica region at the border with Serbia, as well as to some much smaller and more or less isolated enclaves in central and southern Kosovo. The vision of a multi-ethnic Kosovo foreseen by the international community thus never materialized. Rather, the resolve of both communities had hardened. For Albanians, any form of reintegration with Serbia was complete anathema, in much the same way that it was inconceivable for Serbs, especially those living in the Mitrovica region, to agree to living in an independent Kosovo.

These local dynamics, however, are closely linked to developments at other levels. Serbs' resistance to any local arrangements with Albanians, for example the Serb boycott of elections and interim institutions, was actively promoted by Belgrade. Rather than encouraging Serbs in Kosovo to find a modus vivendi with the Albanians, Belgrade did everything possible especially after 2005, to foster closer ties between Kosovo Serbs and the authorities in Serbia, paying local officials' salaries, promoting election boycotts and supporting the abstention of Serbs from the political process in Prishtina. At the same time, public opinion in Serbia was sworn to the mantra of 'Kosovo is Serbia' – in the media, by all parties in every election campaign and by the Serbian Orthodox Church. The public commitment of every leading politician, regardless of their ideological persuasion, left virtually no room for a negotiated solution in the face of similar Albanian intransigence, equally insisting on maximum demands.

By the same token, the region of the Western Balkans as a whole remains riddled by various problems, from slow economic development, to spreading organized crime, and to the persistence of the potentially destructive energies of nationalism. This last in particular is closely related to the fact that at least two self-determination conflicts from the break-up of the Yugoslav federation remain in a very volatile position: the state of Bosnia and Herzegovina is highly dysfunctional, and the Ohrid Agreement of 2001, meant to resolve the conflict between ethnic Albanians and Macedonians, continues to cause resentment on the Macedonian side and leaves many Albanians far from satisfied, even though it has, so far, proved remarkably resilient. On the other hand, the dissolution of the State Union of Serbia and Montenegro in 2006, following a referendum in Montenegro, passed off entirely peacefully. Different parties to the Kosovo conflict, of course, attached different interpretations to all of these situations. While Kosovo Albanians saw Montenegro's independence as a confirmation of the possibility of further changes to existing boundaries in the region, Serbs insisted that this was only possible based on a consensual process. While Kosovo Albanians would refer to their quasi-republic status in the former Yugoslavia and a long track record of violation of their basic human rights by the Serbian state to justify their 'eligibility' for independence, Serbs would point to the concessions they were willing to make (very wide-ranging autonomy for Kosovo within Serbia) and to the precedent that Kosovo's independence would set, especially for the Serb entity in Bosnia and Herzegovina – the Republika Srpska established under the Dayton Accords of 1995. Thus both sides found ample 'regional evidence' to justify their position.

However, what mattered perhaps more than the 'encouragement' that both sides took from the regional dynamics was their perception of how the key international actors interpreted the situation. While the EU, NATO and the US (as the three principal Western powers in the conflict) clearly considered the regional (and wider) implications of Kosovo's drive for independence, they were less worried about a detrimental impact on the region than in the late 1990s. For better or worse, the situation in both Bosnia and Herzegovina and Macedonia had stabilized, there remained an international military presence in the former (the EU Force since 2007), and both countries had been given a clear perspective on EU membership, which was understood to be conditional on, among other things, stability. Moreover, while the population of Republika Srpska may be in favour of joining Serbia, political elites, despite their occasional rhetoric to the contrary, are much more reluctant to support a proposition that would see them end up as municipal officials in small and medium-sized towns in western Serbia rather than retaining their status as power-brokers and influential state politicians in Bosnia and Herzegovina. Moreover, the prospect for the EU, NATO and the US of having to deal with growing discontent among Kosovo Albanians and its likely violent escalation (as seen in the March 2004 riots) was not a scenario that seemed at all attractive to policy-makers in Washington, Brussels and other European capitals. This does not mean that they were intent on worsening relations with Serbia; this was merely seen as the lesser of two evils, especially as the EU in particular anticipated that the membership prospect might sway a majority of Serbs and their political elites eventually to accept Kosovo's independence. Moreover, the supposedly careful management of that independence, through the exercise of pressure on, and the offer of incentives to, the political elites in Kosovo, seemed to offer the prospect of a relatively smooth change of status for the country, despite the absence of a negotiated solution.

The West, moreover, was content with the prospect of Russian resistance. With Vladimir Putin's election to the Russian presidency in 2000, and his attempt to reclaim Russian great power status, relations with Russia had already taken a turn for the worse. The absence of agreement in the UN Security Council on a new resolution mandating independence was not seen as crucial in light of significant Western support for Kosovo. The spectre of the Kosovo precedent, i.e., its leading to a proliferation of successful self-determination movements elsewhere, was not seen as a particularly likely consequence. This also meant that implicit Russian threats to recognize the break-away regions in some of the successor states of the Soviet Union, such as Abkhazia and South Ossetia in Georgia, Transdniestria in Moldova or the Nagorno-Karabakh territory in Azerbaijan, were not considered as particularly credible or, should they indeed occur, to have any consequences.

However, what Russia's policy did was further increase the resolve of Serbia to resist Kosovo's independence. While Russia did not per se rule out independent statehood for Kosovo, it made it clear that it would support such an outcome only if it was achieved on the basis of consensus between Kosovo and Serbia. This gave the government of Serbia an opportunity to reject independence for Kosovo and be assured that no resolution would be passed in the UN Security Council recognizing a unilateral declaration.

In contrast to the situation in 1999, Russia, by 2008, had seriously reasserted its position as a great power on the international scene. What was important for the EU, NATO and the US, however, was that this did not imply that Russia was in favour of, or would support, a military reaction by Serbia to Kosovo's declaration of independence. While this gave Serbia the comfort of knowing that Russia would back the government's resistance to a unilateral declaration by Kosovo, there was, as in 1999, no threat of a military confrontation with Russia.

This suggests that Western backing of Kosovo's independence was undertaken primarily on the basis of cost–benefit and balance-of-power calculations. Such a realist interpretation is further reinforced if one considers the potential alternatives. Delaying a status decision any longer would have further exacerbated what was already a volatile situation in Kosovo and potentially created similar problems in Macedonia, placing in jeopardy in particular plans for eventual integration of the entire Western Balkans into the EU as the best guarantee for stability and security. Reintegration of Kosovo into Serbia was equally inconceivable: not only was this anathema to ethnic Albanians, but Serbian proposals to achieve it were, at best, half-hearted. As we will explore further in subsequent chapters, stable conflict settlements short of secession that involve large, regionally concentrated ethnic groups striving for self-determination, as the Albanians in Kosovo, normally involve self-governance (i.e., autonomy) and shared governance (i.e., some form of power sharing at the centre). Serbian proposals in the negotiations were offering far-reaching concessions on the former but were silent on the latter. Nor would the idea of Albanian participation in any Belgrade government have been palatable to a Serbian public that considers Kosovo, but not necessarily its ethnic Albanian population, a part of Serbia.

Thus, the absence of viable alternatives to Kosovo's independence, and a perception that the international environment, if not supportive, would at least be permissive to Western support for it, strengthened the position of Kosovo Albanians and enforced a perception in the majority of the member states of the EU and NATO that recognizing Kosovo following a unilateral declaration of independence was the most attractive of all options. This, however, does not mean that there were no other considerations beyond crude power politics. It is undeniable that Kosovo Albanians have suffered from serious violations of even their most basic human rights at the hands of Serbia and that they constitute the overwhelming majority of the people in Kosovo, even if one were to reverse the ethnic cleansing of Serbs after 1999, and that this demographic majority overwhelmingly desires not to live in a Serbian state. It is equally undeniable that it would be difficult to find a justification under international law for Kosovo's unilateral declaration of independence. The process of settling the conflict may thus have been flawed. Its outcome, however, does the situation on the ground more justice than any other conceivable option, not least because it holds a greater promise of being sustainable over time.

4 Conclusion

The differences and similarities between the four cases under consideration here are clear. At a most basic level some conflicts have been settled, at least temporarily, while others rumble on. The bulk of the conflicts in Burma are over, albeit in the wake of successful government repression rather than as the result of a genuine peace process. In the DRC, the conflict in the east of the country continued in July 2009 whereas elsewhere the violence has mostly subsided. In Sudan, the conflict between the government and the SPLA is technically at an end, as is with greater probability the conflict in the east of the country, while that in Darfur shows no signs of abating. On the contrary, it appears that it could mutate into a proxy war between Sudan and Chad. In Kosovo, the situation is, superficially at least, well under international control, but there are significantly deeper problems there, in the Western Balkans and more globally that have been partly glossed over and partly lifted to prominence with Kosovo's unilateral declaration of independence – all of which remain unaddressed at the moment.

By employing our levels-of-analysis approach, and identifying the environments within which different actors operate, similarities and differences become clearer. In Burma, the DRC and Sudan, European colonialism was important in terms of the disruption of traditional societies and political arrangements, and most importantly in terms of bequeathing 'nation-states', with populations that had to various degrees been brutalized, that lacked legitimacy and capacity. Kosovo suffered from a different kind of colonialism and colonial legacy, but one that was no less significant in affecting the determination of its local majority Albanian population to seek independent statehood.

In all cases, the involvement of international actors has been prominent in attempting to solve the conflicts. The UN has been especially active, if not particularly successful, if only because warring parties feel they achieve their objectives by continuing to use force. Yet in every case, bar that of Burma, intervention has succeeded in at least encouraging moves towards a peace process, even if that process has not always culminated in the cessation of violence, let alone sustainable settlements. The question of why Burma is different remains. The Burmese government has for years combined internal repression with largely successful attempts to minimize the influence of the 'West', whether that be the influence of Western liberal democratic states or the phalanx of civil society organizations that they spawn. In other words, the configurations that have helped to promote a modicum of peace in Kosovo, Sudan and the DRC simply do not exist in Burma – a fact that highlights equally the importance and the limitations of international intervention.

7

Conflict Settlement in Theory and Practice

1 Introduction

As we have seen in preceding chapters, the democratic governance of multi-ethnic societies can pose particular challenges. This appears to be especially so in cases in which territorially concentrated groups demand to exercise their right to self-determination, which is often (but wrongly) equated by them, the states in which they live, and/or the international community with secession. Since the end of the Second World War alone, '79 territorially concentrated ethnic groups have waged armed conflicts for autonomy or independence, not counting the peoples of former European colonies' (Quinn 2008: 33). By 2006 there were twenty-six ongoing violent self-determination conflicts, as well as fifty-five ethnic groups who pursued their self-determination agenda with non-violent means and an additional forty groups that used both non-violent and violent means. Thus, at the beginning of the twenty-first century there are more than 120 territorially concentrated ethnic groups worldwide that seek a greater degree of independence from their host state, with demands ranging from cultural and territorial autonomy to secession, leading either to independent statehood or unification with another state (ibid.).

While boundary changes after unilateral declarations of independence are generally greeted with some apprehension, there is significantly more enthusiasm in the international community to promote territorial self-governance as a mechanism to resolve underlying conflicts – that is, the legally entrenched power of territorial entities to exercise public policy functions independently of other sources of authority in the state, but subject to the overall legal order of the state.[1] Such promotion of territorial self-governance by the international community normally goes hand in hand with an endorsement of other mechanisms of conflict settlement, including power sharing, human and minority rights legislation, specific participation rights for members of minority groups, etc. As such, recent conflict settlement practice has manifested itself in complex institutional designs combining a range of mechanisms. These are treated separately in most of the existing academic literature on the subject, where certain of them are rejected as morally unacceptable by some and unfeasible by others.

In this chapter, we begin by exploring the institutional design requirements for conflict settlement in divided societies and examine the prescriptions of three main schools of conflict settlement – centripetalism, power sharing and power dividing. We then compare and contrast a number of actual cases of conflict settlement in Europe, Asia and Africa to demonstrate that what appears to be a strong trend in conflict settlement practice is a hybrid model of complex power sharing that has a regime of self-governance at its heart and is complemented by a range of other mechanisms adopted to address, as comprehensively as possible, the variety of claims made by individual conflict parties.

2 Institutional design in divided societies

Advocating the settlement of self-determination conflicts through institutional design assumes that such conflicts can be addressed through an institutional bargain that establishes macro-level structures through which micro-level incentives are provided to elites (and their supporters). This is a rational choice approach which presumes that institutions are chosen and will be stable when the actors involved in them have – and will continue to have – an incentive to adhere to them and thus 'reproduce' them. In other words, one needs to distinguish between incentive structures, i.e., the macro-level frameworks that allow for incentives to be enjoyed by elites and their supporters in a predictable and repetitive way, and the incentives themselves. From this perspective, centripetalism, consociationalism, power dividing and other conflict settlement mechanisms prescribe the macro-level structures which provide incentives such as power, status, security, economic gain, etc. The stability of these macro-level structures, from a rational choice perspective, depends on both the general desirability of the incentives they provide and whether these incentives can be gained through alternative arrangements. If the incentives are desirable and cannot be gained otherwise, existing arrangements would appear to be acceptable and their maintenance desirable, and they would thus be likely to be stable.[2]

As far as conflict settlement in divided societies is concerned, institutional design of macro-level structures needs to address three broad sets of issues. First, the question of the state's overall construction needs to be decided, and here the most important institutional design challenge has to do with the territorial organization of the state. While the principal choice is generally between unitary and federal systems, there is a great deal of variation within these two main categories, and there are a number of hybrid forms as well. Further choices in this area relate to the number of (federal) units and the degree to which these should be ethnically homogeneous or heterogeneous,[3] as well as the extent to which they should have the same or differential powers.

Second, several questions concerning the relationship between the different branches of government need to be addressed, including the nature of the government system – i.e., whether it is a parliamentary, presidential or semi-presidential system. A second dimension is the issue of whether executive power sharing is mandatory and, if so, what the extent of prescribed inclusiveness is. Inclusiveness, at the same time, is also an important feature of legislative design and is realized primarily through the choice of an electoral system.[4] A final issue in this regard is the overall relationship between the three institutions of government – that is, the degree of separation of powers between them. While this relates partially to the choice of government system, it is also about the degree of independence of the judicial branch and its powers of legislative and executive oversight.

A third set of issues concerns the relationship between individual citizens, identity groups and the state. Institutional design in this area is about the recognition and protection of different identities by the state. This relates to human and minority rights legislation, i.e., the degree to which every citizen's individual human rights are protected, including civil and political rights, as well as the extent to which the rights of different identity groups are recognized and protected. While there may be a certain degree of tension between them, such as between a human rights prerogative of equality and non-discrimination and a minority rights approach emphasizing differential treatment and affirmative action, the two are not contradictory, but need to complement each other in ways that reflect the diversity of divided societies and contribute to peaceful accommodation among diverse groups.[5]

While it is important analytically to treat these three areas separately, it is equally important to bear in mind that institutions in practice work as a package – that is, they 'interact in complex ways' (Belmont et al. 2002: 4). Thus, while it may be possible to make a theoretically valid argument about the utility of using the single transferable vote as an electoral system to induce moderation among politicians, district magnitude and local ethnic demography can easily 'conspire' against such an outcome (see Wolff 2005). What matters, therefore, is that different dimensions of institutional design fit each other to enable overall outcomes that are conducive to lasting peace in divided societies. The degree of fit, in part, is dependent on how well institutions represent a viable compromise between competing demands at the local and state levels and how well this is embedded in a supportive regional and global context.

3 Institutional design in existing theories of conflict settlement

Existing theories of conflict settlement generally acknowledge the importance and usefulness of institutional design but offer rather different prescriptions as to the most appropriate models for achieving stable settlements. Three such theories are of particular significance, as they speak directly to the three areas of institutional design identified above: power sharing in the form of its liberal consociational variant, centripetalism and power dividing.

In now discussing the main tenets of these three sets of theories, we focus on their recommendations in each of the three areas of institutional design outlined above. However, we cannot, for reasons of space, claim either to offer a comprehensive examination of these theories or to assess how practically feasible or morally justifiable they are.

3.1 Liberal consociationalism

The term 'consociational democracy' has been associated most closely with the work of Arend Lijphart, as well as more recently with that of John McGarry and Brendan O'Leary. Lijphart began to examine this particular type of democratic system in greater detail for the first time in the late 1960s, when making reference to the political systems of Scandinavian countries and of the Netherlands and Belgium (Lijphart 1968). He followed this up with further studies of political stability in cases of severely socially fragmented societies, eventually leading to his groundbreaking work *Democracy in Plural Societies* (1977). The phenomenon Lijphart was describing, however, was not new. As a pattern of social structure, characterizing a society fragmented by religious, linguistic, ideological or other cultural segmentation, it had existed and been studied (albeit not as extensively) long before the 1960s. These structural aspects were not the primary concern of Lijphart, who was more interested in why, despite their fragmentation, such societies maintained a stable political process, and he identified the behaviour of political elites as the main, but not the only, reason for stability. Furthermore, Lijphart (1977: 25–52) identified four features shared by consociational systems – a grand coalition government (between parties from different segments of society), segmental autonomy (in the cultural sector), proportionality (in the voting system and in public sector employment) and minority veto. These characteristics were exhibited, more or less prominently, by all the classic examples of consociationalism: Lebanon, Cyprus, Switzerland, Austria, the Netherlands, Belgium, Fiji and Malaysia. With some of these consociations having succeeded (Switzerland, Austria, the Netherlands and Belgium) and others having failed (Lebanon, Cyprus, Fiji and Malaysia), Lijphart also established conditions conducive to consociational democracy. These included overarching (i.e., territorial) loyalties, a small number of political parties in each segment, the various segments being of approximately equal size, and the existence of some cross-cutting cleavages with otherwise segmental isolation. The small size of the territory to which a consociational structure is applied and the direct and indirect internal and external consequences of this, as well as a tradition of compromise among political elites, were also emphasized by Lijphart as conditions enhancing the stability of the consociational settlement (ibid.: 53–103).

Lijphart's assumptions and prescriptions, of course, did not go unchallenged. He and other advocates of consociational approaches to ethnic conflict settlement responded in two ways – by offering a robust defence of their views and by gradually developing consociational theory further. Lijphart himself engaged his critics most comprehensively in his book *Power sharing in South Africa* (1985: 83–117) and in his contribution to Andrew Reynolds's *The Architecture of Democracy* (Lijphart 2002b: 39–45). In the latter, he also offers a substantive revision of his original approach, now describing power sharing and autonomy (i.e., grand coalition government and segmental autonomy) as primary characteristics, while proportionality and minority veto are relegated to 'secondary characteristics' (ibid.: 39). Yet, in relation to his grand coalition requirement, Lijphart maintains his earlier position that such executive power sharing means 'participation of representatives of all significant groups in political decision making' (ibid.: 41).

Subsequent developments in consociational theory, especially by John McGarry and Brendan O'Leary (McGarry 2006; McGarry and O'Leary 2004; O'Leary 2005a, 2005b), have made one important modification in particular in this respect. O'Leary contends that 'grand coalition' (in the sense of an executive encompassing all leaders of all significant parties of all significant communities) is not a necessary criterion; rather, he demonstrates that what matters for a democratic consociation 'is meaningful cross-community executive power sharing in which each significant segment is represented in the government with at least plurality levels of support within its segment' (O'Leary 2005a: 13).[6]

In order to appreciate fully the current state of consociational theory, it is useful to examine John McGarry and Brendan O'Leary's *The Northern Ireland Conflict: Consociational Engagements* (a collection of their joint and individual writings on this conflict from 1987 to 2002), in particular its co-authored introduction on the lessons that Northern Ireland holds for consociational theory more broadly.[7] Northern Ireland's 1998 agreement, McGarry and O'Leary maintain, 'highlights six important weaknesses in traditional consociational theory' (McGarry and O'Leary 2004: 5). These are the neglect of external actors; the trans-state nature of some self-determination disputes and the necessary institutional arrangements to address them; the increasing complexity of conflict settlements in which consociational arrangements form an important element but require complementary mechanisms to deal with 'the design of the police, demilitarization, the return of exiles to their homes, the management of prisoners, education reform, economic policy, and the promotion of language and other group rights' (ibid.: 13); terminological and conceptual inaccuracies, associated primarily with Lijphart's grand coalition requirement; the merits of preferential proportional electoral systems, i.e., the Single Transferable Vote (STV); and the allocation of cabinet positions by means of sequential proportionality rules, i.e., the d'Hondt mechanism. In dealing with these weaknesses, McGarry and O'Leary offer both refinements of, and advances to, traditional consociational theory. The refinements relate, first, to the technical side of consociational institutions, where the authors recommend STV instead of list proportional representation as an electoral system, as it militates against the proliferation of micro-parties. Second, McGarry and O'Leary elaborate the usefulness in the allocation of cabinet positions of sequential proportionality rules, such as the d'Hondt mechanism or the Sainte-Laguë method, in order to avoid protracted bargaining between parties and increase parties' incentives to remain part of cross-communal coalitions.

The advances to traditional consociational theory offered, as well as elsewhere in their recent writings (e.g., McGarry 2006), are a significant step forward in that they address both long-standing criticisms of consociationalism and a gap between consociational theory and conflict settlement practice. McGarry's and O'Leary's observations on external actors bring consociational theory in line with an established debate in international relations on the role of third parties in conflict settlement (see, for example, contributions in Diehl and Lepgold 2003; Otunnu and Doyle 1998; Pugh and Sidhu 2003; Thakur and Schnabel 2001; Weller and Wolff 2008). Equally importantly, their discussion of the provisions in the 1998 agreement that go beyond domestic institutions and address the specific 'Irish dimension' of the Northern Ireland conflict reflect a growing awareness among scholars and practitioners of conflict settlement that many ethnic conflicts have causes and consequences beyond the boundaries of the states in which they occur and that, for settlements to be durable and stable, these dimensions also need to be addressed. In the case of the 1998 Agreement for Northern Ireland, McGarry and O'Leary highlight three dimensions: cross-border institutions which formalize cooperation between the Northern Ireland Executive and the Irish government (the so-called North–South Ministerial Council) and renew British–Irish intergovernmental cooperation (the British–Irish Intergovernmental Conference); the explicit recognition by the two governments of the right to self-determination of the people in Northern Ireland and the Republic, i.e., the possibility for them to bring about, in separate referenda, a united Ireland if that is the wish of respective majorities; and new institutions of regional cooperation, incorporating the UK and Irish governments and the executive organs of the other two devolved regions in the UK as well as its three dependent island territories in the Channel and the Irish Sea.

These arrangements have earlier precedents in the history of conflict settlement in Northern Ireland, but they are not unique to this case alone. Institutions of cross-border cooperation have been utilized as part of comprehensive peace settlements elsewhere as well – for example, in South Tyrol and in Bosnia and Herzegovina – and exist, of course, in less conflict-prone situations as part of arrangements between sovereign states and/or substate entities – for example, in the EU's Euroregions. The EU itself, at the same time, is one of the most successful cases of regional integration (albeit among 'equal' partners at the state or local level), while the Nordic Council offers arrangements similar to the British–Irish Council in bringing together sovereign states and self-governing territories within them.

The possibility of future status changes is similarly not unique to Northern Ireland, or indeed to the 1998 agreement. A so-called border poll took place in Northern Ireland in 1973 but was almost completely boycotted by both Nationalists and Republicans. There had also been an initial British commitment to hold such polls at ten-year intervals, but this was unceremoniously and quietly abandoned. Further afield, the people of the Autonomous Republic of Gagauzia in Moldova would have a one-time opportunity to exercise their right to (external) self-determination should Moldova join Romania. The Comprehensive Peace Agreement for Sudan offers the people in the south of the country a referendum on independence after six years, while the Bougainville Peace Agreement includes a clause that envisages a referendum on independence to be held after ten to fifteen years. Crucially, in all these situations, including Northern Ireland, the signatory parties are committed to respecting the outcome of these referenda.

A final, and perhaps the most significant, advance in consociational theory is McGarry and O'Leary's contention that Lijphart's grand coalition requirement is overstated, as 'what makes consociations feasible and work is joint consent across the significant communities, with the emphasis on jointness' (McGarry and O'Leary 2004: 15). On that basis, they distinguish 'unanimous consociations (grand coalitions),[8] concurrent consociations (in which the executive has majority support in each significant segment) and weak consociations (where the executive may have only a plurality level of support amongst one or more segments)' (ibid.).[9] Jointness, more generally, implies equality and cooperation across blocs and some genuine consent among the relevant mass publics for a democratic consociation, and thus excludes just any coalition, as well as cooptation of unrepresentative minority 'leaders'.

The more recent writings by Lijphart, McGarry and O'Leary also indicate a clear move from corporate towards liberal consociational power sharing.[10] The main difference between the two is that a 'corporate consociation accommodates groups according to ascriptive criteria, and rests on the assumption that group identities are fixed, and that groups are both internally homogeneous and externally bounded', while 'liberal . . . consociation . . . rewards whatever salient political identities emerge in democratic elections, whether these are based on ethnic groups, or on sub-group or trans-group identities' (McGarry 2006: 3; see also Lijphart 1995 and O'Leary 2005a). This is another important modification of consociational theory that addresses one of its more profound, and empirically more valid, criticisms, namely that (corporate) consociations further entrench and institutionalize pre-existing, and often conflict-hardened, ethnic identities, thus decreasing the incentives for elites to moderate (e.g., Horowitz [1985] 2000: 566–76; 1991: 167ff.; 2003: 119).

Territorial self-governance is an accepted feature within the liberal consociational approach, emphasizing that the self-governing territory should define itself from the bottom up rather than be prescribed top-down.[11] Liberal consociationalists also support the principle of asymmetric devolution of powers – i.e., the possibility for some self-governing entities to enjoy more (or fewer) competences than others, depending on the preferences of their populations (see McGarry 2007). However, self-governance needs to be complemented with what liberal consociationalists term 'shared rule', i.e., the exercise of power at and by the centre and across the state as a whole. While grand coalitions, proportionality and minority veto rights continue to be favoured by liberal consociationalists, the emphasis is on cooperation and consensus among democratically legitimized elites, regardless of whether they emerge on the basis of group identities, ideology or other common interest. They thus favour parliamentary systems proportional (PR list) or proportional preferential (STV) electoral systems, decision-making procedures that require qualified and/or concurrent majorities, and have also advocated, at times, the application of the d'Hondt rule for the formation of executives[12] (cf. Lijphart 2004; O'Leary 2005a).

This means that liberal consociationalists prefer what O'Leary refers to as 'pluralist federations', in which co-sovereign substate and central governments have clearly defined exclusive competences (albeit with the possibility of some concurrent competences) whose assignment to either level of authority is constitutionally and, ideally, internationally protected; in which decision-making at the centre is consensual (between self-governing entities and the centre, and among elites representing different interest groups); and which recognize and protect the presence of different self-determined identities (O'Leary 2005b).

In order to protect individuals against the abuse of powers by majorities at the state level or the level of self-governing entities, liberal consociationalism offers two remedies – the replication of its core institutional prescriptions within the self-governing entity, and the establishment and enforcement of strong human and minority rights regimes both at the state and the local level. In addition, the rights of communities – minorities and majorities alike – are best protected in a liberal consociational system if its key provisions are enshrined in the constitution and if the interpretation and upholding of the constitution is left to an independent and representative constitutional court whose decisions are binding on both executive and legislature (see O'Leary 2005b: 55–8).

Key to liberal consociational prescriptions of institutional design in divided societies is, therefore, the emphasis on the protection of self-determined (rather than predetermined) identity groups through ensuring both their representation and effective participation in decision-making, especially in the legislature and executive. The underlying assumption here is that representation and participation together will ensure that different identity groups recognize that their aims can be achieved, and their interests protected, by political means and do not require recourse to violence.

3.2 Centripetalism

Centripetalism emphasizes that, rather than designing rigid institutions in which elected representatives have to work together *after* elections, 'intergroup political accommodation' is achieved by 'electoral systems that provide incentives for parties to form coalitions across group lines or in other ways moderate their ethnocentric political behaviour' (Horowitz 2004: 507–8). This school of thought is most prominently associated with the work of Donald Horowitz (1985 [2000], 1990, 1991, 2002), as well as that of Timothy D. Sisk (1996),[13] Benjamin Reilly (2001, 2006) and Andreas Wimmer (2003).

Horowitz remains the standard-setting centripetalist scholar, and his work will be analysed in more detail below. However, it is worth noting significant contributions by other authors as well. Reilly has developed an explicit theory of centripetalism, emphasizing that, in practice, it tries to encourage, among other things,

> (i) *electoral incentives* for campaigning politicians to reach out to and attract votes from a range of ethnic groups other than their own. . .; (ii) *arenas of bargaining*, under which political actors from different groups have an incentive to come together to negotiate and bargain in the search for cross-partisan and cross-ethnic vote-pooling deals. . .; and (iii) *centrist, aggregative political parties* or coalitions which seek multi-ethnic support. (Reilly 2001: 11; emphasis in original)

The empirical evidence offered in support of the utility of centripetal mechanisms in Reilly's 2001 volume was focused primarily on Papua New Guinea,[14] while a much broader study published in 2006 was based on a wider variety of cases across Asia-Pacific. On this basis, he concluded that

> [t]he limited use to date of explicit power sharing requirements, the troubled experiments with grand coalition cabinets in Indonesia and Fiji, and the strong association of such practices with political instability, all underscore aversion towards consociational measures. By contrast, informal power sharing approaches, in which political inclusion is a result of deal-making rather than law, appears to have become successfully institutionalised in a number of cases. (Reilly 2006: 171)

An attempt to apply in practice centripetalist conclusions about which institutional designs can provide lasting peace and stability in divided societies is provided by Wimmer's proposals for the post-war constitution of Iraq. He recommends the introduction of 'an electoral system that fosters moderation and accommodation across the ethnic divides', including a requirement for the 'most powerful elected official . . . to be the choice not only of a majority of the population, but of states or provinces of the country, too', the use of the alternative vote procedure, and a political party law demanding that 'all parties contesting elections . . . be organised in a minimum number of provinces' (Wimmer 2003: 122). In addition, Wimmer advocates non-ethnic federation (ibid.: 123–5), at least in the sense that there should be more federal entities than ethnic groups, even if a majority of those entities would be more or less ethnically homogeneous or be dominated by one ethnic group.

Furthermore, 'a strong minority rights regime at the central level, a powerful independent judiciary system and effective enforcement mechanisms are needed' (ibid.: 125).

In what remains a classic work in the field, Donald L. Horowitz (1985 [2000]) discusses a range of structural techniques and preferential policies to reduce ethnic conflict. Among them, he emphasizes that 'the most potent way to assure that federalism or autonomy will not become just a step to secession is to reinforce those specific interests that groups have in the undivided state' (ibid.: 628). Horowitz also makes an explicit case for federation in his proposals for constitutional design in post-Apartheid South Africa (Horowitz 1991: 214–26) and argues, in a manner not dissimilar to power dividing advocates (see below), for federations based on ethnically heterogeneous entities. In a later study, focused more explicitly on federation as a mechanism for conflict reduction, Horowitz accepts that homogeneous units, too, can prove useful for this purpose, but argues that, rather than the aim being to facilitate group autonomy (the consociational rationale), homogeneous provinces offer the possibility of fostering intra-group competition (Horowitz 2007: 960–1; see also Horowitz 2008: 1218). In an earlier contribution to the debate, Horowitz had recognized the need for federal or autonomy provisions, but cautioned that they could contribute to mitigating secessionist demands only if '[c]ombined with policies that give regionally concentrated groups a strong stake in the center' (Horowitz 1993: 36).[15] In a similar way to Wimmer (2003, see above), Horowitz, citing the Nigerian experience, sees utility in splitting large ethnic groups into several provinces, as this potentially encourages the proliferation of political parties within one ethnic group, resulting in intra-group competition and a lessened impact of relative numerical superiority of one group over others (Horowitz 2007: 960–1; 1985 [2000]: 602–4; see also Horowitz 2008: 1218).

While centripetalism is thus open to engaging with, among others, territorial approaches to conflict settlement, 'its principal tool is . . . the provision of incentives, usually *electoral incentives*, that accord an advantage to ethnically based parties that are willing to appeal, at the margin and usually through coalition partners of other ethnic groups, to voters other than their own' (Horowitz 2008: 1217; our emphasis). In particular, Horowitz emphasizes the utility of electoral systems that are most likely to produce a Condorcet winner – i.e., a candidate who would be victorious in a given constituency in a two-way contest against every other candidate. The most prominent such electoral system is the alternative vote, a preferential majoritarian electoral system,[16] that is said to induce moderation among parties and their candidates, as they require electoral support from beyond their own ethnic group in heterogeneous, single-seat constituencies (Horowitz 2003: 122–5). However, the intended benefits are not always forthcoming, and the consequences of the introduction of electoral systems that aim to encourage moderation through interethnic vote pooling are not always and only the benign ones sought. Horowitz admits that 'there has sometimes been deterioration of interethnic harmony, or the durability of accommodative institutions, or the quality of democracy' (Horowitz 2008: 1223), but, as the debate between him and Fraenkel and Grofman on the case of Fiji and the use of the alternative vote more generally indicates, there is little if any common ground between those who advocate centrepetalist strategies in conflict settlement and those who doubt their utility.[17] The only modest consensus that does seem to exist between the different schools of thought is that preferential electoral systems, majoritarian or proportional, offer benefits in the context of conflict settlement that non-preferential systems cannot provide – that is, they offer at least the theoretical possibility, under context-specific circumstances, that moderation and a degree of inter-ethnic cooperation can be induced.[18]

The debate on electoral systems is also apparent in arguments about whether divided societies are served better by a presidential or a parliamentarian system. The argument here is primarily about whether presidential systems heighten divisiveness. Among consociationalists, Lijphart is an exemplary defender of the parliamentary system, while McGarry and O'Leary accept that especially collective, or multi-member, presidencies can be useful in mitigating divisions, thereby extending consociational principles to presidential systems. For Horowitz, on the other hand, it is the electoral system that is crucial in determining whether the president's election and office unites or divides, and he argues for an electoral system 'that ensures broadly distributed support for the president' (Horowitz 1990: 76). Citing Nigeria and Sri Lanka as examples, he offers two different ways of achieving the election of a president with such broadly distributed support: a combination of total votes cast and votes cast in individual states (Nigerian federation) or a version of the Alternative Vote (AV) in which the two top candidates (those with the highest number of first preference votes) would be put into an instant run-off second round in which lower order preferences cast for eliminated candidates would be redistributed until one of the two top candidates had an overall majority.[19]

In summary of the centripetalist approach, then, it is clear that conflict reduction is to be achieved through inducing inter-ethnic cooperation before and at the polls rather than after elections. This idea permeates centripetalist institutional choices throughout: in relation to the structure and organization of the state as a whole (e.g., federal vs. unitary designs); with regard to the composition and powers of the executive, legislative and judicial branches of government and the relationship between them (e.g., parliamentary vs. presidential systems); and when it comes to the relationship between individual citizens, identity groups and the state (e.g., the degree to which specific groups are to enjoy particular privileges).

3.3 Power dividing

Power dividing, as put forward by Philip Roeder and the late Donald Rothchild in their co-edited volume *Sustainable Peace: Power and Democracy after Civil Wars*

(2005), is the latest contribution to the debate over the utility of different approaches to institutional design in divided societies. For a better appreciation of what distinguishes the theory of power dividing from that of liberal consociational power sharing and centripetalism, we will focus in the following primarily on the conceptual chapters in Roeder and Rothchild's volume, as being so far the most comprehensive treatment of power dividing.

Roeder and Rothchild's main finding is that power sharing is a useful short-term mechanism to overcome commitment problems[20] that may prevent conflict parties in the immediate aftermath of civil wars to agree to and stick with a peace settlement, but that it is detrimental to peace and stability in the long term.[21] Instead, they recommend power dividing as an alternative strategy to manage conflict in ethnically (or otherwise) divided societies. Predicated on the distinction of three types of democracy – Westminster majoritarianism, consociational supermajoritarianism, and power dividing multiple majoritarianism – as institutional options in ethnically divided societies, power dividing is seen as 'an overlooked alternative to majoritarian democracy and power sharing' (Roeder and Rothchild 2005: 6). Three strategies that are said to be central to power dividing – civil liberties, multiple majorities, and checks and balances – in practice result in an allocation of power between government and civil society such that 'strong, enforceable civil liberties . . . take many responsibilities out of the hands of government', while those that are left are distributed 'among separate, independent organs that represent alternative, cross-cutting majorities', thus 'balanc[ing] one decisionmaking centre against another so as to check each majority . . . [f]or the most important issues that divide ethnic groups, but must be decided by a government common to all ethnic groups' (ibid.: 15).

The key institutional instruments by which power dividing is meant to be realized are, first of all, extensive human rights bills that are meant to leave 'key decisions to the private sphere and civil society' (Roeder and Rothchild 2005: 15). Second, separation of powers between the branches of government and a range of specialized agencies dealing with specific, and clearly delimited, policy areas are to create multiple and changing majorities, thus 'increas[ing] the likelihood that members of ethnic minorities will be parts of political majorities on some issues and members of any ethnic majority will be members of political minorities on some issues' (ibid.: 17). Third, checks and balances are needed 'to keep each of these decisionmaking centres that represents a specific majority from overreaching its authority' (ibid.). Thus, the power dividing approach favours presidential over parliamentary systems, bicameral over unicameral legislatures, and independent judiciaries with powers of judicial review extending to acts of both legislative and executive branches. As a general rule, power dividing as a strategy to keep the peace in ethnically divided societies requires 'decisions [that] can threaten the stability of the constitutional order, such as amendments to peace settlements', be made by 'concurrent approval by multiple organs empowering different majorities' (ibid.).

Rejecting the classic options of majoritarian democracy, power sharing, protectorates and partition as long-term solutions that can provide stable democracy after civil wars, Roeder and Rothchild advocate the power dividing arrangements associated with the US constitution: civil liberties, multiple majorities, and checks and balances (Roeder and Rothchild 2005: 15). In order to substantiate this assertion, they and their contributors address five different sets of issues in their volume: the suitability of different power sharing regimes to lead to peace and democracy; their likely success at different stages in the transition from civil war to stable democracy; different factors that condition the success of power sharing arrangements and institutions; whether alternative options are more likely to lead to stability and lasting peace; and whether a comprehensive strategy of intervention with phased institutions appropriate at different stages of the transition from civil war to democracy is possible.

Conceptually based primarily on the Madisonian model of federalism and the American presidential system (and thus perhaps somewhat overstated in its novelty), power dividing is a theoretically interesting alternative to power sharing and centripetalism. While it accepts key premises of the former as necessary to initiate a transition from war to peace, it shares many of the normative assumptions of centripetalism. Empirically, however, power dividing is less convincing as the panacea to ethnic conflict settlement than it is deemed to be, and is evident from Roeder and Rothchild's own volume. For example, Matthew Hoddie and Caroline Hartzell, in their chapter 'Power sharing in peace settlements', find that '[i]n particular. . .both military and territorial power sharing have a positive role to play in fostering post-war peace' and that '[t]hese provisions have the demonstrated capacity to set the stage for the period of transition by enhancing a sense of confidence among former enemies that their interests will not be jeopardised in the context of the postwar state' (Roeder and Rothchild 2005: 103). They also note the importance of thinking beyond power sharing at the level of central government and including other mechanisms, such as military, territorial and economic power sharing, all of which prove important in combination rather than in isolation (ibid.).[22] A very different set of findings regarding the utility of territorial decentralization (i.e., territorial power sharing, in Hoddie and Hartzell's terms) is presented by David Lake and Donald Rothchild, in 'Managing diversity and sustaining democracy'. They argue that three strategic problems – governance, the incompleteness of constitutions, and transient majorities – make it difficult for institutional arrangements of territorial decentralization to provide long-term peace and stability (Roeder and Rothchild 2005: 125–30). The only circumstances in which they are optimistic about territorial decentralization is 'when there are multiple regions with numerous crosscutting political cleavages and relatively balanced capabilities' (ibid.:

130). Additionally, they note that decentralization is not likely to have unintended negative consequences in the face of 'general fatigue with war, the development of a commitment to resolve disputes through bargaining and reciprocity, and the emergence of respect and good will among the parties' (ibid.: 132).

This emphasis on considering conflict settlement mechanisms as a package rather than individually, unsurprisingly, is also one of the conclusions drawn by Valerie Bunce and Stephen Watts in their chapter on the post-communist states of Eurasia. While they also favour a unitary state approach, they find that '[i]ts success depends on whether it is combined with some other key characteristics, such as guarantees of minority rights and cultural autonomy, and separation of powers and proportionality in electoral systems' (Roeder and Rothchild 2005: 139). This proportionality claim, however, is disputed by Benjamin Reilly, whose examination of nine stable democracies in divided societies finds that only four use PR, and further suggests that '[t]here are no examples of an ethnically plural long-term democracy outside the developed world using PR' (ibid.: 171). As Reilly also emphasizes the impact of other factors on what is essentially a question of how well election outcomes reflect the diversity of a given society, such as the geographic distribution of ethnic groups, the question of PR vs. majoritarian/plurality electoral systems seems less relevant anyway. What matters is, again, the right package of institutions, which, as Reilly notes, can in some cases mean a 'combination of plurality elections and federalism' (ibid.: 170).

The individual case studies of Lebanon, India, Ethiopia and South Africa in Roeder and Rothchild's volume all have some good things to say about power sharing but remain largely sceptical of its overall and long-term value. Marie-Joëlle Zahar makes the point that power sharing in Lebanon depended on external guarantors, and as such brought long periods of peace to the country but in the long run inhibited its transition to democracy. Edmond Keller and Lahra Smith, in their study of Ethiopia, have to deal with a rather different experiment in federalization, one that largely failed in its implementation because of a lack of state capacity (limited funds, insufficient qualified personnel and material scarcity) and the emergence of new conflicts.

Amit Ahuja and Ashutosh Varshney describe the success of federalism in India in providing peace and stability in ethnically diverse societies, focusing on a number of factors that facilitated its success, including the technical and structural aspects of the design of the Indian federation and its political process. Yet, perhaps most crucially, they emphasize the importance of India being a nation – that is, the country as a whole and its constituent groups have a clear sense of their joint nationhood. The argument then is that, where belonging to the nation (and, by extension, the state) is by and large not disputed, mechanisms can be found to manage diversity effectively and peacefully. Put more trivially, if people want to live together, they can find ways of doing so.

The final case study, a comparative analysis of South Africa, Northern Ireland, and Bosnia and Herzegovina, by Timothy Sisk and Christoph Stefes, endorses the finding that power sharing is a useful and often a desirable and necessary tool to make the transition from war to peace. Specifically, they argue that the South African experience 'may have lessons for other attempts to build flexibility in institutional design and a deeper base of moderation throughout society' (Roeder and Rothchild 2005: 299). Examining Northern Ireland and Bosnia and Herzegovina in light of the South African experience, Sisk and Stefes assert that 'postwar societies need to move beyond the mutual hostage-taking that a guaranteed place at the decisionmaking table implies, the immobilism it inevitably creates, and the construction of postwar societies around the fixed and unyielding social boundaries of ethnicity' (ibid.: 317). While they see advantages in 'centripetal democratic solutions', they rightly caution that these can succeed 'only if the crosscutting integration in civil society on which they rely can be achieved over time' (ibid.).

Finally, Roeder and Rothchild offer their conclusions and policy recommendations. As they see it, 'nation-state stewardship' seeks to limit 'power sharing to two tactical roles in the initiation phase', i.e., the early period in the transition from civil war to peace. These two roles, according to Roeder and Rothchild, are an 'offer by a majority to reassure minorities about the peace implementation process' and 'a principle of proportionality for one-time, pump-priming decisions, such as the initial staffing of new bureaucracies and the armed forces' (Roeder and Rothchild 2005: 320). They also reiterate an earlier point made in their introduction, and in a similar way by Lake and Rothchild in their chapter on territorial decentralization, namely that, for power sharing to work after civil wars, extraordinary, and thus highly unlikely, circumstances need to be in place, primarily a shared national identity and an abundance of resources (ibid.: 323). As a consequence, they find that power sharing is likely to lead to 'institutional instability, the escalation of conflict, and blocked transitions to democracy' (ibid.: 325). They are equally critical of outside intervention, which they claim 'exacerbates many of the dilemmas of power sharing' and, in fact, introduces additional problems in itself (ibid.: 328).

Instead of endorsing power sharing beyond the initiation phase of peace and democracy, Roeder and Rothchild offer nine policy recommendations for the strategy of nation-state stewardship (Roeder and Rothchild 2005: 337–45): creating or holding together only those states in which constituent groups share a sense of nationhood and agree to live together; limiting government to minimize contentious issues that are decided centrally; delaying intervention until a clear victor emerges; lengthening protectorates to give moderates a chance to emerge; building institutions from the ground up so that local institutions of self-governance can emerge before central ones; phasing withdrawal in accordance with the build-up of local capacity; dividing power between different institutions and arenas such that ethnic stakes in politics are lowered; broadening negotiations for long-term arrangements to include other than just ethnically defined interest groups in the decision-making process; and limiting power sharing in favour of direct rule by the international community.

The main problem with this set of recommendations, however, is that, while they may be normatively appealing to proponents of liberalism, they are based on controversial empirical evidence (the conclusions reached by Roeder and Rothchild are not fully and unambiguously substantiated in the findings offered by their contributing authors), and they draw on a model of political system that contextually bears very little resemblance to the situation in conflict-torn societies (the success of the US model of democracy advocated remains context dependent: just because it works in the US does not mean that it can be successfully replicated elsewhere).

4 Conflict settlement in practice

As indicated in the introduction to this chapter, there are a large number of recent conflict settlements providing evidence for a trend towards favouring territorial self-government as part of an overall institutional design that seeks to square the circle between self-determination of identity groups, on the one hand, and territorial integrity and sovereignty of existing states, on the other. Evidence for this trend can be found across the globe: in Canada, Central and South America (Panama, Colombia, Mexico, Ecuador and Nicaragua), Africa (Sudan, Zanzibar),[23] Asia (Iraq, Indonesia, Papua New Guinea and the Philippines),[24] and Europe (Belgium, Bosnia and Herzegovina, Macedonia, Moldova, Russia, Serbia and Montenegro,[25] Ukraine and the United Kingdom).[26] From among these cases we selected ten different instances in which territorial self-governance regimes were established as part of a settlement: Bosnia and Herzegovina,[27] Bougainville (Papua New Guinea),[28] Brussels,[29] the Crimea,[30] Gagauzia,[31] Macedonia,[32] Mindanao (the Philippines),[33] Northern Ireland,[34] South Sudan,[35] and South Tyrol.[36]

The point of the following empirical analysis is to illustrate how institutional arrangements combining territorial self-governance and power sharing manifest themselves in practice. While this analysis, therefore, focuses primarily on local and state-level factors, we must not forget that even such settlements have a regional and global context in which they are negotiated, implemented and operated.[37]

4.1 State construction

The first element to consider in the context of questions about state construction is the actual existence of multiple layers of authority, or the extent to which conflict settlement practice reflects theoretical preferences for or against territorial self-governance designs. Table 7.1 illustrates that self-

Table 7.1 Variation in the vertical layering of authority[38]

Two-layered structures	Three-layered structures	Multi-layered structures
Macedonia	Bougainville	Bosnia and Herzegovina
	Crimea	Brussels
	Northern Ireland	Gagauzia
		Mindanao
		South Sudan
		South Tyrol

governance regimes rely predominantly on more than two layers of authority. In the cases of Bougainville, Northern Ireland and the Crimea, the three layers are central, substate and local government. In Macedonia, on the other hand, the middle level of government is missing. The functions and powers of the central and local governments are detailed in the constitution and in relevant legislation. There also exists a legally guaranteed opportunity for citizens to develop a further layer of government at the neighbourhood level, but this is regulated by by-laws of the individual local governments and is thus a matter of local decision-making rather than of state construction.

In the cases of Bosnia and Herzegovina, Brussels, Gagauzia, Mindanao, South Sudan and South Tyrol, more than three levels of government exist. In Bosnia and Herzegovina, this is a result of the interplay of domestic (i.e., state and local), regional and international factors in the process of state creation at Dayton, leading to a federal–confederal structure of the state. However, we need to be aware of the fact that cooperation between the two entities remains limited and often occurs as a consequence of the intervention of the High Representative, who has the power to veto decisions taken by the various local organs of administration. Analysis of voting behaviour also indicates that these complex arrangements have not yet been wholly effective in reducing inter-communal hostility. The basic rule of thumb is that, the higher the order of election, the less likely voters are to support parties that attempt to appeal to all communities. The complexity of domestic divisions and the process of federalization, leading to a structure in which regions and communities are simultaneously components of the overall federal structure, accounts for the four-layered structure of the Belgian system. In the case of Mindanao, an existing four-layered structure of government was altered with the creation of a specific and unique fifth layer – the legal–political entity of the Autonomous Region of Muslim Mindanao – to which powers were devolved. Similar to the case of Gagauzia, where a pre-existing three-layered structure was amended to accommodate the creation of the Territorial Autonomous Unit of Gagauzia, South Sudan has an additional level between central and state governments expressing the distinct, common identity of the southern states.

Table 7.2 Structural and functional symmetry and asymmetry of institutions

	Structures			Functions	
	Symmetric	Single asymmetric	Multiple asymmetric	Symmetric	Asymmetric
Bosnia and Herzegovina			X		X
Brussels	X				X
Bougainville	X				X
Crimea		X			X
Gagauzia			X		X
Macedonia	X			X	
Mindanao		X			X
Northern Ireland			X		X
South Sudan		X			X
South Tyrol	X				X

Another way of looking at structural types of vertically layered authority is to examine the degree to which these cases represent institutions that are structurally and/or functionally symmetric or asymmetric,[39] as this perspective provides a more comprehensive picture of the structure of the entire polity concerned and the place and status of territorial self-governance institutions within it.

Table 7.2 indicates that there is no clear-cut predominance of symmetric or asymmetric forms of institutional structures across the case studies, but that, from a functional perspective, i.e., the way in which powers and functions are distributed horizontally at the relevant levels of government in a polity, asymmetry is more frequent. In other words, the vertical layering of authority, regardless of whether or not it is structurally 'coherent' across a given state, facilitates asymmetric distribution of powers and functions, thus enabling central governments and specific regions to create a special relationship, in the sense that more powers and functions or parts thereof are devolved to a particular region, which thereby acquires greater autonomy in a wider range of policy areas compared to other territorial entities in the same country. Furthermore, while symmetric structures and symmetric functions may be correlated (Macedonia), symmetric structures do not preclude asymmetric functional capacities (Bougainville, Brussels, South Tyrol).

From a theoretical point of view, it is worth noting that consociational power sharing and centripetalism, albeit to differing degrees, allow for asymmetric structures and functions. While liberal consociational power sharing is principally in favour of territorial configurations reflecting the expressed wishes of self-defined communities (whatever the basis of such self-definition), centripetalists are not opposed to the use of territorial self-governance arrangements in either symmetric (federation) or asymmetric (autonomy) forms. However, crucially in this respect, centripetalists and advocates of power dividing prefer territorial self-governance to be based on 'administrative' rather than 'ethnic' criteria, in an effort to prevent the institutionalization of group identities and to enable coalitions of interest based on policy rather than identity (centripetalists) or to facilitate multiple and changing majorities (power dividers). Nevertheless, it is evident that, in the cases that form the basis of this empirical comparison, the entities of territorial self-governance are exclusively those in which group identities form the basis of boundaries.

One of the key questions to ask of any self-governance regime is where powers rest – i.e., how different competences are allocated to different layers of authority and whether they are their exclusive domain or have to be shared between different layers of authority. Naturally, there is a certain degree of context-dependent variation across the cases under examination, primarily with regard to the way in which powers are allocated and the degree of flexibility concerning new fields of policy-making not relevant or not included at the time a specific agreement was concluded.

The principal mechanism to handle the distribution of powers is the drawing up of lists that enumerate precisely which powers are allocated to which levels of authority and/or which are to be shared between different such levels. These lists can be very specific for each layer of authority (Bougainville, Mindanao, South Sudan and South Tyrol)[40] or they can be specific for one or more layers and 'open-ended' for others (Bosnia and Herzegovina, the Crimea, Gagauzia, Macedonia and Northern Ireland). The key difference in the latter case is which layer of authority has an 'open-ended' list and retains residual authority for any partly devolved power or any other policy area not explicitly allocated elsewhere.

As table 7.3 illustrates, in Brussels, the Crimea, Gagauzia and Macedonia, the centre holds residual authority over all matters not expressly devolved to the lower layers of authority, while in South Tyrol and Bosnia and Herzegovina the two entities retain all the competences not explicitly assigned to the centre.

The multi-layered system of public authority that is in place in Mindanao has very specific lists of powers allocated to the individual levels within it, even though the central government remains the original source of all authority – i.e., the reverse of the situation in South Tyrol (since 2001). This is also the case in Northern Ireland, but here the system of allocating powers operates on the basis of three different lists, enumerating devolved, reserved (with the

Table 7.3 Power allocation in self-governance regimes

Specific lists	Combination of specific and 'open-ended' lists	
	Open-ended list at centre	Specific list at centre
Bougainville	Brussels	Bosnia and Herzegovina
Mindanao	Crimea	South Tyrol
Northern Ireland[41]	Gagauzia	
South Sudan	Macedonia	

future possibility of devolution) and excepted (without the future possibility of devolution) matters. In Bougainville, which also operates a system of specific power allocation to the different layers of public authority, an additional feature is that there are specific arrangements as to how to deal with emerging policy areas (a joint commission that will resolve disputes over the allocation of new powers). Another distinctive feature of the Bougainvillean system is that, initially, all powers allocated to the autonomous province are retained at the central level and are, albeit almost automatically, devolved to Bougainville upon application to the central authorities by the provincial authorities. In the case of South Sudan, notably, specific lists of powers exist for the centre, the government of South Sudan and state governments, as well as a list of so-called concurrent powers whose exercise falls into the competence of more than one layer of government.

None of the three theories of conflict settlement discussed above offers much specific guidance on this issue of power allocation to different vertical layers of authority. Some inferences can nevertheless be made. Power-dividers, who express a certain preference for the American model of federalism (e.g., Roeder 2005), favour strong central governments and are thus likely to opt for residual authority to remain with the central government. A similar tendency can be observed for advocates of centripetalism (e.g., Wimmer 2003). For the liberal consociational school, it is important that power sharing is a more attractive option to conflict parties than recourse to violence; hence it advocates that substantive powers be transferred to territorial self-government entities by assigning residual authority to these entities or by drawing up specific lists.

The distribution and separation of powers, horizontally and vertically, in complex power sharing systems requires mechanisms for the coordination of law- and policy-making. This is generally an important issue in the operation of any multi-layered system of government, but in the context of self-determination conflicts it assumes additional significance, as coordination failures not only have an impact on the effectiveness of government but also have repercussions for the perception of the usefulness of a particular institutional structure to resolve a conflict. Although there is a wide spectrum of individual coordination mechanisms, these can be grouped into four distinct

Table 7.4 Coordination mechanisms in self-governance regimes

Cooptation	Joint cttees and implementation bodies	Judicial review and arbitration	Direct intervention by the international community
Brussels	Bougainville	Bosnia and Herzegovina	Bosnia and Herzegovina
Gagauzia	Brussels	Bougainville	
Mindanao	Gagauzia	Brussels	
	Macedonia	Crimea	
	Mindanao	Gagauzia	
	Northern Ireland	Macedonia	
	South Sudan	Mindanao	
	South Tyrol	Northern Ireland	
		South Sudan	
		South Tyrol	

categories: cooptation, joint committees and implementation bodies, judicial review and arbitration processes, and direct intervention by the international community.

As demonstrated in table 7.4, with the exception of the Crimea, all the cases exhibit at least two different coordination mechanisms, with one of them always (in the case of the Crimea, the only one) being judicial review and arbitration processes. This suggests that there is a strong reliance upon the legal regulation of relationships between different layers of public authority and an emphasis on the separation of powers between different branches of government, creating an independent judiciary.

Cooptation, adopted in Belgium, Moldova and the Philippines, is a mechanism to ensure the representation at the centre of local-level officials (from Brussels, Gagauzia, and the Autonomous Region of Muslim Mindanao (ARMM), respectively). In all cases, local-level officials are *ex officio* members of relevant central government departments. This arrangement is symbolic and emphasizes the special relationship between central government and autonomous region. In the cases of Gagauzia and Mindanao, it is also necessary as the two autonomous entities are artificial constructions from an administrative-territorial point of view and do not fit into the pre-existing structures of authority in Moldova and the Philippines. Cooptation thus becomes a potential mechanism to deal with this kind of irregularity and to ensure that the special circumstances of the autonomous regions are borne in mind in the process of state-level law- and policy-making. Cooptation is notably absent in the similar cases of the Crimea and South Sudan, but well compensated for in the latter through extensive power sharing mechanisms. In the Crimea, the Representative Office of the President of Ukraine acts, in part, as a coordination mechanism with oversight, but without executive powers.

The need for joint committees and implementation bodies often arises from two sources – to find common interpretations for specific aspects of agreements and regulations and to coordinate the implementation of specific policies at state and local levels. Examples of the former are Bougainville and Gagauzia, while the latter can be found in Macedonia (inter-ethnic relations), Mindanao (development), Northern Ireland (cooperation between Northern Ireland and the Republic of Ireland and among all entities party to the British–Irish Council) and South Sudan (constitutional review, application of Shari'a Law, human rights, elections, referendum, fiscal and financial allocation). Such bodies usually hold regular meetings (Bougainville, Macedonia, Mindanao, Northern Ireland, South Sudan); and they can be in their nature domestic centre–periphery bodies (Bougainville, Macedonia, Mindanao, South Sudan) or reflect the international dimension of a particular self-determination conflict (Northern Ireland). They may be prescribed in agreements between the conflict parties (Bougainville, Mindanao, Northern Ireland, South Sudan) or arise from actual needs (Gagauzia and Macedonia).

In the case of South Tyrol, significant aspects of the original negotiations of the autonomy statute in the 1960s were carried out by the so-called Commission of Nineteen, involving representatives of South Tyrol and the Italian government. Subsequently two separate commissions were created to facilitate and oversee the implementation of the statute in relation to provincial and regional aspects of autonomy. Since 1997 a further commission, required according to Article 137 of the autonomy statute, has been operational which deals specifically with questions of minority protection and economic, social and cultural development of the ethnic groups in South Tyrol. This commission must be consulted in the event of any planned changes to the autonomy statute. A further special commission was created in 2001 to deal with the implementation of changes resulting from the reforms that year of autonomy statute and Italian constitution. A standing commission at the office of the Italian prime minister, created to monitor the implementation of the statute, has been in place since 1972. In addition to policy coordination at the level of commissions, South Tyrol's autonomy also benefits from a strong and independent judicial system. Its role, however, has changed significantly in the operation of the system, especially the function of the constitutional court in protecting South Tyrol's legislative acts from undue interference by the central government.

Unique to Bosnia and Herzegovina is the previously mentioned continuing and apparently open-ended direct intervention of the international community as a mechanism to coordinate law- and policy-making. Here, powerful international officials retain significant powers, enabling them to intervene directly in the political processes of the two entities. This results primarily from the unprecedented involvement of the international community in the process of resolving the three underlying self-determination conflicts within Bosnia and Herzegovina and the responsibility that international agents thereby assumed for post-conflict state construction, as well as from the particularly bitter nature of the disputes concerned.

The three theories of conflict settlement discussed above offer some limited guidance on coordination mechanisms. All three generally emphasize the importance of a law-based system and thus of the role played by independent judicial institutions. Liberal consociationalists further allow for additional coordination mechanisms, the presence of which is in fact a key characteristic of 'regional consociations' (see Wolff 2004b). Centripetalists, even where they explicitly discuss federal-type arrangements (e.g., Horowitz 1991: 214–26; Wimmer 2003), say very little on how policy can best be coordinated in multi-layered systems of authority.

4.2 The institutions of government

As illustrated in table 7.5, there is a slight predominance of parliamentary systems, at both central and, where applicable, substate level of government. Of these, the UK, Papua New Guinea,[42] Bougainville,[43] and the Crimea use plurality electoral systems, and all others rely on PR systems for the election of members of their respective parliaments. Noteworthy, however, is the use of preferential systems in Northern Ireland (STV) and South Tyrol (open party list system). Such preferential systems are generally linked more closely to centripetalism, even though Horowitz's clear inclination is towards majoritarian preferential systems. The fact that consociationalists have also come to appreciate preferential systems indicates both a greater openness towards the potential benefits of preferential systems (i.e., election of more moderate leaders) and a 'liberalization' and 'democratization' of consociationalism away from Lijphart's earlier preference for the elite cartel.

In presidential systems, at both central and substate levels of government, the method of electing presidents is by simple majority vote with a second-round run-off between the two candidates topping the first-round ballot. The lower chambers of parliament at the central level are elected by plurality systems in single-seat constituencies (Sudan), parallel mixed systems (the Philippines, Ukraine) or list PR (Bosnia and Herzegovina). At substate level, the electoral system for parliament in Mindanao is a parallel mixed system, while in Gagauzia it is plurality in single-member districts. No elections have yet taken place in South Sudan and no electoral system has been determined.

One element of the complexity of self-governing regimes as a mechanism to resolve self-determination conflicts stems from the fact that constitutional engineers have developed innovative ways to combine traditional structures of horizontal power sharing and vertical power dividing. As the cases of Macedonia and Mindanao demonstrate (see table 7.6), the absence of formal

Table 7.5 Parliamentary vs. presidential systems

Central parliamentary system	Central presidential system	Substate parliamentary system	Substate presidential system
Belgium		Brussels	
Italy		South Tyrol[44]	
	Bosnia and Herzegovina*	Federation of Bosnia and Herzegovina	
Bosnia and Herzegovina, Macedonia			
Moldova			Gagauzia
Papua New Guinea			Bougainville
	Philippines		Mindanao
	Sudan		South Sudan
	Ukraine*	Crimea	
United Kingdom		Northern Ireland	

* Denotes semi-presidential system

Table 7.6 Horizontal executive power sharing at central and substate levels of authority

No horizontal power sharing	Horizontal power sharing at the centre	Horizontal power sharing at substate level only	Horizontal power sharing at the centre and substate level
	Macedonia[45]	Crimea[47]	Bosnia and Herzegovina/ Federation of Bosnia and Herzegovina[49]
	Moldova[46]	Northern Ireland	
		South Tyrol[48]	Papua New Guinea/ Bougainville[50]
			Belgium/Brussels
			Philippines/ Mindanao[51]
			Sudan/South Sudan[52]

structures of power sharing at the centre does not preclude power nevertheless being shared to some extent. This is more obvious in Macedonia, as the country's demographic balances and the structure of the party and electoral systems combine in a way that make the formation of government coalitions between ethnic Macedonian and ethnic Albanian parties likely (they have indeed been a reality since 1992). In Mindanao, on the other hand, since the 1996 peace agreement between the Philippines government and the Moro National Liberation Front (MNLF) and the establishment of the ARMM (ICG 2008), there is a somewhat greater degree of formality in power sharing arrangements at the centre, as members of the substate level governments are coopted into respective branches of the central government. Cooptation, however, limits the extent of the influence that can be exercised by the region at the centre, as substate-level cooptees are outnumbered by other members of the central government and have little, if any, leverage when compared with a situation in which a substate-level party is a member of a governing coalition and can potentially exercise veto powers. Critics, however, argue that, owing to ARMM's lack of revenue raising capacity, the region's autonomy is more notional than real; fighting between government forces and the (communist) New People's Army (NPA) continues, and on the island of Jolo the Islamic fundamentalist movement Abu Sayyaf, which first emerged in the early 1990s (ICG 2005), is still active.

Horizontal power sharing at the substate level exists in all those cases where there is significant ethnic or other diversity within the region, i.e., where mere devolution of powers to a lower level of authority would simply replicate the conflict at the state level. This is clearly the case in Bosnia and Herzegovina (Federation level), Brussels, Mindanao, Northern Ireland and South Tyrol.[53] More specifically, the South Tyrol arrangements can be described as a 'nested consociation', that is, consociational structures exist at both the provincial (South Tyrol) and the regional[54] (Trentino-South Tyrol) level. This reflects the territorial organization of the Italian state into regions and (normally) subordinate provinces. On the other hand, Germans are a minority at the regional level, while Italians are in a minority position in the province. Given that, until the 2001 reforms, the region was a much more important political player in relation to the exercise of South Tyrol's competences, concerns of German-speakers about political influence could be addressed by their mandatory inclusion in the regional cabinet. At the same time, the Italian minority in South Tyrol required similar protective mechanisms. To achieve a stable equilibrium in the face of this dual minority situation required the establishment of an interlocking consociational mechanism that would recognize and protect both main linguistic groups within the existing structure of territorial-political organization.

In contrast to the 'abundance' of power sharing arrangements in the case of South Tyrol, mandatory state and substate horizontal power sharing mechanisms are lacking in Macedonia, but their absence can also be explained with reference to territorial, demographic and political factors. The territorial concentration of ethnic Albanians, the range of powers devolved to the municipal level, and the opportunity for citizens to establish a further layer of authority at the neighbourhood level address a wide range of self-government concerns among ethnic Albanians. In addition, the numerical strength of ethnic Albanians in the Macedonian polity and the structure of its party and electoral systems guarantee significant representation of ethnic Albanian parties in the Macedonian parliament and make their participation in a coalition government at least highly likely. As of 2008, three Albanian parties were represented in parliament. At present the most important is the Democratic Party for Prosperity (PPD), which sits in government with a number of Macedonian parties. The Democratic Union for Integration (BDI) and the Democratic Party of the Albanians (PDSH) both form part of the opposition. While the Ohrid Agreement clearly recognizes and privileges the two largest ethnic communities in Macedonia, it is not traditionally consociational in the institutional design it prescribes. In fact, one could argue that, in the specific context of Macedonia's demography and party-political system, it facilitates pre-election inter-ethnic coalitions on the basis of ideological affinity at the centre. The high degree of compactness of the Albanian community allows them to benefit fully from the implementation of local autonomy, as foreseen in the Ohrid Agreement, and makes the implementation of formal territorial autonomy less important for them. This, in turn, allays some of the fears among Macedonians that autonomy would be just a first step to the partition of the country.

This indicates that, under certain conditions – relative territorial concentration of ethnic communities, sufficient levels of devolution, and a minimum degree of representation at the centre – vertical division of powers can function as a useful substitute for formal structures of horizontal power sharing at both central and substate level and suffice in addressing institutional dimensions of power (re)distribution in self-determination conflicts. The fact that vertically divided powers can substitute for horizontal levels of power sharing only under very specific conditions is also highlighted by the example of Bosnia and Herzegovina, where, despite wide-ranging devolution, horizontal power sharing remains mandatory at the level of state institutions and at the level of the Bosnian-Croat Federation.

It is important to note, however, that the absence of formal power sharing structures, i.e., the lack of a consociational requirement for a cross-community representative executive, should not be equated with either the complete absence of power sharing or the derogation of communal identities from the public to the private sphere. Furthermore, voluntary executive power sharing arrangements that emerge do not necessarily do so on the basis of a specific electoral system. The centripetalists' favourite AV model is absent in all relevant cases – deputies to the Crimean Supreme Council have, since 1998, been elected on the basis of a single-seat non-preferential majoritarian system, and Macedonia's members of parliament are elected by a parallel mixed system.

4.3 The relationship between individual citizens, identity groups and the state

Relevant human and minority provisions exist in all cases covered in this analysis, albeit to differing degrees. Applicable law includes international

Table 7.7 International human and minority rights instruments[55]

	UN membership	Convention on the Prevention and Punishment of the Crime of Genocide*	International Convention on the Elimination of All Forms of Racial Discrimination*	International Covenant on Economic, Social, And Cultural Rights*	International Covenant on Civil and Political Rights*	Optional Protocol to the International Covenant on Civil and Political Rights*	UNESCO membership	UNESCO Convention against Discrimination in Education
Belgium	Yes	1951	1975	1983	1983	1994	Yes	–
Bosnia and Herzegovina	Yes	1992	1993	1993	1993	1995	Yes	1993
Italy	Yes	1952	1976	1978	1978	1978	Yes	1966
Macedonia	Yes	1994	1994	1994	1994	1994	Yes	1997
Moldova	Yes	1993	1993	1993	1993	2005	Yes	1993
Papua New Guinea	Yes	1982	1982	–	–	–	Yes	–
Philippines	Yes	1950	1967	1974	1986	1989	Yes	1964
Sudan	Yes	2003	1977	1986	1986	–	Yes	–
Ukraine	Yes	1954	1969	1973	1973	1991	Yes	1962
UK	Yes	1970	1969	1976	1976	–	Yes	1962

Note: * Status as of 1 November 2006

and regional standards and more specific statewide, and in some cases local, human and minority rights legislation, as summarized in tables 7.7 to 7.9.

There are no regional human and minority rights instruments applicable to the Asian case studies in this analysis (Papua New Guinea and Philippines). Sudan ratified the African Charter for Human and People's Rights[56] in 1986.

This is not the place to examine in detail the legal provisions contained in any of these documents or the degree to which law translates into policy and is enforced in the countries covered by this comparative analysis. The general trend in legal provisions for human and minority rights, however, is obvious in that constitutional human rights provisions are universally present and in that, with the exception of Papua New Guinea, all countries are states parties to the key international conventions. There seems to be significantly greater reluctance to include minority rights provisions in constitutions or even provide for separate minority rights legislation at both the state and the local level. This emphasis on individual human rights over (group-specific) minority rights is consistent with recommendations of power-dividers and centripetalists. Consociationalists, too, appreciate the value of individual

Table 7.8 Regional human and minority rights instruments: Europe[57]

	Council of Europe membership	(European) Convention for the Protection of Human Rights and Fundamental Freedoms	(European) Framework Convention for the Protection of National Minorities	European Charter for Regional or Minority Languages
Belgium	Yes	1955	(2001)	–
Bosnia and Herzegovina	Yes	2002	2000	(2005)
Italy	Yes	1955	1998	(2000)
Moldova	Yes	1997	1998	(2002)
Macedonia	Yes	1997	1998	(1996)
Ukraine	Yes	1997	1998	2006
UK	Yes	1953	1998	2001

Table 7.9 Domestic and local human and minority rights provisions

	Constitutional human rights provisions	Constitutional minority rights provisions	Statewide minority rights legislation	Local human rights legislation	Local minority rights legislation
Belgium/Brussels	Yes	No	No	Yes	Yes
Bosnia and Herzegovina	Yes	Yes	Yes	Yes	Yes
Italy	Yes	Yes	Yes	Yes	Yes
Moldova	Yes	Yes	No	Yes	No
Macedonia	Yes	Yes	Yes	n.a.	n.a.
Papua New Guinea	Yes	No	No	Yes	No
Philippines	Yes	No	Yes	No	No
Sudan	Yes	Yes	No	Yes	No
Ukraine	Yes	Yes	Yes	Yes	No
UK[58]	Yes	No	No	Yes	No

human rights provisions, but their recommendations do not caution against the parallel use of minority rights provisions, which is consistent with their generally more pronounced emphasis on the recognition and protection of (self-determined) group identities.

When it comes to the relationship between individual citizens, groups and the state, it is also important to clarify the boundaries of authority. While rights protect individuals (and groups) from undue state interference, such stipulations are only meaningful inasmuch as the legitimate exercise of political power has clearly defined boundaries, i.e., to whom and where these rights apply. Such boundaries normally relate to a specific territory and/or a defined group of people. The degree to which both of these categories shape the boundaries of authority of specific institutions of government contributes to an assessment of the degree to which group identities are institutionally recognized and protected.

A national government has the authority to exercise its power within the territorial confines of the state it is governing and over the residents of this territory (with the exception of foreign diplomats, for example). Some elements of a national government's authority may also extend beyond the territorial boundaries of its state, but then they will normally be limited to that particular state's citizens, for example in the field of tax collection. In terms of self-governance regimes, the extent of these two limitations placed on the exercise of authority is similar. Regional territorial self-governance regimes are spatially confined. The powers devolved to them apply only within the territorial boundaries of the region and, by extension, to (permanent) residents of the region. Analogous to authority extending beyond territorial boundaries are instances of personal autonomy in which the autonomous body has authority over all individuals belonging to it, no matter where they live in the territory of the state or region concerned.[59]

These observations are particularly relevant in two of the cases examined here. The territories of Gagauzia and of the Autonomous Region of Muslim Mindanao were determined by a referendum at the local level, giving the population an opportunity to express in a free vote whether they wanted to live under the authority of a newly created substate government or continue being governed within the existing structure of vertically layered institutions. In Mindanao, this vote took place at the level of provinces and towns, and in Moldova at that of local communities, thus allowing for a much more 'precise' gauging of popular will and the degree to which minority identities express themselves, in part, through a desire for self-governance. In both cases, the result was that the autonomous territory thus created is not in fact a contiguous area, but is made up of a number of patches of territory. Early indications suggest that this is not necessarily detrimental to the exercise of authority at the level of the autonomous territory. Additionally, a degree of personal autonomy exists in the Autonomous Region of Muslim Mindanao with regard to judicial affairs, as Shari'a and tribal courts have authority alongside lower-order courts of the statewide judicial system in religious and family affairs to cater for the specific needs of the different religious, ethnic and tribal communities in these areas. In the third case, South Sudan, the relevant territory comprises the southern states as they existed at Sudan's independence. Special provisions apply to two disputed areas: Abyei and the Southern Kordofan/Nuba Mountains and the Blue Nile States. The former is defined as the area of the nine Ngok Dinka chiefdoms, which were transferred to Kordofan in 1905. Both territories were accorded special status during the interim period prior to the referendum on independence for South Sudan and have different options in this referendum.[60]

The cases of Gagauzia and Mindanao suggest that there is an additional degree of differentiation available that goes beyond the traditional territorial delimitation of authority, in that it incorporates a public consultation process for the definition of the territorial boundaries of the autonomous area. If combined with levels of personal autonomy in specific policy areas, the range of authority that a self-governance entity enjoys can be tailored to the specific demographic and geographic situation, taking account of settlement patterns and ethnic, religious, cultural and other types of heterogeneity. While such 'fine-tuning' increases the complexity of self-governance regimes, it may also make them more suitable in particular contexts and thus more acceptable. In other words, careful territorial and personal delimitation of self-governance potentially increases the belief in the authority of the institutions established among those governed by them, and is thus likely to contribute to greater stability of these same institutions and the political process of which they are part. However, as we have previously indicated, adding a further layer of authority to those already existing within the structure of an established state increases the complexity of institutional design, places greater demands on policy coordination, and has the potential to undermine the authority of the territorial entity created specifically to increase the degree of self-governance enjoyed by a particular population group.

However, what is striking about the arrangements in both Gagauzia and Mindanao[61] is the fact that, while the relevant local government units can decide in a referendum as to whether or not they want to belong to the newly created autonomous entity, there seems to be no provision for the reverse process, i.e., to allow units to leave the autonomous entity. In case of significant changes in the population balance in one or more such units, a new minority would be created within the autonomous entity (whose demands would have to be accommodated). Demographic developments always have implications for security perceptions and the stability of settlements of complex self-determination conflicts, but it is reasonable to assume that their implications would be even more severe in cases where territorial (re)arrangements are recent, precisely because they will imply a degree of fluidity which is threatening to both majorities and minorities. On the other hand, given reasonably and rationally acting political elites, there is nothing to say that significant demographic shifts could not be addressed constructively.

Two further cases are worth mentioning. In Macedonia, devolution of significant powers to the local layer of authority was accompanied by boundary revisions to take better account of ethnic settlement patterns and render local municipalities more ethnically homogeneous, especially along the 'internal' Albanian–Macedonian border. In South Tyrol, the boundaries of the autonomous province were determined largely on the basis of its historical entity, but some 'adjustments' were made to incorporate some predominantly German-speaking municipalities that would otherwise have been part of the province of Trentino.

Thus, in half of the cases considered in our comparative analysis, the recognition and protection of group identities went beyond the application of mere territorial principles. This is not to say that in the other cases identities are not institutionally recognized or protected. After all, self-governance in all cases is applied to territories inhabited, wholly or in part, by ethnically or otherwise distinct groups. Furthermore, in most cases, power sharing arrangements exist that explicitly acknowledge group identities and afford them a measure of institutional protection precisely because of the inclusiveness of resulting governance arrangements at various levels. What is important, though, is to realize that, among some of the complex power sharing arrangements discussed here, the recognition and protection of group identities extends beyond the application of these principles and establishes territorial entities, or adjusts pre-existing ones, to facilitate the inclusion of the maximum possible number of members of one particular ethnic group into self-governance regimes – without, of course, engaging in their (involuntary) resettlement. The recent use of local referenda, moreover, means that there is no automatic, predetermined equivalence of identity and territory.

This issue of privileging group identities is one in which liberal consociationalist views dominate in conflict settlement practice – territorial boundaries of self-governing entities are self-defined by their populations. The resultant 'ethnic' entities run counter especially to the recommendations of power-dividers, who generally prefer administrative, heterogeneous entities to ethnically self-defined ones with particular group majorities or pluralities.

5 Conclusion

From the degree of institutional variation across the case studies examined above, one can draw a number of both analytical and empirical conclusions. Empirically, there are four important lessons for the role that complex power sharing regimes have in conflict settlement. First, dividing power along a vertical structure of institutions can serve as a useful substitute for formal horizontal power sharing at either state or substate level, provided that statewide or substate ethnic demographies create suitably homogeneous territories and that substantial powers are devolved from the centre. In other words, such cases lend themselves to the application of forms of territorial autonomy or of the subsidiarity principle, instead of the use of executive co-decision-making as foreseen by power sharing institutions. Moreover, a reasonable degree of representation of minority groups at the relevant 'central' level (substate in the case of the Crimea, central state in the case of Macedonia), in addition to these other two conditions, also seems to facilitate this kind of institutional structure.

Second, no attempt was made in any of the cases studied to *create* heterogeneous entities as subjects of territorial self-governance or to divide large pre-existing ethnic entities into smaller units. Heterogeneity, where it exists, was addressed by means of consociational power sharing within the self-governing territorial entity. This means that some key recommendation by advocates of centripetalism and power dividing – to encourage heterogeneous territorial entities – was not followed by practitioners of conflict settlement in any of the cases studied. At the same time, institutional designers did not, except in the case of Bosnia and Herzegovina, rush to create larger territorial entities on the basis of ethnic identities where these did not pre-exist, as the example of Macedonia demonstrates.

Third, coordination between different vertical layers of authority and the establishment of a clear division of powers are important to ensure that vertical layering of authority remains meaningful and can contribute to the long-term sustainability of a particular conflict settlement. Where there is a danger of eroding the degree of self-governance enjoyed by specific territorial entities and their populations created as a particular layer of authority with the specific purpose of conflict settlement (such as Gagauzia, Mindanao, South Sudan and, with some qualifications, the Crimea), conflict settlements may not be sustainable in the long term.

This means, fourth and finally, that, without safeguards against arbitrary government interference, it is unlikely that the conflict parties will develop a sense of satisfactory permanence and predictability in relation to a particular settlement. Legal and constitutional entrenchment and effective dispute resolution mechanisms, possibly alongside international guarantees, are thus important mechanisms for the stabilization of institutional structures. These and other power dividing strategies that provide checks and balances on the exercise of power serve to ensure that principles of liberal democratic state construction shape complex power sharing regimes and enhance their longer-term legitimacy. These strategies, of course, are also fully compatible with liberal consociational power sharing and centripetalism.

Analytically, it appears that none of the three theories of conflict settlement fully captures the current practice of complex power sharing. That said, liberal consociationalism emerges as the one theory that is most open to the incorporation of elements of centripetalism and power dividing. Within a liberal consociational framework, there is room (and a recognized need) for a range of power dividing strategies, including a strong role for judicial entrenchment and enforcement mechanisms, and universally applicable and enforceable human rights legislation. Liberal consociationalism is also open to a vertical division of power on the basis of non-ascriptive (i.e., non-ethnic) criteria, but in contrast to power dividing and centripetalism does not rule it out either, should self-determined entities on that basis emerge and desire territorial or corporate self-governance. Liberal consociationalists and cen-tripetalists share some common ground in terms of the principle of preferen-tial electoral systems, even though they disagree about whether preferential PR or majoritarian systems are better suited to achieve outcomes conducive to stable settlements in the long term. In support of power sharing more generally, the empirical evidence presented in our analysis also indicates that executive inter-ethnic power sharing is a component of all institutional designs discussed – either as a mandatory requirement or as an outcome of the application of certain institutional design features (especially the use of specific electoral systems) to particular (territorial-demographic) contexts.

The second point worth emphasizing is related to the stability of the set-tlements discussed. In other words, is complex power sharing a feasible alternative to the purist implementation of existing theories, or is it the result of misguided and ill-informed diplomats and policy-makers making choices of short-term convenience rather than long-term prudence? There is little point in making immodest claims at this stage about the feasibility of complex power sharing, as conceptualized and analysed here, as a conflict settlement strategy equal, if not superior to, what existing theories prescribe. While complex power sharing practice *may* eventually lead to a synthesis of existing theories in a complex power sharing framework, there is as yet not enough real-world evidence about how stable such regimes can be under varying conditions. The cases examined in this chapter were all similar to the extent that they comprised self-determination claims by territorially concen-trated identity groups that lent themselves to the establishment of complex power sharing regimes with territorial self-governance arrangements at their heart. Some of them have proven relatively stable over time (i.e., over ten years): Brussels, Bosnia and Herzegovina, the Crimea, Gagauzia and South Tyrol. Macedonia's Ohrid Framework Agreement of 2001 has proved resilient enough to provide a stable institutional structure and political process for more than eight years now. Northern Ireland has, despite significant delays, achieved a remarkable institutional compromise. Bougainville and South Sudan are too short-lived to provide reliable data as to their long-term stabil-ity, while the agreement in Mindanao has achieved only partial success in bringing peace to a troubled region of the Philippines.

8

'Alternatives' to Consensual Conflict Settlement

1 Introduction

The preceding chapters have illustrated various aspects of international conflict regulation and have paid special attention to the theory and practice
of conflict settlement. The settlements that we have analysed fall broadly
into the category of 'methods for managing ethnic differences' (McGarry
and O'Leary 1993: 4), yet, as we illustrated in chapter 7, a close-up analysis of
conflict settlement practice led us to acknowledge that settlements are true
hybrids in practice, including at least some 'methods for eliminating differences' (ibid.) as well. What they all have in common – from power sharing
agreements to the creation of autonomous regions – is that they are reached
by consensus.[1] In the following, we therefore turn to the alternatives to such
consensual conflict settlement. The most commonly mentioned policies to
'resolve' ethnic conflicts in a non-consensual way involve genocide, ethnic
cleansing, hegemonic control, forced assimilation and partition/secession.[2]

2 The track record of the alternatives

What is striking about these so-called alternatives is that they have no obvious track record of success, yet they nonetheless continue to be pursued by
conflict parties. Take the case of genocide, for example. The major incidents
of genocide in the twentieth century all failed to achieve their stated aims,
namely the extermination of an entire population group.[3] The Holocaust,
although horrific in its scale of industrialized mass slaughter of European
Jews, did not result in the Nazis' aim of total extermination of the Jewish
population. Nor did the regime succeed in eliminating all Roma. The reasons
for this failure are related to the sheer scale of the undertaking, the lack of
'cooperation' extended to the effort by the various countries and populations
under Nazi control, and the defeat that the Germans suffered at the hands of
the Allies. It is argued conventionally that, half a century later, the genocide
in Rwanda, which killed around 800,000 minority Tutsi (and moderate Hutus
opposed to it), failed to achieve its ultimate aim not because of an international intervention, but because Tutsi rebels invading Rwanda from neighbouring Uganda defeated the Hutu regime before the latter could complete
its mission. On the other hand, if the Ugandan government had not allowed

the Rwandan Patriotic Front to operate on its territory, and had not actively engaged in supporting and equipping that movement from the point of its inception in 1990, there might well have been an outcome very different from the genocide that ensued. In fact, the actions of the Museveni government in Uganda demonstrate that outside intervention was crucial to the overthrow of the Hutu ruling elite and their allies.

During the disintegration of Yugoslavia in the first half of the 1990s, especially in the war in Bosnia and Herzegovina, killings of Bosniaks occurred on a massive scale. Yet, while judges of the International Court of Justice accepted that Bosniaks had been specifically targeted and had become victims of systematic 'massive mistreatment, beatings, rape and torture causing serious bodily and mental harm, during the conflict and, in particular, in the detention camps', they failed to find conclusive evidence that there was an intent, on the part of Serbs, to destroy Bosniaks as a whole and as a group, and thus did not find that Serb policies in Bosnia and Herzegovina amounted to genocide except in the specific case of Srebrenica, where, in July 1995, some 8,000 Bosniak men and youths were killed.[4]

While the events in Bosnia and Herzegovina thus present yet another example of the senselessness of genocide, they also indicate how closely some of these alternative policies are linked to each other. Leaving aside, for the moment, the question of whether genocide was indeed committed in Bosnia and Herzegovina, there can be no doubt that killings, rape and torture occurred on an enormous scale and induced the mass flight of people. The ethnic homogenization of large parts of Bosnian territory – that is, the forcible removal of people from another ethnic group, paved the way towards the quasi-partition of Bosnia and Herzegovina into today's two entities (the Republika Srpska and the Federation of Bosnia and Herzegovina) and the relative ethnic homogeneity of the cantons in the federation. While genocide may, legally speaking, not have taken place in Bosnia and Herzegovina, the consequences of what happened are not dissimilar: the social fabric of an erstwhile multi-ethnic society in which groups coexisted peacefully, and in urban areas intermarried, has been destroyed and has given way to a system of self-segregation and ghettoization. To be sure, the events in Bosnia and Herzegovina are nowhere near on the same scale as the Holocaust or the genocide in Rwanda, but they illustrate just as much as these the lengths to which ethnic groups – leaders and followers alike – are prepared to go when it comes to ridding themselves of what they argue are threats to their own physical and cultural survival.

Of course, in times of crisis, ethnic groups do not respond in a uniformly violent manner. Genocide is the exception rather than the rule. Other 'alternative solutions' to ethnic conflict, however, have a track record that is no better. Forced assimilation has been attempted under many different guises but hardly ever been successful as a policy to eliminate an ethnic group's sense of distinctiveness. Roma in Central and Eastern Europe, for example, have been subjected to many forms of forced assimilation for hundreds of years. From the days of the Habsburg empress Maria Theresa, who in the eighteenth century established designated settlements and sought to create jobs and school places for 'Gypsies', to communist attempts in Czechoslovakia to curb high birth rates by financially rewarding Roma women who were willing to be sterilized, Roma have been at the receiving end of policies based on prejudice and stereotype. But their case also highlights another important aspect of 'alternative solutions' to ethnic conflicts. Policies of forced assimilation are often couched in terms of social progress – that is, attempts to help 'socially backward' populations attain the same standards of living, education, employment, and so on, as the rest of the population. Ill-informed and patronizing as these may be, they are not always, per se, meant to do harm to the ethnic groups at which they are aimed. Once these policies fail, however, because ethnic groups resist attempts at forced assimilation, a backlash occurs, manifesting itself in deliberate exclusion, discrimination and abuse. Today, the result of this is a situation in which government efforts in Central and Eastern Europe to improve the situation of Roma populations, supported, for example by the European Union, are systematically undercut by persisting deep-seated prejudice among the wider population. Attempts to integrate Roma children into mainstream education, for example, then fail because parents, children and teachers resist the implementation of such programmes, while human and minority rights legislation aimed at giving Roma formally equal status in society and offering affirmative action measures falter in the face of police abuse and failure to investigate violations of their rights.

Another example of failed forced assimilation attempts is the programme of rapid Italianization introduced by Mussolini in South Tyrol immediately after the fascist takeover of 29 October 1922. South Tyrol, a predominantly German-speaking area in northern Italy, had not, until the 1919 peace settlement of St Germain, been part of Italy, and the resistance of its population to incorporation was considerable. Italianization was hence seen as a way to break this resistance, and the assimilation programme – extended to the three main areas of culture, economy and administration – aimed at the systematic destruction of the linguistic, religious and demographic foundations of the ethnic identity of the population.

Italian became the official language in public life, including the courts (with the exception of a small number of civil cases where both parties were German), and a compulsory language in schools. The use of German in public was prohibited; all communities received Italian names; all public inscriptions in German, those on tombstones among them, had to be removed and replaced with their Italianized version. Similarly, family names were Italianized. With regard to religion, the lighting of the so-called Heart of Jesus fires was prohibited, an essential ritual and symbol of the traditional Tyrolese devotion to the Sacred Heart of Jesus, officially recognized as early as 1796. This cult symbolically underlines the self-perceived role of the Tyrolese as a chosen people, which becomes manifest in the postulate of a special 'covenant' between them and

Christ. This concept has remained a central and vital part of Tyrolese identity (both north and south of the Brenner Pass). The annual lighting of the fires on the mountain tops on the third Friday after Pentecost has remained a symbol of Tyrolese ethnic identity and political unity ever since, and was used in 1961 as the setting for the first major wave of violence. Economic measures to destroy the conditions in which South Tyrolese identity had developed over the centuries included the abrogation, in 1929, of the ancient legislation guaranteeing impartibility of inheritance in land and the forced sale of German land to Italians. Massive industrialization, which began in 1924, encouraged a significant influx of Italians to South Tyrol. The alteration of the demographic balance of the region was a crucial element of Italianization, and the South Tyrolese thereafter perceived immigration as a state-administered attempt to change the ethnic character of their traditionally German homeland. Since 1946, control over immigration has been one of the persistent demands of South Tyrolese politicians. In connection with the immigration policies of the 1920s, a comprehensive land appropriation began in 1926 to acquire the necessary space for industrialization, housing projects and the regulation of the Adige and Isarco rivers. In the political and administrative sectors South Tyrol was initially incorporated into the larger region of Venezia Tridentina, but soon afterwards it was given separate status as the province of Bolzano and placed under the direct control of Rome. The elected local government system was replaced by a provincial prefect, who was appointed by Rome and who selected all mayors and communal secretaries. Traditionally independent small communities were integrated into larger administrative units. Most German-speaking South Tyrolese officials were either dismissed from their offices or sent to other parts of Italy and replaced with Italians. The police and security forces in the area were reinforced and German-speakers dismissed. A law of 1937 gave the Italian authorities the power to expropriate land for the settlement of Italian peasants; in 1939, these powers were extended to urban property.

Despite all this, forced assimilation failed. South Tyrolese opposition to the Italianization programme was initially and primarily cultural, and political only through the implications of cultural resistance. With official political representation of the German-speaking population abolished, the rural clergy, as occurred in Alsace in the 1920s and 1930s, became an essential part of the opposition movement against Italianization. They continued to assert their right to deliver sermons in German and played a major part in the preservation of the German language through the organization of clandestine schools and through clerical newspapers, recognizing that the preservation of German as the native language of South Tyrolese of ethnic German descent was an essential element in the effort to maintain a community identity and a sense of solidarity. A further aspect of resistance was the hope that many South Tyrolese put in Hitler and the Nazis and their pan-German aspirations. However, in the light of political developments in Italy and the importance of the country as an ally for Germany, Hitler made it very clear that he was not willing to sacrifice his global interests for the fate of 300,000 German-speaking South Tyrolese.[5]

In an attempt to solve the South Tyrol question, the so-called Option was designed, representing an example of escalating 'conflict settlement' efforts from forced assimilation to forced migration. In 1939, the German-speaking population in South Tyrol had to choose between remaining in Italy and being subjected to further Italianization or to relocate to the German Reich. Of the 267,265 German-speaking South Tyrolese eligible to participate, 43,626 abstained. Of the 223,639 participants in the plebiscite, 183,365 voted to leave and 38,274 to stay (Cole and Wolf 1974: 57; see also Alcock 1970: 45ff.).

Whereas Hitler tried to get rid of an obstacle to a lasting political and military alliance with Italy, the Italian rationale for the Option was slightly more complex. Italy aimed at a partial resettlement of only 60,000 to 80,000 South Tyrolese, among whom were about 10,000 so-called Reichsdeutsche, who were suspected of spearheading South Tyrolese resistance against Italianization, as well as the valley farmers and the urban craftsmen and intelligentsia, who were thought to be easily replaceable by Italian immigrants. In this way the Italians hoped that the economic prosperity of South Tyrol could be maintained and the remaining South Tyrolese, now in a minority position in the province, more easily and successfully subjected to Italianization. Italian efforts to prevent a massive exodus of the South Tyrolese agricultural workforce, especially of mountain farmers, in addition to the unfavourable resettlement conditions in the German Reich, resulted in a much lower percentage of the population actually leaving than had originally opted for resettlement. The reason for this must also be seen in the traditionally strong bonds between the South Tyrolese and their native soil. For many this bond was, and still is, a non-negotiable part of their identity. Thus it is not surprising that, of all those who opted for Germany, only about 70,000, or less than 40 per cent, actually left. As a consequence, both forced assimilation and forced migration failed to settle the conflict, while a combination of territorial autonomy and power sharing provided a compromise solution in the decades after the Second World War, as we have seen in chapter 7.[6]

Finally, partitions and secessions[7] have not fared much better in terms of providing stable settlements to ethnic conflicts. As Sambanis (2000) has demonstrated in a survey of eighty cases of ethnically or religiously motivated civil war, partitions occurred in only thirteen countries,[8] including merely temporary ones such as Russia (Chechnya) and multiple ones such as Georgia (South Ossetia and Abkhazia). Apart from not being widespread 'solutions', partitions and secessions have several other problems that make them unsuitable. Sambanis (ibid.: 477ff.) notes that, in the course of partitions, forced population movements are more likely than not to occur, that these often bear the seeds of future war, and that recurrence of war is more likely after partition than after a negotiated settlement. These findings are similar to those of O'Leary (2006). Discussing four cases of partition – India, Palestine,

Ireland and Cyprus – O'Leary identifies several common problems that make partitions undesirable strategies for resolving ethnic conflicts, particularly the high likelihood of disorder and violence, the need for comprehensive expulsions to achieve the goal of ethnic homogeneity, and the institutional and other weaknesses inflicted on at least one of the successor states of the partitioned entity.

3 Examining alternative solutions in detail: ethnic cleansing

In the following, we examine one so-called alternative solution to ethnic conflict – ethnic cleansing – in greater detail. As in previous chapters, we focus on specific cases and analyse at local, state, regional and international level the factors that have made ethnic cleansing possible. Choosing ethnic cleansing as a specific case study is deliberate. It is a frequent strategy and tactic in ethnic conflict, and, even where it is not a specific goal of one or more of the conflict parties, large numbers of refugees and IDPs are one of the most frequent consequences. Moreover, ethnic cleansing is closely related to a number of other 'alternatives' to settling ethnic conflicts: genocide, partition/secession and forced assimilation all too often involve involuntary population movements on a grand scale.

While in the remainder of this chapter we focus on Europe, we do not want to deny that ethnic cleansing has occurred elsewhere as well. The partition of India in 1947 resulted in approximately 14 million people leaving their traditional homelands in search of security among their own religious group: some 7 million Muslims 'moved' to Pakistan, and approximately the same number of Hindus and other non-Muslims 'relocated' to India. The very fact that several hundred thousand people died in the violence surrounding partition and migration illustrates that this mass movement of people was everything but voluntary. Only one year later, the first Arab–Israeli war, when the Arab states surrounding Israel tried to prevent, with military force, the creation of the state of Israel, resulted in approximately 850,000 Palestinian refugees in Jordan, Lebanon, Syria, and the West Bank and Gaza Strip. Together with internally displaced Palestinians in Israel and those affected by the 1967 Arab–Israeli war, the total number of Palestinian refugees and their descendants has grown to around 4.5 million. Around one-third of these remain in fifty-eight refugee camps administered by the United Nations Relief and Works Agency for Palestine Refugees in the Near East (UNRWA). Most recently, the UN-administered referendum for independence in East Timor in 1999 was accompanied by massive intimidation and violence of East Timorese by Indonesian regular and irregular forces, which further increased once the results (a clear vote for independence) were made public. As a consequence, some 200,000 people were forced to flee. Moreover, as a result of the destruction that occurred at this time, what little infrastructure East Timor possessed was all but destroyed, and most of the better educated residents, who were overwhelmingly non-Timorese, withdrew with the Indonesian forces. For a variety of reasons, some of which are not in any substantive way related to the period of occupation, to this day East Timor, although independent, barely functions as a state. This example, moreover, highlights the fact that in certain circumstances the mere act of self-determination does not solve basic existential questions.

At the beginning of the twenty-first century, the global figure for internally displaced persons stands at between 20 and 25 million and that for refugees (those that manage to escape abroad) at just under 10 million. While this might be seen as a positive reversal in terms of the potential spillover effect from refugee crises, it also implies an ever greater humanitarian urgency to address the conflicts that cause internal displacement. The main contributors to these numbers are conflicts in Africa: in Uganda, the DRC and Sudan alone, UNHCR estimated IDP numbers in 2006 at 1.4, 1.5 and 6 million respectively, while refugee numbers were comparatively smaller, at around 30,000, 500,000 and 700,000. These three countries alone thus contribute about 40 per cent of the world's IDPs and about 10 per cent of its refugees.[9]

These broad statistics and the human misery that they barely convey notwithstanding, the twentieth-century European experience with ethnic cleansing merits more detailed analysis, not least because of the lessons that can be learned from it for our understanding of, and responses to, ethnic conflict. From Northern Ireland to the Caucasus, from the Basque country to the Åland Islands and from Kosovo to Silesia, the competing claims of distinct ethnic groups to self-determination have been the most prominent sources of ethnic conflict in Europe. Striving to achieve internal stability and external security in the face of such demands, many states have sought to minimize the political impact of ethnic minorities with an affiliation to other, often neighbouring, states or parts of their population by expelling them or exchanging them against ethnic kin of their own. Such forced population transfers in Europe are linked primarily to two phenomena which in themselves are interrelated: the collapse and dissolution of (multinational) states and the redrawing of state boundaries. From the First and Second Balkan Wars to the First and Second World Wars, and finally to the violent break-up of Yugoslavia, Europe has seen numerous expulsions and exchanges of populations that did not fit into the concept of 'relatively homogeneous wholes' which states which had gone to war with each other 'at the high noon of ethnic nationalism' sought to create (Brubaker 1995: 192). As a consequence of the ethnic mobilization of polities, and because of the hostilities that existed between them before and during wars – and that continue to exist after an often unstable peace had been made – 'the ethnic mosaics which were the pride of empires became liabilities' (Barkey 1997: 102).

Apart from discussing the 'modalities' of ethnic cleansing, it is thus important to explore whether this particular strategy in ethnic conflict has any real conflict regulation potential. In other words, if 'properly executed', would the creation of ethnically homogeneous states, regions and neighbourhoods contribute in any way to inter-ethnic peace – i.e., can these adequately address the causes and consequences of ethnic conflicts?

Following Bell-Fialkoff (1996: 3), we understand ethnic cleansing as a 'planned, deliberate removal from a certain territory of an undesirable population' on the basis of ethnic criteria. Naimark (2001: 4f.) has pointed to the dual meaning of cleansing in its Slavic and German usages as purging 'the native community of foreign bodies' and 'one's own people of alien elements', the latter of which 'accounts in some measure for the fearsome up-close killing and barbarous mutilation of neighbours and acquaintances that characterises a number of cases of ethnic cleansing'. Kramer (2001: 1f.) slightly narrows the meaning of ethnic cleansing in the context of post-Second World War population movements in Central and Eastern Europe to 'the involuntary transfer of entire ethnic groups from one country to another' and, like Naimark, points to the 'widespread atrocities and violent excesses committed' in their course. Ethnic cleansing thus comprises policies resulting in the forced transfer of members of an ethnic group from territories exclusively claimed for and by other ethnic groups, which can happen across established, new or perceived future borders to territories inhabited predominantly by members of the same ethnic group as those transferred and/or through the refusal to allow refugees to return. As such, these policies violate norms of international law, as they 'are collective in nature . . . carried out by force or threat of force, . . . are involuntary, . . . deliberate on the part of the . . . party conducting [them], . . . systematic, . . . discriminatory, and . . . take place without due process' (UN Commission on Human Rights 1997: § 10).

The goal of such ethnic cleansings is to rid states of allegedly troublesome minorities that are considered (mostly on the basis of selectively interpreting historical and recent evidence) as threats to the internal stability and/ or external security of their pre-cleansing host state, on whose territory they may have lived for some time or by whom they may have been 'acquired' as part of war and/or post-war territorial gains. The two predominant forms taken by ethnic cleansing in this context are population exchanges and expulsions. A population exchange implies an agreement between at least two states involved, while an expulsion is usually the unilateral act of one state. In many cases, both forms of ethnic cleansing have the explicit consent, or at least tacit approval, of relevant regional and world powers. In this sense, ethnic cleansing is occasionally interpreted as a conflict prevention strategy, at least in the sense of preventing the resurgence or escalation of past inter-ethnic tensions.[10]

So much for the conceptualization of ethnic cleansing. In practice, the first relevant European cases were the minority exchanges in the Balkans after the 1912–23 Balkan wars and the territorial reorganization of the region after the First World War, between 1919 and 1923. The first instance in this context was the Bulgarian–Turkish exchange of populations agreed by the two states in an Annex to the Peace Treaty of Constantinople on 15 November 1913. Together with the Treaty of Bucharest, this resulted in the second partition of Bulgaria after its brief existence as Greater Bulgaria following the treaty of San Stefano in 1878. A third partition followed in November 1919 with the Treaty of Neuilly between Greece and Bulgaria, and again this included a convention that affected a massive cross-border migration of Bulgarians to their kin state. The relevant convention annexed to this treaty was concluded with Greece and effectively stipulated the reciprocal migration of Greeks and Bulgarians. It was implemented over a period of thirteen years and involved the migration of 92,000 Bulgarians and 46,000 Greeks (Koufa and Svolopoulos 1991: 281).[11] Bulgaria was ill-equipped to integrate the refugees, many of whom were housed in camps for years and burdened the public purse. The loss, within forty years, of significant territories considered part of a Greater Bulgaria, and its consequence, that by 1919 approximately 1 million Bulgarians (or 16 per cent of all Bulgarians at the time) lived outside the country (Crampton 1997: 149), has been a source of Bulgarian irredentism ever since. Despite the fact that the forced population transfers before and after the First World War rectified this part of the problem only marginally, Bulgarian irredentism has never posed a serious threat to regional stability, although relations between Bulgaria and Macedonia were uneasy for a number of years before the two countries finally signed a series of bilateral treaties and agreements in 1999. However, the incompleteness of the population transfers up to 1919 kept the issue of emigration on the agenda: Bulgaria and Turkey signed various bilateral agreements after 1945. Almost 270,000 'Turks' left Bulgaria for Turkey between 1950 and 1978 (Eminov 1997: 78). The extent to which this process was voluntary is debateable, given the Bulgarian (communist) government's strident nationalism, and how many of these 'Turks' were actually Turkish as opposed to being Slav Muslims (Pomaks) is similarly open to question. The wave of migration received a further stimulus in 1989 with the collapse of communism in Eastern Europe. In that year around 370,000 Turks left the country when the opportunity to do so arose (Brubaker 1995: 194). Many of these migrants, together with those from the pre-1989 cohort, have subsequently returned to Bulgaria, partly for economic reasons, and partly because of their unease in what is in essence a completely alien society.

The third population exchange in the context of the Balkan wars was formally agreed in the Convention Concerning the Exchange of Greek and Turkish Populations of 30 January 1923. Religious affiliation, rather than mother tongue, was used as the definition of ethnic/national provenance in this case. Approximately 1.1 million Greeks from Asia Minor and Eastern Thrace were expelled to Greece and between 350,000 and 500,000 Muslims, primarily from the Greek provinces of Macedonia, Epirus and Crete, were expelled to Turkey. Certain categories of people who professed the 'wrong' religion were exempted. These included, for example, Muslims from Western

Thrace and Christians living within the municipal boundaries of Istanbul. However, of this latter group some 150,000 migrated to Greece, regardless of their wishes (Mango 1999: 390). Both countries thereby acquired newly arrived co-nationals who had little knowledge of the national language. The implementation of the convention showed that at least some effort, although how much is disputed, was made to handle the whole exchange with efficiency and a minimum loss of dignity. The transferred individuals automatically lost the citizenship of the country they left but gained that of their country of destination. Despite the fact that many, especially arrivals to Turkey, had little knowledge of the national language, neither state charged duty on possessions carried by those involved in the exchange; property left behind (houses, land) was either exchanged or became part of a lengthy and not wholly satisfactory compensation process; and both governments provided transport facilities and sought to administer the exchange as quickly as possible (Koufa and Svolopoulos 1991: 290f.). Furthermore, both governments agreed to the setting-up of a mixed commission, including representatives of the League of Nations, to supervise and facilitate the population exchange and to liquidate the property left behind by the affected populations.

International efforts to ease the transfer and its domestic consequences extended particularly to Greece, which had to deal with the far larger number of people transferred. An international loan worth £12.3 million was granted for the resettlement of those transferred in 1923–4, resulting, within two years, in half of that section of the population being resettled and economically self-sufficient (Pentzopoulos 1962: 75ff.). Additionally, Greece received a stabilization loan of £7.5 million in 1928, and organizations such as the Red Cross funded aid projects of various kinds throughout Greece (ibid.). Nevertheless, the integration process was difficult and prolonged. In Greece, for example, the resettlement programme continued throughout the 1960s, and the housing situation of many of the children and grandchildren of those transferred from Turkey still remains unsatisfactory (Hirschon 1989).

Similar situations in post-1919 Eastern Europe – the territorial losses incurred by Hungary following the Treaty of Trianon in 1920, particularly in relation to Transylvania, Vojvodina and southern Slovakia, and the incorporation of the predominantly German-speaking Sudetenland into the newly established Czechoslovak state – did not lead to forced population transfers. The cases of Transylvania and southern Slovakia would have allowed population exchanges, the former probably in connection with further border revisions. In Vojvodina and the Sudetenland a lack of 'sufficient' numbers of Serbs in Hungary, and even more so of Czechs in Germany or Austria, would have left the measure of expulsions only to create ethnically more homogeneous polities. For various reasons, neither the Great Powers nor the states involved had a particular interest at the time in pursuing a policy of ethnic cleansing, either against Hungarians or against Germans. If one accepts, and there is little convincing evidence to do so, that ethnically homogeneous nation-states are the only alternative to permanent civil strife and internal and external instability, the consequences of the 'failure' to create homogeneous nation-states in this instance could be argued to have been devastating: the Munich Agreement of 1938 dismembered Czechoslovakia, annexing to Germany the Sudetenland, which had already 'united' with Austria earlier the same year. The two Vienna Awards of 1939 and 1940 granted Hungary large parts of southern Slovakia and led to a north–south partition of Transylvania between Hungary and Romania. However, it needs to be borne in mind that the failure to create homogeneous nation-states in these cases was merely a convenient pretext for the execution of irredentist policies. The existence, and alleged maltreatment, of minorities in the areas coveted by Germany and Hungary may have given their demands additional 'credibility', but it is unlikely that population transfers would have prevented the forced cession of territory. On the contrary, post-1945 developments in relation to the expulsion of Germans from Poland and Czechoslovakia indicate that irredentism persists regardless.

Since the end of the Second World War, Europe has witnessed three major forced population transfers: those occurring immediately after the end of the war, primarily in an effort to create ethnically homogeneous states in Central and Eastern Europe as bulwarks against another war; the internal displacement of more than 200,000 people in Cyprus after 1974; and the ethnic cleansing in the former Yugoslavia in the 1990s.

Although exact figures remain disputed, it is safe to say that about 15 million people were affected by policies of forced population transfers at the end of the Second World War. These included:

- approximately 11 million Germans from Poland, Czechoslovakia and today's district of Kaliningrad in the Russian Federation, who were expelled or fled to Germany;
- another 500,000 ethnic Germans from Hungary, Romania and Yugoslavia who were expelled or fled to Germany;
- over 500,000 Ukrainians and Belorussians expelled from Poland to the Soviet Union;
- over 2 million Poles expelled from the Soviet Union to Poland;
- about 75,000 ethnic Hungarians and 75,000 ethnic Slovaks who were exchanged between Hungary and Czechoslovakia;
- several thousand Italians who fled or were expelled from Yugoslavia.

In addition, about 3 million Poles were internally transferred to resettle in areas from which the Germans had been removed, and a significantly smaller number of Czechs was resettled within Czechoslovakia for the same reason.

With the exception of the expulsion and flight of ethnic Germans from Southeastern Europe (Romania, Yugoslavia and Hungary), all of these transfers were directly connected to border changes: either the re-establishment of pre-1939 borders (Czechoslovakia–Germany and Czechoslovakia–Hungary) or the creation of entirely new borders (Poland–Soviet Union, Poland–Germany, Czechoslovakia–Soviet Union, Germany–Soviet Union – the Kaliningrad/ Königsberg area of former East Prussia – and Italy–Yugoslavia).

The Second World War, some minor post-war adjustments in favour of Poland notwithstanding, resulted in an alteration of the Polish–Soviet border and created the context in which some 3 million Poles and Ukrainians were forcibly uprooted from their homelands and moved across borders. This particular case is unique in two ways. First it occurred against the backdrop of a pre-existing insurrection by the Ukrainian Insurrectionary Army (UPA), which was directed against the Polish and Soviet governments. Second, Operation Wis a (Akcja Wis a), designed to break the back of this insurrection, deliberately used forced displacement as a tactic to defeat the insurgents, leading to about 140,000 Ukrainians being internally displaced in Poland. In addition, Operation Wis a thus also prepared the ground for subsequent attempts to promote the forced assimilation of surviving Ukrainians into Polish society.

In many other ways, however, this case of forced population transfers is similar to many others in this era. Although regulated by a treaty between Poland and the Soviet Union, the transfer was often chaotic and accompanied by violence against people and property. Authorities in the receiving areas were unprepared, compensation for lost property was slow and insufficient, and the reception towards the newcomers on the part of the indigenous population and the authorities was often hostile, their integration taking many years. In addition, Polish–Ukrainian relations in the period after the end of the Cold War were marred initially by unresolved issues resulting directly and indirectly from the forced transfers, including the fact that these transfers were incomplete – i.e., groups of Poles and Ukrainians (as well as Belorussians) were left behind in the expelling states. In the post-communist era, however, the pattern of relations between the three states concerning this issue has been very different. In the case of Poland and Ukraine, despite initial difficulties, the two sides have not allowed the issue to cloud bilateral cooperation, and successive Polish governments have sought to consolidate an independent liberal democratic Ukraine that is clearly linked to Western Europe. In the case of Belarus, where liberal democratic forces are much weaker, both the Lukashenka regime and successive Polish governments have instrumentalized minority issues.

The expulsion of Germans from Poland and Czechoslovakia can be seen to have its origin in three distinct but related policy considerations: to prevent the instrumentalization of external minorities for an irredentist foreign policy; to accommodate the westward shift of Poland; and to punish ethnic German minorities for the role they had played in the German occupation policy in Central and Eastern Europe. The Allies gave their consent at the Potsdam Conference to the 'humane and orderly transfer' of ethnic Germans from the Sudetenland and the 'formerly German territories' of Poland, as well as from other parts of Poland and the Free City of Danzig.[12] As a consequence of flight and expulsion, approximately 2 million ethnic Germans died from exhaustion, starvation, and attacks by local mobs and regular and irregular military units.

About two-thirds of the refugees and expellees were resettled in the American and British occupation zones; of the remaining third, sent to the Soviet zone, approximately 40 per cent left for West Germany before 1961. The integration problem was initially one of housing, food and employment, and the reception that many refugees and expellees received was accordingly hostile. Subsequently, however, the positive contribution to the economic and social modernization, especially of relatively backward and underdeveloped areas in the later West Germany such as Bavaria and Schleswig-Holstein, was both appreciated and publicly acknowledged, and contributed to the overall successful economic and social integration of the expellees. Apart from a brief period in the 1950s, expellees never had their own political party. By the early 1960s their integration in the political process of West Germany helped its stabilization and consolidation into a three-party system. The experience of repeated injustices during the expulsions and of the loss of home and property, however, also meant that the older generation in particular held deep feelings of resentment against Poland and Czechoslovakia and resisted, until the early 1990s, any form of reconciliation. Younger generations, who had only vague or no memories of flight and expulsion, have proven to be more flexible and open to the idea of constructive reconciliation.

In the case of Cyprus, the competing interests of Greece and Turkey deeply affected the country once it had achieved independence from Britain in 1960. Competition between the two outside powers fuelled inter-communal strife between Greek and Turkish Cypriots, and intra-community tensions among the Greek Cypriots destabilized and finally led to the collapse of a power sharing arrangement between the two communities. As a consequence, and based on its interpretation of the Treaty of Guarantee,[13] Turkey invaded Cyprus in July 1974, quickly capturing about 37 per cent of the island, where it subsequently established the Turkish republic of Northern Cyprus, which has not been recognized internationally by any country except Turkey.

The 1974 invasion provided the pretext for the creation of two ethnically homogeneous parts of the island, in the course of which some 200,000 people, an estimated third of the population of Cyprus, became internally displaced.[14] The completeness of the population transfer becomes obvious from the following census figures: 78 per cent of the island's population are ethnically Greek, and of these 99.5 per cent live in the Greek Cypriot area. The ethnically Turkish population of Cyprus is about 18 per cent, of whom 98.7 per cent live in the Turkish Cypriot area. Other ethnic groups make up some 4 per cent of the population, and 99.2 per cent of them live in the Greek Cypriot area. This means that on either side of the buffer zone there are fewer than 1,000 people who are not of the same ethnic origin as the rest of the population in the area.

Relations between the two communities remain difficult and dependent upon the relations between Greece and Turkey. Despite recently renewed efforts to achieve a comprehensive settlement in the context of Cyprus's EU accession, major progress has yet to be achieved. This is also due to a number of internal factors. There has been quite extensive settlement of mainland Turks in the northern part of the island, mostly in properties that had to be abandoned by Greek refugees from the area. Matters remaining to be resolved are the property question in general, a return of refugees and the cases of more than 1,500 mostly Greek Cypriot individuals that have been missing since 1974. The partition of, and the forced population transfers in, Cyprus has led to the involvement of a variety of international governmental organizations in order to establish a just settlement of issues related to the conflict, including the UN and a variety of European institutions. While these have been successful in stabilizing the situation and preventing further military confrontation, their efforts to resolve the underlying conflict have so far been futile.

The ethnic cleansing that occurred in the context of the disintegration of Yugoslavia in the 1990s was the latest in the long history of forced population transfers in twentieth-century Europe. In scale and ferocity it is second only to the events in East Central Europe at the end of the Second World War.[15]

Forced population transfers occurred linked to two distinct events – the wars in Bosnia and Herzegovina and Croatia and the Kosovo conflict. The former produced approximately 2.8 million refugees and IDPs. The bulk of internal displacement occurred in Bosnia and Herzegovina (1.1 million) and Croatia (200,000), while the three largest refugee contingents went to Serbia (650,000), Western Europe (616,000, of whom more than half went to Germany) and Croatia (187,000). Fewer people sought refuge in Slovenia (22,000), Hungary (9,000) and Macedonia (9,000).

Forced population transfers in the Kosovo conflict occurred in two waves: initially some 850,000 mostly Kosovo Albanians were forced from their homes as a result of the Serbian campaign against the Kosovo Liberation Army before and during the NATO air strikes in the first half of 1999. Subsequent retaliation against the Serb and other non-Albanian population groups in Kosovo produced almost a quarter of a million IDPs from Kosovo who went to Serbia and Montenegro and an additional quarter million refugees (approximately 15,000 Albanians from southern Serbia), IDPs (35,000 Albanians), other 'residents at risk' (100,000 Serbs, 30,000 Roma, 5,000 members of other minority groups) and some 65,000 returnees from the Albanian majority (50,000), as well as various, predominantly Serb, minorities (15,000) in Kosovo itself.

This whole episode raises some uncomfortable questions that illustrate the nature of 'moral hazard' in such situations. For example, to what extent did NATO, pushed as it was by 'world public opinion', allow itself to become a tool of the KLA? Moreover, to what extent did KLA commanders calculate that their actions would lead to an indiscriminate and disproportionate response on the part of their Serb enemies, which would turn 'world public opinion' further against the Serbs. Neither should we forget that, as is so often the case in such instances, the desire for revenge outweighed all other considerations on the part of the former victims: hence the later ethnic cleansing of non-Albanians from most of Kosovo.[16]

As the previous sections illustrate, the overall situation in the region is complex at a number of levels. This complexity results from the large-scale forced population transfers and their consequences, including the policies applied to address them. In turn the transfers and their consequences also add to the difficulties that still exist in dealing with the aftermath of the violent disintegration of Yugoslavia. The two predominant problems are the devastation of almost the entire regional economy and the political and institutional instability and uncertainty that engulfs most of the successor states of the former Yugoslavia and some of their neighbours. The former has meant that it has been impossible so far to create conditions under which the refugees and IDPs could achieve a certain level of economic self-sufficiency; rather they continue to depend on humanitarian aid provided primarily by UNHCR, whose annual budget for Kosovo-related programmes alone is close to $80 million. The political and institutional instability, in particular in Bosnia and Herzegovina, Serbia, Macedonia and Kosovo, has so far made it extremely difficult to devise, let alone implement, any long-term solution. Because of the regional dimension of the problem and the strained relations between the different political entities, any such solution must be conceived at a regional rather than a country level. However, at the same time, no regional solution will be possible without cooperation at the level of the different entities involved.

With international actors seeking to undo the forced population transfers that have occurred, the fact that very little return migration has taken place testifies to the failure so far to achieve a comprehensive solution. On the contrary, refugees and IDPs seem to 'settle' for the permanent loss of their homes, thus adding to the difficulties international actors face in their relations with local political elites and administrations in the implementation of return strategies. At the same time, the large number of refugees and IDPs serves as a constant reminder of the atrocities committed. Moreover, the forcibly transferred population groups pose additional risks to regional political stability, as they are the most likely to be radicalized by ethno-nationalist ideologues. In Serbia in particular, the arrival of large numbers of refugees in the mid-1990s led to an aggravation of local tensions between ethnic groups in Kosovo and in some instances to the displacement of locally resident minorities. Reasons for the failure of such strategies can, of course, be located within the attitudes of the very people affected. Resources, or the lack thereof, comprise another potential issue. In addition, there is a need for any international involvement to be credible, otherwise it will be ignored or manipulated, and the states concerned must be obliged into engaging in serious negotiations and reforms that will end any such impasse (UNPO 2006).

The temporary acceptance of refugees in Western Europe, adopted in the context of the war in Bosnia and Herzegovina and to a lesser extent also in the Kosovo conflict, was quite a novel strategy to deal with the immediate impact of ethnic cleansing, but it could not, nor was it supposed to, provide a long-term solution. On the contrary, it led to additional difficulties in relation to refugee repatriation, as this has occurred often against the refugees' will and under conditions far from conducive to success. Refugees often returned to their homes only to find them destroyed or now situated in areas under the control of hostile ethnic groups, thus merely adding to the number of IDPs and further aggravating the already difficult humanitarian and security situation in the region.

Bosnia and Herzegovina was the worst affected country in the region, and, despite a massive international effort to address the consequences of the forced population transfers that occurred, progress has been slow and painful. This is best illustrated by the difficult process of the Property Law Implementation Plan, which had been designed to enforce the rights of those rightfully owning or otherwise entitled to properties occupied by others. While decisions on rightful ownership and occupancy were made, it was estimated in 2000 that, at the then rate of implementation, it would take another twenty-two years in the Bosnian-Croat federation (at an implementation rate of just under 29 per cent) and another forty years in the Republika Srpska (at an implementation rate of just over 13 per cent) to resolve the issue. Even though figures had improved considerably by January 2002, to an implementation rate of just over 32 per cent in the Republika Srpska and to just under 51 per cent in the federation, this is still a far cry from resolving the problem of displacement, in particular because it runs the risk of prolonging temporary solutions rather than addressing the crucial issue of property rights comprehensively. Overall, the magnitude of the problem becomes clear if one considers that, since the Dayton Agreement which ended the war in Bosnia and Herzegovina, a long-term solution has yet to be found for up to 600,000 refugees and IDPs from this country. Until such issues are resolved in a manner acceptable to all parties, even if that means they have to settle for something less than the optimal arrangement, tolerance, mutual respect and understanding between estranged groups will continue to be in short supply (UNPO 2006).

The previous short studies of major incidents of forced population transfers in Europe in the twentieth century have highlighted a number of factors that cause problems in the short, medium and long term for the states directly affected by the transfers, but also for international actors concerned with their humanitarian and security aspects.

Violence: Forced population transfers always involve high levels of violence, regardless of whether they are carried out by regular or irregular armed forces. This has resulted in some cases in unprecedented casualty rates. The often purposeful humiliation of those to be transferred has long-term negative implications for return and/or bilateral and inter-community relations.

Economic devastation and material losses: Most of the cases of forced population transfers outlined above occurred in the context of war. Added to the damage caused by military actions, the large-scale removal of populations from one socio-economic environment to another brings with it economic difficulties, such as the disruption of economic processes, the destruction of privately owned enterprises and farms, and the creation of population groups that are not economically self-sufficient. In addition, most of those forcibly transferred will have suffered material losses exceeding the compensation offers and capacities of the states involved. Thus, apart from the brain and skills drain, forced population transfers are mostly accompanied by a loss of capital that is necessary for the economic reconstruction in both receiving and expelling states.

Instability in the receiving state: This occurs usually as a consequence of the large-scale and often poorly regulated and coordinated influx of refugees. In most cases studied, tensions exist between the resident population and the newcomers and between both communities and the authorities of the host state. In some cases, the refugee influx has also led to follow-on displacement of previously resident populations and to the escalation of already existing tensions between different ethnic groups in a particular area, whose numerical and power balance was altered as a consequence of the arrival of refugees. Such a contagion effect is particularly likely when the ethnic demography of a particular region or of individual countries within it prevents the proponents of forced population transfers from achieving the creation of ethnically homogeneous territorial entities. Large-scale population influxes can also change political balances in the receiving state, especially if refugees enjoy voting rights at different levels of government and can be mobilized as a single constituency rather than integrating into an existing party political system. Pakistan provides us with one such example: to this day, Urdu-speaking Mohajir, who fled India after partition, often remain ghettoized and largely alienated from the society of which they are notionally a part.

Instability in the expelling state: This normally arises when the forced population transfer remains incomplete, i.e., when significant numbers of members of the population groups transferred remain in their original host country. The original 'problem' is not then solved, but merely reduced in scale. Contrary to the propagated aims of the population transfer, the problem can actually be intensified by a politically more active kin state and a resentful and committed irredentist movement made up of the transferred section of the original population group. Within this context, Burma is an illustrative case. Despite campaigns in recent years to solve the minorities issue through the implementation of policies designed to force people out of the state, various insurrections rumble on, based largely in refugee camps on the Thai–Burmese border.

Citizenship: Failure to resolve the citizenship issue for those affected by the forced population transfer can add to the instability in both receiving and expelling states. Long-term uncertainty about their actual status in the receiving state diminishes the ability of refugees to integrate and be integrated, while it also leaves open the possibility of their return to their places of origin, thus potentially creating a constant level of tension between the states involved. The fate of thousands of so-called asylum seekers who have in recent years fled to various Western European states is an instructive example of this particular issue.

Bilateral relations between receiving and expelling state: These are often characterized by mutual recrimination and high levels of tension. The actual forced transfer of populations is one but often not the only issue in bilateral relations. However, it often serves as a catalyst for rising levels of tension and is easily exploitable in mobilizing public opinion for confrontational foreign policies. Relations between the Federal Republic of Germany and Poland between 1949 and 1970 are a textbook example of how such issues can thwart moves to establish normal inter-state relationships, and contribute to the propagation of negative stereotypes.

Many of these problems have their sources in the following two factors, which also appear to be a common feature of forced population transfers.

1. *Incompatibility of goals sought to accomplish with forced population transfers*: While the 'official' justification of forced population transfers is often the creation of ethnically homogeneous states because of their alleged greater viability and stability, the actual transfers themselves are often driven by a desire for revenge. This leads to high and indiscriminate levels of violence against the people affected and their property. While it may achieve ethnically homogeneous states, it intensifies problems in other areas, such as the economy of the expelling state and its bilateral relations with the receiving state. In other words, contrary to proclaimed goals, it is more likely that internal stability is endangered and external security diminished. In recent years, one of the most apposite examples we have of this phenomenon is the various wars of Yugoslav secession, where Serbia, Bosnia and Herzegovina and Kosovo remain blighted by the consequences of forced population transfers.

2. *Combination with partition or other boundary changes leading to territorial disputes*: Decreased external security often also has its reasons in the combination of forced population transfers with partition or other boundary changes, which lead to long-term international territorial disputes. Once

again, the example of the Federal Republic of Germany is instructive, as are, albeit to a lesser extent, the disputes between (Czecho)Slovakia and Hungary and Hungary and Romania.

In the face of these problems, it is, to say the least, astonishing that forced population transfers are occasionally still advocated as a means of providing durable solutions to self-determination conflicts.[17] Quite apart from the fact that both the populations transferred and those allegedly benefiting from the transfer because of the creation of ethnically more homogeneous entities hardly ever experience a real increase in self-determination, not least because the transfer occurs against their will and they continue to live in conditions they would normally not have chosen for themselves, states rarely see a net increase in internal stability and external security. At best, the constellation of threats to which they are exposed changes, requiring that different policies and mechanisms for their management be found. On the other hand, the apparent 'success' of some forced population transfers seems to provide evidence that such policies can work, i.e., provide internal stability and external security for the states affected and thus also contribute to a larger set of conditions under which people can exercise their right to self-determination.

Forced population transfers are a clear violation of the human and civil rights of their victims. Moreover, given the human suffering occurring in the course and as a consequence of forced population transfers and the fact that the trade-offs in internal stability and external security are at best marginal, the twentieth-century European experience suggests that ethnic cleansing is immoral and should be prevented wherever possible. However, it would be unwise to expect that prevention will always be possible. Therefore, it is equally important to review the previous examples again and examine whether and under what conditions forced population transfers once they have occurred can contribute to the internal stability and external security of the states involved. That is, how can it be avoided that gains in internal 'ethnic' stability (prevention of ethnic strife and of minorities being used as instruments of irredentist foreign policies) are offset by other social, economic and political problems that occur as a consequence of the forced population transfers both at a domestic and an international level? The most common 'solutions' to the problems frequently occurring in the context of forced population transfers are detailed below, and as we will see, the results are mixed.

Reciprocal population exchanges instead of unilateral expulsions: The advantages of this are often seen in serving the interests of two states at the same time, i.e., creating two ethnically homogeneous and therefore internally more stable states, which then have a shared interest in preserving a newly attained status quo. In addition, reciprocal exchanges offer ways of dealing with the issue of compensation by exchanging properties between transferees on an equally reciprocal basis. The aforementioned example of Greece and Turkey offers some evidence of the efficacy of such a strategy. However, the evidence is at best both patchy and disputed. Despite a rapprochement in recent years, neither state appears to be willing to pursue a bilateral relationship that is based above all on the contemporary situation, as opposed to one that has more than half an eye to mutually incompatible versions of their shared history.

International facilitation of the transfer and of the subsequent integration of the transferees in their new host societies: The involvement of international actors is considered as beneficial in two ways – contributing to a 'humane and orderly transfer' of the populations concerned and subsequently providing sufficient levels of aid to avoid humanitarian disasters and contributing to the successful long-term integration and thus economic self-sufficiency of the refugees in the receiving and expelling states. The UNHCRs 'repatriation' of millions of displaced persons, refugees and concentration camp survivors in Europe between 1945 and 1949 provides us with an example of the successful implementation of such an objective. However, we should not lose sight of the fact that huge numbers of those who were repatriated to various communist states, and in particular the Soviet Union, faced immediate imprisonment and in many cases summary execution.

Integration of transferees: Rather than insisting on their eventual return and thus creating an often prolonged period of uncertainty and dependency on aid, the permanent economic, political and social integration of transferees in the receiving states is meant to prevent their internal instability and to contribute to a rapid stabilization of their bilateral relationship. This is what in effect occurred in both parts of Germany after 1945, the early rhetoric of return to and recovery of the 'lost territories' by the federal government to one side.

Reconciliation between states and populations involved: In the long term, the goal of increasing states' external security on the basis of forced population transfers can be achieved only if there is a process of reconciliation between the states involved in, and the populations affected by, the transfers. This has to include a permanent settlement of any territorial disputes and (symbolic) gestures of acknowledgement, apology and compensation in relation to the suffering and losses of those transferred. The wider process of reconciliation between Germany and the peoples and states that fell victim to the Nazis is instructive here.

Supra-regional integration of states involved: Further stabilization and prevention of open hostilities between the states involved can also be achieved through their integration in supra-regional organizations and the use of the latter's mechanisms and procedures to resolve outstanding issues. Europe, through the vehicles of the EU and, to a lesser extent, the Council of Europe and the OSCE, illustrates how regional integration may act to dissipate injurious legacies.

The foregoing discussion of policies to cope with the problems that accompany forced population transfers should not be construed as an argument in support of ethnic cleansing as a viable policy to settle ethnic conflicts. If anything, these policies should be considered as alternatives if efforts aimed at preventing ethnic cleansing have failed or if attempts to undo them are unlikely to succeed and/or contribute to the internal stability and external security of the states involved. The unambiguous verdict, however, remains: it is less costly in terms of human suffering, material losses and long-term instability to seek alternatives to forced population transfers.

4 Conclusion

Tempting as it may be at times when consensual conflict settlement efforts are frustrated by an inability and/or unwillingness of local parties to compromise and regional and global actors to support an ensuing peace process, there is no evidence that would suggest that the so-called alternatives explored in this chapter are indeed viable or feasible. This is not only because they are morally reprehensible but also because they must be rejected on pragmatic grounds, as they do not provide frameworks in which ethnic conflicts can be sustainably settled.

This is not to say that there may not be occasions in which such 'alternatives' are pursued by local parties, with or without international complicity. If that happens, the question arises of what should be (un)done. Clearly, episodes of genocidal violence cannot be undone, but every effort must be made to avoid their recurrence, precisely by finding a consensual settlement to the underlying conflict. Forced assimilation may offer opportunities for undoing, but care needs to be taken that well-intentioned efforts in this respect do not in fact constitute forcible dissimilation. When it comes to ethnic cleansing, here, too, some undoing is possible. However, international prerogatives for not rewarding those who carry out the ethnic cleansing in the first place by accepting 'facts on the ground' may be misguided. Undoing ethnic cleansing may very well place individuals at great risk, either by their being sent back to areas in which they are personally endangered or by their being kept in refugee camps for prolonged periods of time because not doing so might accept the results of ethnic cleansing. Yet, while such a supposedly principled approach might suit the relevant players in the international community, it is not necessarily in the best interests of the people affected. Nor does it contribute to security and stability in the state(s) and regions affected: a permanently temporary settlement always bears an element of uncertainty that can easily be exploited for the purposes of radicalization and polarization of the groups involved.

Importantly, then, looking at the picture in its whole complexity of actors and structures involved at local, state, regional and global level is essential to weigh the options available in response to certain consequences of ethnic conflict. Where 'alternative solutions' such as the ones explored in this chapter have been pursued, careful consideration needs to be given to the implications of accepting or rejecting them. In this context, again, our levels-of-analysis approach allows us not only to understand why such alternatives were pursued but also to assess their future consequences.

9

Conclusion

At the beginning of our intellectual journey into ethnic conflict stood a series of questions about its causes and consequences, and about the responses to it: Who fights in ethnic conflicts, and why do they do it? Why do ethnic conflicts cause often seemingly random and excessively cruel violence to civilians? What drives people to inflict such suffering, or at least support those who do? Why are international organizations and powerful states often indifferent to the security threat that ethnic conflicts pose until a major crisis has developed? What is it that makes many an ethnic conflict so difficult to settle?

Empirically, we found answers to all of these questions, but they are not always satisfactory. To know that some prefer violent confrontation over peaceful cooperation because material gain and personal gratification are more easily obtained at the barrel of a gun is difficult to comprehend, especially if it puts innocent civilians at risk of death or displacement, as in many of the cases we have examined in more detail. In terms of the sheer magnitude of suffering, the Democratic Republic of Congo stands out, with millions killed and displaced in the last decade alone. Nor is it any easier to buy into the logic of those governments who brutally repress some of their citizens because they belong to a different ethnic group, speak another language or practise a particular religion. The denial of basic rights and opportunities, including the ability to express, preserve and develop one's ethnic identity, in turn, leads to situations in which individuals belonging to the oppressed group see no other way to improve their lot, and sometimes even to prevent it from worsening, than to take up arms – despite the consequences of this. The attempt to impose Shari'a law in South Sudan in 1983 serves as an example. In many of the cases that we discussed, little, if any, comfort can be taken from the response of the international community. Be it misjudgement or mismanagement, lack of will or resources, or pure self-interest, international and regional organizations and individual third-party states do not have a convincing track record in preventing, managing or settling ethnic conflicts. In this context, the war between Georgia and Russia over South Ossetia in August 2008 serves as a reminder of how various forms of peaceful international engagement may still give way to military 'solutions', regardless of the patchy track record that they might have. Russia's military victory thus has solved little, if anything, given that the continuing instability in the wider Caucasus region continues and given the failure of the Abkhazian and South

Ossetian regimes to obtain even a modicum of wider international recognition. This war also serves to remind us that we ignore the state as a political actor at our own peril.

Attributing a share of responsibility for the failure of conflict prevention to international organizations and other external actors is not to suggest that they are complicit in mass killings and displacements: nothing can, or should, let us forget that the primary responsibility for killing lies with those who pull the trigger or wield the knife. Yet internal failings of the UN did make it possible for the Rwandan genocide to run a long stretch of its course. The case of Rwanda also illustrates how decisions not to intervene can sometimes have incalculable long-term consequences. Failure to engage quickly not only facilitated genocide in Rwanda but created a dynamic whereby the entire Great Lakes region became ever more volatile, to the point where the then already unstable Zaire became the sanctuary of defeated *interahamwe* units. The subsequent inability of Kinshasa to deal with this problem in turn led to an attempt by Uganda and Rwanda to force regime change and install a government of their own liking. The combined consequences of inaction and unsuccessful regime change are all too obvious in the situation in the DRC today.

A few cases, though, offer hope. While there has been a proliferation in ethnic conflict since the end of the Cold War – in the sense of a range of new conflicts escalating violently in a relatively short span of time in the 1990s – a significant number of settlements have been achieved in this period. Often providing innovative and complex institutional designs, the practice of contemporary conflict settlement has emphasized the accommodation of conflicting interests through power sharing and self-governance, as well as in a few select cases the option of independence, as in Kosovo (where it has been exercised), South Sudan and Bougainville. Moreover, conflict management has had a few successes, too, indicating that not every conflict needs to escalate, or relapse, into full-scale civil war. The experience of the Western Balkans, and especially of Macedonia, is instructive here: prolonged and determined international engagement does have positive effects. Even if it may not be able to prevent all violence, it can stop a downward spiral into ethnic conflict and enable the parties to find an institutional compromise to resolve their differences. The ensuing settlements may not be perfect, but they are doubtless preferable to ongoing violent confrontation, and gradually the parties – from Northern Ireland to Mindanao and from South Tyrol to Gagauzia – can learn to live and work with them. Yet the fragility of such settlements is illustrated by both Northern Ireland and Mindanao, where the continued existence of 'spoilers', either for reasons of personal gain or as the consequence of total alienation from the state in which they live, works to destroy any gains made. Even if such individuals do not succeed in derailing a peace process, as in Northern Ireland, they are nonetheless capable of inflicting unnecessary harm and suffering.

As with the causes of ethnic conflict, there is no uniformity of explanation when it comes to account for the specific design of conflict settlements or the degree of sustainability that peace may, or may not, enjoy in a given case. At first sight, this may seem analytically dissatisfying. While we never had the ambition to develop a theory of ethnic conflict or conflict settlement that could offer such a comprehensive explanation, our book is not without an argument that we believe has analytical merit. Rather than privileging any one theory – of ethnicity, inter-ethnic relations or international relations – we developed an analytical framework that was broad enough to integrate several such theories and allowed us to offer comprehensive accounts of the causes and consequences of ethnic conflict and the responses to it in specific cases. To the extent that we found any consistency across the wide range of different ethnic conflicts that we analysed in this way, it was that it always takes insights from several theories to produce any kind of comprehensive picture. We cannot explain the onset and duration of the conflict in Mindanao without reference to the grievances of its Moro population, the greed of criminal networks such as Abu Sayyaf, and the jihadist tendencies of some of the militias still holding out on a peace deal. Nor would it be possible to account for the long duration of the conflict in the DRC without considering the interests of local parties, the central government and neighbouring states, as well as the response by the international community, initially and significantly limited in terms of the numbers of peacekeepers and the adequacy and robustness of their mandate.

In a more abstract way, what we developed conceptually, and found empirically, is that the motives, means and opportunities of the immediate conflict parties are dependent upon a wide range of factors at the local, state, regional and global level, and that we need to examine these factors and their interplay in order to understand why Rwanda experienced a genocide while Macedonia saw very little violence, why there has been widespread Western recognition of Kosovo's unilateral declaration of independence but not of those by South Ossetia and Abkhazia just six months later, why international intervention is acceptable to the government of the DRC but not to the military regime in Burma, and why the 1999 UN mandate for Kosovo was exceptionally strong while that in Darfur was exceptionally weak and took a long time to be agreed upon. Different theories can help us understand specific dimensions of the particular problem at hand, and we need their combined analytical power to make sense of what shapes the actions of the parties to a given conflict – to prevent violence where possible, contain it locally where necessary, and shape successful international interventions to improve the plight of fellow human beings in conflict zones. International intervention is, in most cases of ethnic conflict, necessary in order to establish conditions for sustainable peace. As many of our cases indicate, it is a long-term, costly and often risky endeavour, but one that is without much credible alternative. Where it fails, it does so rarely because of bad intent but rather because it ends too soon.

The most successful international interventions are those that are sustained at a high level of commitment and credibility beyond the negotiation of a peace agreement. The 'alternatives' we discussed in the previous chapter are seldom if ever morally defensible. The fact that we accept the consequences of such actions does not make them right. The message that we have tried to convey in this volume is that, if conflicts are to be resolved in a manner that does not involve us constantly reliving history, sustained engagement on the part of external actors in concert with national and substate actors is necessary in order for seemingly intractable conflicts to be resolved. Such settlements allow the populations concerned to move towards a situation that transcends those of simple ceasefires and armed peace. No matter how distant it may seem, the ultimate objective of conflict settlement strategies should be to create an environment within which a sustainable peace can be created, and where the lessons of history are learned, as opposed to being utilized as a rationale for further rounds of conflict. As this volume has demonstrated, settling ethnic conflict is a continuous challenge in war-torn societies, and post-conflict reconstruction is a complex yet necessary task that is integral to the successful settlement of any conflict. But this is a story for another book.

Notes

CHAPTER 1 INTRODUCTION

1 We borrow the term 'conflict regulation' from the title of a volume co-edited by John McGarry and Brendan O'Leary (1993), who use it in an inclusive way and understand it to cover 'both conflict termination and conflict management' (McGarry and O'Leary 1993: 4). Our own usage of the term involves three dimensions: conflict prevention, conflict management and conflict settlement. Other authors use 'conflict management' in a similarly inclusive manner (cf. Carr and Callan 2002; Coakley 2003; and Rothchild 1997).

CHAPTER 2 THE STUDY OF ETHNIC CONFLICT

1 Rogers Brubaker and David D. Laitin, 'Ethnic and nationalist violence', *Annual Review of Sociology*, 24 (1998), p. 425.

2 This also means that violent riots or protest demonstrations in themselves do not 'qualify' as ethnic conflicts. They may be part of an ongoing ethnic conflict, but they can also occur in situations where there are tensions or disputes, i.e., where a situation may occasionally escalate into violence, but where its use is not part of the normal repertoire of interaction among ethnic groups and/or between them and state institutions.

3 Another valuable analysis of the regional dimension of ethnic conflicts is Lake and Rothchild (1996).

4 The reasons why an initially promising initiative to this effect did not succeed are analysed in Wolff (2001).

5 Here, and below, we draw on a range of original and synthetic sources, including Adamson (2005), Brown (1996), Buzan and Wæver (2003), Carr and Callan (2002), Collier and Hoeffler (1998), Cordell and Wolff (2004), Fowkes (2001), Horowitz ([1985] 2000), Kaufman (2001), Lake and Morgan (1997), Lake and Rothchild (1996), Rotberg (2004), Rubin (2001), Scherrer (2003) and Tellis et al. (1997).

6 A third school of IR theory – social constructivism – has emerged since the early 1990s. Constructivists emphasize the intersubjective aspects of human behaviour and interaction, i.e., the ability and willingness to establish certain norms and values of conduct and allow themselves to be guided by it. However, social constructivism so far has remained by and large at the level of a meta-theory. Social constructivism as a school of thought within the social sciences emerged long before and independently of its application in the field of international relations. One of its most significant early contributions – Berger and Luckmann (1966) – appeared more than a quarter of century before Wendt's groundbreaking article 'Anarchy is what states make of it' (Wendt 1992). More recently there have been some attempts to develop social constructivist theories of foreign policy analysis, e.g., Boekle et al. (2001) and Cordell and Wolff (2005). We will return to social constructivist theories briefly below and in the section on theories of ethnicity.

7 There has been a massive increase in civilian casualties as a result of this shift from

inter-state warfare between regular armed forces to internal and regional conflicts involving, if not exclusively, a large number of irregular and often poorly disciplined and controlled non-state forces. While at the beginning of the twentieth century only about 10 per cent of war casualties were civilians, by the end of the century the figure was closer to 95 per cent. On the character of these so-called new wars, see Kaldor (2006).

8 The subsequent deterioration of the situation in East Timor in 2007–8 cannot be directly attributed to the intervention.

9 On regimes, see also Krasner (1983).

10 The various debates are captured, among others, in Horowitz (1991), Noel (2005), McGarry and O'Leary (2004), O'Flynn and Russell (2005), and Reynolds (2002).

11 Occasionally, the following terms are used synonymously: essentialism and perennialism for primordialism, and instrumentalism or modernism for constructivism.

12 Rogers Brubaker (e.g., 1996) and Russell Hardin (e.g., 1995) may be the two most prominent exceptions here. Arguably, Collier and Hoeffler (1998) and Fearon and Laitin (2000) also subscribe to a very strong constructivist tradition.

13 On the role of ethnic activists and political entrepreneurs, see Lake and Rothchild (1996) and below. More general examples of this kind of constructivist approach are Aronoff (1998), Brass (1980) and Laitin (1998).

14 Among some US-based political scientists, Connor and Smith are not considered mainstream constructivists, but rather find themselves at the '[e]xtremes within this general perspective' of constructivism. See Lustick (2000: § 1.1).

15 In contrast to this distinction between theories of ethnicity and theories of inter-ethnic relations, Horowitz (1998) includes both sets of theories into 'ten explanations' of ethnic conflict. The two are inherently linked, but there is reasonable doubt about the extent to which theories of ethnicity can be used to explain the occurrence of ethnic conflict other than by assuming that the mere existence of different ethnic groups inevitably leads to conflict between them. This is a point that Horowitz makes in relation to primordialism (Horowitz 1998: 5).

16 We are excluding control regimes from the following discussion as these are only temporary and inherently unstable approaches to manage conflict rather than to settle it. According to Schneckener (2004), control regimes include coercive domination (Israeli policy in the occupied territories, the Apartheid system in South Africa and Serb policy vis-à-vis Kosovo throughout most of the 1990s are examples of this kind of control regime, as was Indonesian policy in Aceh and as remains Sri Lankan policy vis-à-vis the Tamil minority), coopted rule (e.g., the Russian, Habsburg and Ottoman empires of past centuries and the colonial empires of the British and French in Africa and Asia) and limited self-rule (e.g., the Ottoman millet system, the ghettos established by the Nazis for Jews, the so-called homelands created by white South Africans for the country's black majority, and the reservations in the United States to which Native Americans were sent).

17 Interestingly, O'Leary originally suggested (re-)partition as an option for Northern Ireland in 1989 in the light of the failure by then of consociationalist solutions, but he recognized later that this was not a viable solution either.

18 In a speech on 30 January 2006, the Russian president, Vladimir Putin, said that the future status of Kosovo must not become a potentially dangerous precedent for conflicts in the post-Soviet periphery, telling a meeting of the Russian cabinet that a 'universally applicable' solution must be found for Serbia's UN-administered, predominantly ethnic Albanian province, which he considered to be in the interest of international law, as well as in 'the practical interests in the post-Soviet space' (RFE/RL 2006). This has been variously interpreted as support for Serbia's anti-independence position and as a threat to the territorial integrity of Georgia, Moldova, Azerbaijan and potentially even Ukraine (Socor 2006).

19 Evidence for this transformative capacity is so far admittedly sketchy – Weller and Wolff (2006) base their analysis on the case of Bosnia and Herzegovina. An earlier analysis of South Tyrol arriving at a similar conclusion is by Wolff (2001). Note that McGarry and O'Leary share some of this optimism in relation to Northern Ireland (McGarry and O'Leary 2004: 36).

CHAPTER 3 THEORIES OF ETHNIC CONFLICT

1 In part, Lake and Rothchild draw on Fearon (1995).
2 Horowitz, too, operates with the concept of fear. See below.
3 Interestingly, this seems to point in the direction of grievances rather than greed, but it is not discussed further by the authors.
4 For a comprehensive critique of these two models of ethnic conflict, see Sambanis (2004).
5 We will return to the case of Kosovo in the context of Kuperman's (2008; see also Crawford and Kuperman 2006) moral hazard argument below.
6 Milton J. Esman (1994a) identified five transnational expressions of ethnic politics: irredentism, diaspora politics, strategic interventions, international organizations and transnational networks.
7 See, among others, Bieber and Daskalovski (2003), Bose (2002), Brown (1996), Danspeckgruber (2002), Hechter (2000), McGarry and Keating (2006), Noel (2005), Paris (2004), Rotberg (2004), Schneckener and Wolff (2004), Walter and Snyder (1999) and Weller and Wolff (2005, 2008).

CHAPTER 4 MOTIVE, MEANS AND OPPORTUNITY

1 Cf. Kaufman (2001), as discussed previously, and Romano (2006), who offer somewhat different versions of the means–motive–opportunity nexus.
2 We refer to this country by its constitutional name as of 31 July 2009.
3 Shevardnadze was later elected Georgia's president, which post he held until he was overthrown in the so-called Rose Revolution in October 2003 and replaced by Mikhail Saakashvili.
4 This section does not concern itself with the New People's Army, which although active in Mindanao eschews religion as an ideological or motivational force.
5 The figure for the Roma must, as elsewhere in the region, be treated with extreme caution. It is almost certainly an underestimate.
6 According to an ESI report of 2002, based on figures from the disputed 1994 census, 'ethnic Albanians make up 22.7 percent of the population, but they account for only 20.2 percent of the overall state administration. In the critical area of security, Albanians make up only 2.9 percent of army officers and defence ministry personnel . . . In the interior ministry, they constitute 8.7 percent of employees' (ESI 2002: 5). Similar patterns of underemployment of ethnic Albanians exist in the private sector (ibid.).
7 For further details and an in-depth analysis of the role of education in the conflict in Macedonia, see Petroska-Beska and Najcevska (2004).
8 According to Ackermann (1996), however, Belgrade, assuming roughly 300,000 Serbs living in Macedonia in 1991 (ten times the official census figures), tried to encourage them to increase their demands vis-à-vis the government in Skopje.
9 For a detailed discussion of the historical and contemporary aspects of the Macedonian question, cf. Pettifer (2001), Poulton (2000) and Roudometof (2000). A useful summary of key events and developments can be found in Engström (2002).
10 Note, however, that Bulgaria celebrates its national day on 3 March, the day of the

signing in 1878 of the Treaty of San Stefano, which saw modern-day Bulgaria reach its greatest territorial extent. Despite its short-lived nature – until the Treaty of Berlin later the same year – this is an almost mythical event in Bulgarian history, and one that is sometimes seen as an example of territorial revisionism.

11 For example, Macedonia is placed in the UN next to Thailand, as Greece rejected its placement under 'M' (for Macedonia) and Macedonia refused being seated under 'F' (for former).

12 Far from putting all blame on Greece in this dispute, the fact that Macedonia renamed its capital airport 'Alexander the Great' did not contribute to more cordial relations with Athens either.

13 For a detailed timeline of events, see Ilievski (2007).

14 Arguably, the OSCE High Commissioner on National Minorities was a similarly significant figure in his efforts to mediate a compromise on Albanian-language higher education and to establish the private, trilingual Southeast European University in Skopje. On the work of the High Commissioner, see Kemp (2001).

15 UNPROFOR, the United Nations Protection Force, was created through Security Council Resolution 743 (1992), of 21 February 1992, and initially intended for deployment in Croatia. Its mandate was subsequently extended to Bosnia and Herzegovina and Macedonia. In 1995 the Security Council decided to create three separate missions, the one for Macedonia being called UNPREDEP and operating until 1999.

16 See for example, Security Council Resolution 1345 (2001), of 21 March 2001, condemning the escalation of violence and the 'external' support it received, and Security Council Resolution 1371 (2001), of 26 September 2001, supporting full implementation of the OFA and the establishment of a multinational security presence.

17 This happened primarily through using mechanisms of NATO's Partnership for Peace, of which Macedonia has been a member since 1995.

18 President Trajkovski had convened a first round of talks on 2 April (a week before the conclusion of the Stability and Association Agreement). By 23 April (two weeks after), agreement on major issues was announced, and a new government was formally agreed upon on 11 May.

19 The name dispute had also delayed the EU's recognition of Macedonia in the 1990s. Although the country was deemed to have fulfilled the EU's recognition criteria of 1991, formal diplomatic recognition could only be extended in 1993 in the context of resolving the name issue before the UN (see above).

20 None of the 'issues' identified in our conceptual exploration in chapter 2 are of consequence for Macedonia. Hence we omitted them from our analysis in the following.

21 The UN and the US are truly international actors, so their inclusion at the global level requires no great justification. NATO and the EU are, in terms of their membership, regional rather than international organizations, yet because of their *global reach* we discuss them as part of the global level of analysis.

CHAPTER 5   THE PREVENTION, MANAGEMENT AND SETTLEMENT OF ETHNIC CONFLICTS

1 There are some exceptions to this rule: successful, voluntary assimilation is rarely based on a formally negotiated agreement, and the same holds true for forced assimilation, forced population transfers and genocide. See chapter 8 below.

2 On genocide prevention in Burundi, see Weissman (1998).

3 A good Western European example of this is the marching season in Northern Ireland. Some of the most contentious parades have been banned or rerouted over the past several years to avoid violent clashes between the two communities; yet this often resulted

in violent protests by Loyalists not only against the Nationalist/Republican community, but also against the British authorities.

4 Threats perceived by minorities comprise all of the features in both boxes. Depending on the specificity of the situation, it is not always possible for the minority (or the outside observer) to determine the source of the threat with absolute accuracy. In particular, in situations where the host nation has complete control over the institutions of the state and uses them against the minority, distinctions between host state and host nation are blurred, and to some extent even irrelevant.

5 Horowitz (1985: 229–88) has emphasized the variety of factors that make successful, or even desirable, irredentas very unlikely.

6 Concerning Germany and her minorities, see Wolff (2000: 183–203).

7 One of the underlying assumptions here is that demography shapes demands: a peripheral territorially concentrated group is more likely to ask for increased levels of self-governance (including, possibly, an independent state of its own) than a dispersed group. Relative size of groups will additionally determine the feasibility of any demands for power sharing and wealth-sharing at the centre.

8 In one, perhaps unusually prolonged, experience, the 137 different measures contained in the 1969–72 special autonomy statute for South Tyrol took more than thirty years to implement, while the core institutions, regional and provincial governments and parliaments were fully operational from the start (see Wolff 2003a).

9 See Wolff (2009); on commitment issues, see also Fearon (1998), Van Houten (1998) and Walter (2002).

10 This has been observed by one of us at close range. At one capacity-building seminar with representatives of the 'western movements', the main problem was for them to achieve a common stance about what their grievances were before being able to discuss different options on how to address these. Some time later, at a joint workshop, including also representatives of the government of Sudan, disunity among representatives of the movements made it easy for the government to reject any of the proposed compromises, insisting that it was far from clear that any compromises made would deliver peace.

11 This is both because of the less antagonistic structure of the international system, at least throughout the 1990s, and because of the proliferation of a relatively large number of severe ethnic conflicts in a relatively short period of time. See Danspeckgruber (2002: 5ff.), Diehl (2008: 52–5), Doyle (2001), Weiss (2007: chs 2–3).

12 These are the missions in Kashmir, Cyprus, the western Sahara, Georgia, Kosovo, the DRC, Sudan, Darfur and the Central African Republic (CAR)/Chad.

13 These are the operations in Bosnia and Herzegovina (2), Kosovo, Georgia, the Palestinian Territories (2), Iraq, CAR/Chad, and DRC (2).

14 For different approaches, see, among others, Brown (1996), Cochrane (2008: 43–63), Crocker et al. (2001), Doyle (2001), Esman and Herring (2001), Halperin et al. (1992: 95–111), Rothchild (1997), Safran (2004), Wallensteen (2007: ch. 10), and Weller and Wolff (2008).

15 For more details on this and follow-up initiatives, see www.ecmikosovo.org/.

16 See section 5 in this chapter, 'Explaining success and failure of international conflict regulation'.

17 Regarding the impact of Iraq on the case for non-consensual military interventions, see Bellamy (2004).

18 Normative arguments for and against intervention are explored at great length in, among others, Finnemore (2003), Hoffmann (1996), Holzgrefe and Keohane (2003), Kaldor (2007), Lang (2003), Smith (1998), Weiss (2008) and Wheeler (2000). The classic text on just war remains Walzer (1977).

19 This influence can be, and has been, brought to bear during negotiations of late. The

ability of the EU, together with NATO, in 2001 to make political parties in Macedonia accept the Ohrid Framework Agreement is a good example of the success of this strategy, while the rejection of Serbia to recognize the status of Kosovo as an independent country illustrates its failure.

20 On recent World Bank efforts to 'mainstream' conflict regulation concerns into development policy, see Van Houten (2007).

21 Two recent volumes have begun to address this gap: Kronenberger and Wouters (2004) and Tocci (2007).

22 Smith (2004); Cannizzaro (2002); Dannreuther (2003); Ginsberg (2001); Mahncke et al. (2004); Marsh and Mackenstein (2005); H. Smith (2002); K. E. Smith (2003).

23 Comelli et al. (2007); Dodini and Fantini (2006); Dannreuther (2006); Kelley (2006).

24 One notable, albeit now somewhat dated, exception is Duke (2003).

25 For example, Lake and Morgan (1997); Thakur and Schnabel (2001); Pugh and Sidhu (2003); Diehl and Lepgold (2003); Otunnu and Doyle (1998).

26 For example, Coppieters et al. (2004); Diez et al. (2002); Holliday et al. (2004); Hughes et al. (2004); Toggenburg (2005); Vachudova (2005).

27 There have been few systematic studies of this relationship: Gilligan and Stedman (2003) and Fortna (2004) offer evidence that international intervention most often takes place in cases of severe violent conflict, i.e., a very difficult situation on the ground shapes the prospects of success and failure. Caplan (2005b) similarly distinguishes between the capabilities of the intervening actor and the local context in which the intervention occurs. Diehl (2008) ascribes success to operational, contextual and behavioural factors. Pushkina (2006) explores these factors specifically in the context of post-Cold War UN peace missions.

28 This is sometimes already obvious in book titles: King and Mason (2006) subtitle their empirically very rich analysis 'How the World Failed Kosovo', while Chandler (2000) offers his view on the situation in Bosnia and Herzegovina in 'Faking Democracy after Dayton'.

CHAPTER 6 INTERNATIONAL INTERVENTION

1 The final award in this so-called Abyei arbitration was delivered on 22 July 2009 by a five-member tribunal constituted to rule on the dispute between the government of Sudan and the Sudan People's Liberation Movement over the delimitation of the Abyei area. For details of the proceedings and award, see www.pca-cpa.org/showpage.asp?pag_id=1306.

2 The involvement of NGOs in Kosovo goes back to the 1980s, when Amnesty International and other human rights organizations began to monitor, and report on, the situation in Kosovo. See, for example, Amnesty International (1989).

3 See UN Economic and Social Council (1996); US Department of Justice (1996, 1997).

4 As early as 1993 there were also reports by independent human rights organizations that Serbs were subjected to intense ethnic discrimination and intimidation on the part of Albanians in Kosovo. See IHFHR (1993).

5 An English translation of the petition is reprinted in Magas (1993: 49).

CHAPTER 7 CONFLICT SETTLEMENT IN THEORY AND PRACTICE

1 The definition of self-governance has been adapted from Wolff and Weller (2005).

2 This can then also be tested using certain empirical indicators, such as absence of violent conflict and/or absence of non-violent conflict about the arrangements (macro-level structures) per se, no violations of specific aspects of arrangements, absence of political parties opposed to the arrangements ('weighed' by the popularity of these parties), and

evidence available from relevant public opinion surveys. This argument is developed more fully in Wolff and Van Houten (2007).

3 Another element of institutional design as far as overall state construction is concerned relates to coordination mechanisms between different layers of authority, including the establishment of dispute resolution arrangements. This is related primarily to the different types of such mechanisms (e.g., cooptation, joint committees, judicial review) and their leverage (consultative vs. legally binding). For a more detailed examination of this issue, see Wolff (2008: 436–8).

4 Power sharing features and inclusiveness may also extend to the judicial branch, primarily in relation to provisions for the appointment of judges and prosecutors.

5 The relationship between individuals, groups and the state is of course also about the degree to which institutional design favours particular groups and excludes others – that is, the degree to which different groups are given different status (e.g., constituent nations vs. minorities) and the political, economic and resource implications of this (e.g., mandatory inclusion in government, participation in proportional public sector job allocation, reception of public funding, etc.). In other words, the question here is about the degree to which specific group identities are recognized and protected and how this manifests itself in the way in which the boundaries of authority are shaped by territory or population groups. We discuss this in greater detail in relation to the overall organization of the state and the branches of government.

6 We elaborate this point in more detail below.

7 The arguments put forward by McGarry and O'Leary here have also been rehearsed elsewhere (e.g., McGarry and O'Leary 2004a, 2004b). See also Choudhry (2008).

8 O'Leary (2005a: 12) later refers to this also as 'complete consociations'.

9 The subsequent assertion, also repeated in other writings, that '[c]onsociations become undemocratic when elites govern with factional or lower levels of support within their segments' (McGarry and O'Leary 2004: 15) is less convincing in our view. Assuming that 'support' means electoral support, a consociation is democratic if its executive emerges in free and fair elections, not if it fulfils certain numerical tests. Implicitly, what seems to be at stake is less the democratic credentials of the arrangement than its consociational nature, especially the criterion of jointness. By extension, such an arrangement might also prove less stable compared to one in which an executive can rely on broader levels of support. Insisting that plurality support is a minimum requirement for democratic consociations is also empirically not without difficulties. In South Tyrol, for example, the only formal requirement for the provincial executive is that it must reflect the numerical strength of the linguistic groups as represented in the provincial parliament. This means that an Italian party with less than plurality support can become a coalition partner of a German party as long as it sends into the provincial cabinet sufficient numbers of ministers that reflect the total numerical strength of all Italian parties in the provincial parliament, and provided that this government commands the required majority in parliament.

10 Corporate consociationalism, however, is still evident to some extent in political practice: for example, Bosnia and Herzegovina, under the original Dayton Accords, Northern Ireland under the 1998 agreement, Lebanon under the National Pact and under the 1989 Ta'if Accord, and Cyprus under the 1960 constitution and proposed (but rejected) Annan Plan all display features of predetermined arrangements based on ascriptive identities.

11 In the context of Iraq, McGarry (2006: 6–7) explains how this process has been enshrined in the Iraqi constitution: 'Kirkuk can choose to join Kurdistan if its people want. Governorates in other parts of the country are permitted to amalgamate, forming regions, if there is democratic support in each governorate. In this case, a twin democratic threshold is proposed: a vote within a governorate's assembly and a referendum. . . . It is also possible for Shi'a dominated governorates that do not accept

SCIRI's vision to remain separate, and, indeed for any governorate that may be, or may become, dominated by secularists to avoid inclusion in a sharia-ruled Shiastan or Sunnistan.'

12 For details on the d'Hondt rule, see O'Leary et al. (2005).

13 Sisk (1996) uses the terms 'integrative' and 'integration' when referring to centripetalism, which Horowitz (2008: 1217) rejects as misleading.

14 See also Reilly (2006) for a comparative study of preferential voting.

15 This need for centripetal elements in territorial designs for conflict settlement is also echoed in some corners of the consociational school: see Weller and Wolff (2005).

16 The Coombs rule provides another such system, but one that is rarely used. There is one crucial difference between them. Under AV, lower-order preferences are redistributed among candidates by eliminating the candidate with the lowest number of first preference votes in each round until one candidate with more than 50 per cent emerges. Under the Coombs rule, candidate elimination is based on the highest number of last-preference votes achieved. That means, under AV the least popular candidate is eliminated in each round, while under Coombs it is the most *un*popular one.

17 Compare Fraenkel and Grofman (2004) with Horowitz (2004) on AV more generally, and Fraenkel and Grofman (2006) with Horowitz (2006) on the case of Fiji specifically. For an attempt to bridge the divide between those advocating majoritarian preferential systems (such as AV) and proportional preferential systems (such as STV or open PR lists), see Wolff (2005). On Fiji, see also Horowitz (2008: 1235–6).

18 This consensus is not fully embraced by Lijphart, who remains a staunch defender of PR list systems. See Lijphart (2002a, 2002b).

19 This model presumes that no candidate has an instant majority in the first round of voting.

20 On commitment problems, see Fearon (1995, 1998) and Lake and Rothchild (1998).

21 This is remarkably similar to Horowitz's (2008: 1220) observation that '[c]ivil wars . . . can sometimes be brought to an end with consociational arrangements, but the desirability and durability of such agreements are often in doubt.'

22 This basic endorsement of power sharing is confirmed in later work (Hartzell and Hoddie 2008) by findings that the most durable negotiated settlements of civil wars are those that include economic, military, political and territorial power sharing arrangements. While these findings can be read as a combination of power sharing and power dividing mechanisms, they are not generally in line with Roeder and Rothchild's recommendations, which emphasize power dividing over power sharing as a precondition for sustainable peace.

23 Proposals for decentralization/federalization also exist in Ethiopia, Nigeria and the Democratic Republic of Congo, but in all three cases lack serious implementation efforts.

24 In India, one could include the so-called Union Territories, such as Pondicherry (Puduchery).

25 The 2003 constitution of the Union of Serbia and Montenegro provided for a binational federation between the two entities and included an option for Montenegrin independence after three years if at least 55 per cent of people participating in a referendum would opt for it. The referendum was held on 21 May 2006, and Montenegro declared its independence on 3 June after the country's referendum commission confirmed as official the preliminary result, which had already been recognized by all five permanent members of the UN Security Council on 23 May. For the text of the Constitutional Charter of the State Union of Serbia and Montenegro, see www.mfa.gov.yu/facts/const_scg.pdf.

26 This is not meant to be a comprehensive list of cases. For an analysis of some examples

and general trends in the spread of territorial self-governance regimes as part of conflict settlements, see contributions in Weller and Wolff (2005).

27 'General Framework Agreement for Peace in Bosnia and Herzegovina', www.intstudies. cam.ac.uk/centre/cps/documents_bosnia_dayton.html.

28 'The Bougainville Peace Agreement, www.intstudies.cam.ac.uk/centre/cps/documents_ bougainville_final.html; 'The Constitution of the Autonomous Region of Bougainville', www.vanuatu.usp.ac.fj/library/Paclaw/Papua%20New%20Guinea%20and%20 Bougainville/Bougainville.htm.

29 'The Constitution of Belgium', www.fed-parl.be/constitution_uk.html.

30 'The Constitution of Ukraine', www.rada.kiev.ua/const/conengl.htm; 'The Constitution of the Autonomous Republic of Crimea', www.rada.crimea.ua/index.html.

31 The Law on the Special Status of Gagazuia, www.intstudies.cam.ac.uk/centre/cps/ documents_moldova_law.html.

32 'Framework Agreement', www.intstudies.cam.ac.uk/centre/cps/documents_macedonia_ frame.html; 'Law on Local Self-government of the Republic of Macedonia', www.urban.org/ PDF/mcd_locgov.pdf.

33 'Peace Agreement', www.intstudies.cam.ac.uk/centre/cps/documents_philippines_final. html.

34 'The Agreement Reached in the Multi-party Negotiations', www.intstudies.cam.ac.uk/ centre/cps/documents_ireland_peace.html.

35 'Protocol between the Government of Sudan (GOS) and the Sudan People's Liberation Movement (SPLM) on Power sharing', www.intstudies.cam.ac.uk/centre/cps/documents_ sudan_powersharing.html.

36 'Special Statute for Trentino-Alto Adige', www.provinz.bz.it/lpa/service/publikationen. asp?redas=yes&somepubl_action=300&somepubl_image_id=116246.

37 Moreover, this wider context in applicable cases also finds an institutional expression in the form of cross-border/transnational links and in the phenomenon of para-diplomacy (for more detailed discussions, see Wolff 2007b).

38 This classification ignores purely or mostly ceremonial heads of state as well as the fact that for all West European cases the European Union is an additional layer of authority.

39 Structural asymmetry is meant to signify the existence of territorial entities that do not 'fit' the overall construction of the state, i.e., an autonomous territory in an otherwise unitary state, as is the case with the Crimea. Functional asymmetry is meant to signify that some territorial entities enjoy a different measure of competences, e.g., have wider legislative powers than others. 'Multiple asymmetry' simply means that more than one such structural and/or functional asymmetry exists, and that the asymmetric entities in themselves are different from one another in terms of territorial status and/or competences. For an excellent discussion of the usefulness of asymmetric designs for conflict settlement, see McGarry (2007).

40 Since the 2001 constitutional reforms, South Tyrol is in the unusual situation of having both specific lists of competences allocated to different layers of authority, as well as a general clause assigning all not specifically mentioned policy areas automatically to the legislative competence of the province.

41 In case it is requested by the Assembly in Northern Ireland, the regional power sharing institutions could enjoy an open-ended list of powers allocated to them, with only specifically excepted matters retained by the Westminster government.

42 Elections to the parliament of Papua New Guinea involved a version of AV, the so-called limited preferential vote (LPV), between 1964 and 1975. A single member plurality system was in operation from 1975 to 2002, when LPV was restored.

43 According to the Bougainville constitution, there are three reserved seats each for former combatants and women, representing the three regions of the Autonomous Region of

Bougainville. Mandatory representation of former combatants can be abandoned by a two-thirds majority vote in the regional parliament.

44 According to the 2001 revised autonomy statute, the *Landeshauptmann* can now be elected directly, but will at the same time remain head of the provincial government, which needs to be elected by the provincial parliament. South Tyrol's system of government is thus an unusual type of parliamentary system with a directly elected prime minister who at the same time is head of 'state'.

45 Even though there is no mandatory power sharing at any level in Macedonia, the power balance of national politics makes coalitions at the centre between ethnic Macedonian and ethnic Albanian parties highly likely. In fact, so far ethnic Albanian parties have been present in all coalition governments since Macedonia's independence, except for the 1990–2 'government of experts', which was not structured around political parties but included three ethnic Albanians. Our thanks to Eben Friedman and Zoran Ilievski for providing this information.

46 To the extent that members of the executive committee of Gagauzia are coopted into the corresponding structures of the central government, there is a certain degree of power sharing at the centre.

47 Power sharing at regional level is not mandatory, but is a likely outcome of the regional demographic and power balances.

48 The self-governance arrangements in South Tyrol combine horizontal power sharing at the level of the province (South Tyrol) and the region (Trentino-South Tyrol).

49 Mandatory power sharing at regional level applies only to the federation and cantons within it.

50 The regional constitution of Bougainville determines mandatory inclusion of representatives of Bougainville's three regions into the regional government.

51 To the extent that certain members of the government of the Autonomous Region in Muslim Mindanao are coopted into structures of the central government, there is a certain degree of power sharing at the central level in addition to the mandatory power sharing at regional level.

52 In the period prior to elections.

53 Crimea's constitution does not provide for formal structures of power sharing, but local demographic and power balances make voluntary inter-ethnic power sharing at least likely.

54 The Italian system distinguishes between regions and provinces as second- and third-order levels of territorial administration.

55 The 2005 UNESCO Convention on the Protection and Promotion of the Diversity of Cultural Expressions has not yet been signed by any of the countries concerned.

56 For the text of the Charter, see www.achpr.org/english/_info/charter_en.html.

57 Dates in parentheses indicate that the country has not yet ratified.

58 The UK does not have a single constitutional text, in accordance with the doctrine of parliamentary sovereignty.

59 In reverse, this means that all members of the ethnic group concerned can enjoy the rights accorded to them in the autonomy arrangement anywhere in the territory of the relevant state. This form of autonomy is particularly useful in instances where groups are more dispersed. It is also used to complement territorial forms of autonomy in specific policy areas (culture, religious affairs, education, etc.) when autonomous territories are ethnically heterogeneous.

60 For further analysis of this issue, see Weller (2005b).

61 In Mindanao, an initial referendum took place in 1989 in which four of the twenty-two provinces and cities opted for inclusion in the ARMM. In 2001, a second referendum was held, and one further province and one further city joined the ARMM.

CHAPTER 8 'ALTERNATIVES' TO CONSENSUAL CONFLICT SETTLEMENT

1 We note, however, that consensus does not always mean that the settlement reached reflects parties' first preferences. Internationally mediated settlements, such as the Dayton Accords for Bosnia and Herzegovina, are often achieved because the alternatives are even less agreeable to the conflict parties on the ground.

2 It goes without saying that nothing in the following is an endorsement of any of these policies, all of which ultimately indicate the failure of consensual conflict settlement.

3 Valentino (2004: 1, 10) uses the term 'mass killings' ('intentional killing of massive numbers of non-combatants') and attributes to them between 60 and 150 million victims, compared to 34 million battle deaths in civil wars. Similarly, Chirot and McCauley (2006) make an argument that genocides have occurred throughout history, regardless of any geographical, religious, ethnic or political distinctions in the societies in which they were perpetrated.

4 For the full judgement of the International Court of Justice, see ICJ (2007).

5 Gruber (1974: 171) gives the following 1922 quote from Hitler: 'Germany has to join forces with Italy, which experiences a time of national rebirth and has a great future ahead of itself. In order to accomplish this, a clear and final renunciation of all claims to South Tyrol is necessary.'

6 See also Wolff (2008).

7 Partitions can be defined as divisions of existing states in such a way that at least one of the ethnic groups which is a party to the conflict perceives the border change as a division of its homeland, while secessions describe a state of affairs in which an ethnic group wishes to withdraw, together with the territory on which it lives, from an existing state. Partition and secession can be followed by either independent statehood or unification with an existing state. There are grey areas in the definition of partition and secession: Kosovo, from an Albanian perspective, is a secession but from a Serb perspective a partition, while a future 'detachment' of Northern Kosovo would be interpreted as partition from the Albanian perspective. For similar definitions and a discussion of definitional issues, see Horowitz ([1985] 2000: ch. 6). Partition and secession can be consensual (Ethiopia/Eritrea, Czechoslovakia) or contested (Bangladesh, Kosovo). They have also occurred in the context of decolonization (most recently, East Timor, and still pending, Western Sahara) and of state dissolution (Yugoslavia and the Soviet Union).

8 Note that Sambanis (2000: 445) does not distinguish between partitions and secessions, but defines partitions as 'a war outcome that involves both border adjustment and demographic changes'.

9 All the figures in this paragraph are taken from UNHCR (2006: ch. 7).

10 In the case of the expulsion of Germans from Central and Eastern Europe in the post-1945 period, this has been analysed and documented in Cordell and Wolff (2005) and Wolff (2005).

11 However, it should be noted that this Greek–Bulgarian Convention on Reciprocal Emigration recognized the *right* of emigration and emphasized the *voluntary* character of any emigration in its context; it was drafted by the Commission on New States and for the Protection of the Rights of Minorities and subsequently accepted by Greece and Bulgaria (Ladas 1932: 40ff.)

12 The introductory paragraph to section XII, 'Orderly Transfer of German Populations', of the Potsdam Agreement reads as follows: 'The Three Governments, having considered the question in all its aspects, recognize that the transfer to Germany of German populations, or elements thereof, remaining in Poland, Czechoslovakia and Hungary, will have to be undertaken. They agree that any transfers that take place should be effected in an orderly and humane manner.'

13 The Zurich–London agreements, signed in London on 19 February 1959, provided legitimacy to actions taken jointly or individually by Greece and Turkey, as well as by Britain, to uphold the constitution of Cyprus.

14 In this section we are drawing primarily on reports by UNHCR on its activities in Cyprus (UNHCR 1975, 1976, 1977, 1998).

15 In this section we are drawing primarily on reports from UNHCR (1997) and fieldwork, including interviews with former UNHCR staff in Belgrade.

16 This issue of moral hazard has been examined in great detail in Crawford and Kuperman (2006). See also chapter 3 above.

17 The debate on the viability of forced population transfers (and partitions) was reignited by Posen (1993) and Mearsheimer and Pape (1993). The most prominent advocate is probably Chaim D. Kaufmann (1996a, 1996b, 1998). See also Byman (1997) and, for a book-length treatment from an international law perspective, Henckaerts (1995).

References

Abuza, Z. (2003) *Militant Islam in Southeast Asia: Crucible of Terror*. Boulder, CO: Lynne Rienner.

Ackermann, A. (1996) The former Yugoslav Republic of Macedonia: a relatively successful case of conflict prevention in Europe, *Security Dialogue*, 27/4: 409–24.

Ackermann, A. (2000) *Making Peace Prevail: Preventing Violent Conflict in Macedonia*. Syracuse, NY: Syracuse University Press.

Ackermann, A. (2003) The idea and practice of conflict prevention, *Journal of Peace Research*, 40/3: 339–47.

Adamson, F. B. (2005) Globalisation, transnational political mobilisation, and networks of violence, *Cambridge Review of International Affairs*, 18/1: 31–49.

Alcock, Antony E. (1970) *The History of the South Tyrol Question*. London: Michael Joseph.

Amnesty International (1989) *Yugoslavia: Recent Events in the Autonomous Province of Kosovo*. London: AI.

Amnesty International (2008) *Annual Report: Philippines*; www.amnesty.org/en/region/philippines/report-2008.

Aronoff, M. J. (1998) The politics of collective identity, *Reviews in Anthropology*, 27/1: 71–85.

Asiimwe, A. (2004) Rwanda census puts genocide death toll at 937,000: Reuters Alert Net. www.alertnet.org/thefacts/reliefresources/108117321274.html.

Ballentine, K., and Sherman, J. (2003) *The Political Economy of Armed Conflict: Beyond Greed and Grievance*. Boulder, CO, and London: Lynne Rienner.

Barany, Z., and Moser, R. G. (eds) (2005) *Ethnic Politics after Communism*. Ithaca, NY: Cornell University Press.

Barkey, K. (1997) Thinking about consequences of empire, in *After Empire: Multi-Ethnic Societies and Nation-Building*, ed. K. Barkey and M. von Hagen. Boulder, CO: Westview Press, 99–114.

Baze, Mero (n.d.) The risk of misleading knowledge on the 'Albanian dimension of the crisis' in Kosovo, *Independent Albanian News Agency*.

Bellamy, A. J. (2004) Ethics and intervention: the 'humanitarian exception' and the problem of abuse in case of Iraq, *Journal of Peace Research*, 41/2: 131–47.

Bell-Fialkoff, A. (1996) *Ethnic Cleansing*. London: Macmillan.

Belloni, R. (2006) The tragedy of Darfur and the limits of the responsibility to protect, *Ethnopolitics*, 5/4: 327–46.

Belmont, K., Mainwaring, S., and Reynolds, R. (2002) Introduction: institutional design, conflict management, and democracy, in *The Architecture of Democracy: Constitutional Design, Conflict Management and Democracy*, ed. A. Reynolds. Oxford: Oxford University Press, pp. 1–11.

Berger, P. and Luckmann, T. (1966) *The Social Construction of Reality*. New York: Anchor Books.

Bieber, F., and Daskalovski, Z. (2003) *Understanding the War in Kosovo*. London: Frank Cass.

Billig, M. (1976) *Social Psychology and Intergroup Relations*. London: Academic Press.

Boekle, H., Rittberger, V., and Wagner, W. (2001) Constructivist foreign policy theory, in *German Foreign Policy since Unification: Theories and Case Studies*, ed. V. Rittberger. Manchester: Manchester University Press.

Bose, S. (2002) *Bosnia after Dayton: Nationalist Partition and International Intervention*. London: Hurst.

Brass, P. R. (1980) Ethnic groups and nationalities: the formation, persistence, and transformation of ethnic identities over time, in *Ethnic Diversity and Conflict in Eastern Europe*, ed. P. F. Sugar. Santa Barbara, CA: ABC Clio, pp. 1–68.

Brown, M. E. (1996) Internal conflict and international action, in *The International Dimensions of Internal Conflict*, ed. M. E. Brown. Boston: MIT Press.

Brubaker, R. (1995) Aftermaths of empire and the unmixing of peoples: historical and comparative perspectives, *Ethnic and Racial Studies*, 18/2: 189–218.

Brubaker, R. (1996) *Nationalism Reframed: Nationhood and the National Question in the New Europe*. Cambridge: Cambridge University Press.

Buzan, B., and Wæver, O. (2003) *Regions and Powers: The Structure of International Security*. Cambridge: Cambridge University Press.

Byman, D. L. (1997) Divided they stand: lessons about partition from Iraq and Lebanon, *Security Studies*, 7/1: 1–29.

Cannizzaro, E. (ed.) (2002) *The European Union as an Actor in International Relations*. The Hague and London: Kluwer Law International.

Caplan, R. (2005a) *Europe and the Recognition of New States in Yugoslavia*. Cambridge: Cambridge University Press.

Caplan, R. (2005b) *International Administration of War-Torn Territories: Rule and Reconstruction*. Oxford: Oxford University Press.

Carr, F., and Callan, T. (2002) *Managing Conflict in the New Europe: The Role of International Institutions*. Basingstoke: Palgrave Macmillan.

Caspersen, N. (2004) Good fences make good neighbours? A comparison of conflict regulation strategies in post-war Bosnia, *Journal of Peace Research*, 41/5: 569–88.

Chandler, D. (2000) *Bosnia: Faking Democracy after Dayton*. London: Pluto Press.

Chirot, D., and McCauley, C. (2006) *Why Not Kill Them All? The Logic and Prevention of Mass Political Murder*. Princeton, NJ: Princeton University Press.

Choudhry, S. (ed.) (2008) *Constitutional Design for Divided Societies: Integration or Accommodation?* Oxford: Oxford University Press.

Coakley, J. (ed.) (2003) *The Territorial Management of Ethnic Conflict*. London: Frank Cass.

Cochrane, F. (2008) *Ending Wars*. Cambridge: Polity.

Cohen, J. (2002) Regional introduction: struggling to find peace, in *Searching for Peace in Europe and Eurasia: An Overview of Conflict Prevention and Peacebuilding Activities*, ed. P. van Tongeren, H. van de Veen, and J. Verhoeven. Boulder, CO: Lynne Rienner, pp. 404–15.

Cole, J., and Wolf, E. R. (1974) *The Hidden Frontier*. New York and London: Academic Press.

Collier, P. (2001) Economic causes of civil conflict and their implications for policy, in *Turbulent Peace: The Challenges of Managing International Conflict*, ed. C. A. Crocker, F. O. Hampson and P. Aall. Washington, DC: United States Institute of Peace Press, pp. 143–62.

Collier, P. and Hoeffler, A. (1998) On economic causes of civil war, *Oxford Economic Papers*, 50/4: 563–73.

Collier, P., and Hoefller, A. (2001) On the incidence of civil war in Africa, *Journal of Peace Research*, 38/4: 429–44.

Comelli, M., Greco, E., and Tocci, N. (2007) From boundary to borderland: transforming the meaning of borders through the European Neighbourhood Policy. *European Foreign Affairs Review*, 12/2: 203–18.

Connor, W. (1994) *Ethnonationalism: The Quest for Understanding*. Princeton, NJ: Princeton University Press.

Coppieters, B. (1999) The roots of the conflict, in *A Question of Sovereignty: The Georgia–Abkhazia Peace Process*, ed. J. Cohen. London: Conciliation Resources; www.c-r.org/our-work/accord/georgia-abkhazia/conflict-roots.php.

Coppieters, B., et al. (2004) *Europeanization and Conflict Resolution: Case Studies from the European Periphery*. Flensburg: ECMI; www.ecmi.de/jemie/special_1_2004.html.

Cordell, K., and Wolff, S. (eds) (2004) *The Ethnopolitical Encyclopaedia of Europe*. Basingstoke: Palgrave.

Cordell, K., and Wolff, S. (2005) *German Foreign Policy towards Poland and the Czech Republic: Ostpolitik Revisited*. London: Routledge.

Cornell, S. E. (2001) *Small Nations and Great Powers: A Study of Ethnopolitical Conflict in the Caucasus*. London: Curzon Caucasus World.

Crampton, R. J. (1997) *A Concise History of Bulgaria*. Cambridge: Cambridge University Press.

Crawford, T.W., and Kuperman, A. (eds) (2006) *Gambling on Humanitarian Intervention: Moral Hazard, Rebellion and Civil War*. London: Routledge.

Crocker, C. A., Hampson, F. O., and Aall, P. (eds) (2001) *Turbulent Peace: The Challenges of Managing International Conflict*. Washington, DC: United States Institute of Peace Press.

Dannreuther, R. (ed.) (2003) *European Union Foreign and Security Policy: Towards a Neighbourhood Strategy*. London: Routledge.

Dannreuther, R. (2006) Developing the alternative to enlargement: the European Neighbourhood Policy, *European Foreign Affairs Review*, 11/2: 183–201.

Danspeckgruber, W. (ed.) (2002) *The Self-Determination of Peoples: Community, Nation, and State in an Interdependent World*. Boulder, CO, and London: Lynne Rienner.

DCWEU (Defence Committee of the Western European Union) (1998) *Europe and the Evolving Situation in the Balkans*, WEU Document 1608, 13 May. Paris: Assembly of the Western European Union.

de Figuero, R. J. P., and Weingast, B. R. (1999) The rationality of fear: political opportunism and ethnic conflict, in *Civil Wars, Insecurity and Intervention*, ed. B. Walter and J. Snyder. New York: Columbia University Press, pp. 261–302.

Deutsch, K. W. (1953) *Nationalism and Social Communication: An Inquiry into the Foundations of Nationality*. Cambridge, MA: MIT Press.

Diehl, P. F. (2008) *Peace Operations*. Cambridge: Polity.

Diehl, P. F., and Lepgold, J. (eds) (2003) *Regional Conflict Management*. Lanham, MD: Rowman & Littlefield.

Diez, T., et al. (2002) *Enlargement and Reconciliation: EU Accession and the Division of Cyprus*. Flensburg: ECMI.

Dodini, M., and Fantini, M. (2006) The EU Neighbourhood Policy: implications for economic growth and stability, *Journal of Common Market Studies*, 44/3: 507–32.

Doyle, M. W. (2001) War making and peace making: the United Nation's post-Cold War record, in *Turbulent Peace: The Challenges of Managing International Conflict*, ed. C. A. Crocker, F. O. Hampson and P. Aall. Washington, DC: United States Institute of Peace Press, pp. 529–60.

Duke, S. (2003) Regional organisations and conflict prevention: CFSP and ESDI in Europe, in *Conflict Prevention: Path to Peace or Grand Illusion?*, ed. D. Carment and A. Schnabel. Tokyo: United Nations University Press, pp. 91–111.

Eminov, A. (1997) *Turkish and Other Muslim Minorities in Bulgaria*. London: Hurst.

Engström, J. (2002) The power of perception: the impact of the Macedonian question on inter-ethnic relations in the Republic of Macedonia, *Ethnopolitics*, 1/3: 3–17.

ESI (European Stability Initiative) (2002) *The Other Macedonian Conflict*, www.esiweb.org/pdf/esi_document_id_32.pdf.

Esman, M. J. (1994b) Ethnic actors in international politics. *Nationalism and Ethnic Politics*, 1/1: 111–25.

Esman, M. J. (1994b) *Ethnic Politics*. Ithaca, NY: Cornell University Press.

Esman, M. J., and Herring, R. (2001) *Carrots, Sticks, and Ethnic Conflict*. Ann Arbor: University of Michigan Press.

Father Sava (1998) The interview to 'Blic' Daily by Hiermonk Sava from Decani Monastery, www.balkanpeace.org/index.php?index=/content/balkans/kosovo_metohija/articles/kam11.incl.

Fearon, J. (1995) Rationalist explanations for war, *International Organization*, 49/3: 379–414.

Fearon, J. D. (1998) Commitment problems and the spread of ethnic conflict, in *The International Spread of Ethnic Conflict: Fear, Diffusion, and Escalation*, ed. D. Lake and D. Rothchild. Princeton, NJ: Princeton University Press, pp. 107–26.

Fearon, J., and Laitin, D. (1996) Explaining interethnic cooperation, *American Political Science Review*, 90/4: 715–35.

Fearon, J. and Laitin, D. (2000) Violence and the social construction of ethnic identity, *International Organization*, 54/4: 845–77.

Fink, C. (2001) *Living Silence: Burma under Military Rule*. London: Zed Books.

Finnemore, M. (2003) *The Purpose of Intervention: Changing Beliefs about the Use of Force*. Ithaca, NY: Cornell University Press.

Fortna, V. P. (2004) Does peacekeeping keep peace? International intervention and the duration of peace after civil war, *International Studies Quarterly*, 48/2: 262–92.

Fowkes, B. (2001) *Ethnicity and Ethnic Conflict in the Post-Communist World*. Basingstoke: Palgrave.

Fraenkel, J., and Grofman, B. (2004) A neo-Downsian model of the Alternative Vote as a mechanism for mitigating ethnic conflict in plural societies, *Public Choice*, 121: 487–506.

Fraenkel, J., and Grofman, B. (2006) Does the Alternative Vote foster moderation in ethnically divided societies? The case of Fiji, *Comparative Political Studies*, 39/5: 623–51.

Frost, F., Rann, A., and Chin, A. (2003) *Terrorism in Southeast Asia*. Parliament of Australia: Parliamentary Library; www.aph.gov.au/library/intguide/FAD/sea. htm.

Gellner, E. (1983) *Nations and Nationalism*. Ithaca, NY: Cornell University Press.

Georgieff, A. (1998) Macedonia: local Albanian leader complains of discrimination, *RFE/RL Feature*, 23 February.

Gilligan, M., and Stedman, S. J. (2003) Where do the peacekeepers go? *International Studies Review*, 5/4: 37–54.

Ginsberg, R. H. (2001) *The European Union in International Politics: Baptism by Fire*. Lanham, MD: Rowman & Littlefield.

Gruber, A. (1974) *Südtirol unter dem Faschismus*. Bozen: Athesia.

GSO (Global Security Org) (2008) The Lord's Resistance Army, www.globalsecurity. org/military/world/para/lra.htm.

Halperin, M. H., Scheffer, D. J., and Small, P. L. (1992) *Self-Determination in the New World Order*. Washington, DC: Carnegie Endowment for International Peace.

Hardin, R. (1995) *One for All: The Logic of Group Conflict*. Princeton, NJ: Princeton University Press.

Hartzell, C., and Hoddie, M. (2008) *Crafting Peace: Power sharing and the Negotiated Settlement of Civil Wars*. University Park: Pennsylvania State University Press.

Hechter, M. (2000) *Containing Nationalism*. Oxford: Oxford University Press.

Henckaerts, J.-M. (1995) *Mass Expulsions in Modern International Law and Practice*. The Hague: Martinus Nijhoff.

Hirschon, R. (1989) *Heirs of the Greek Catastrophe: The Social Life of Asia Minor Refugees in Piraeus*. Oxford: Clarendon Press.

Hoffmann, S. (1996) *The Ethics and Politics of Humanitarian Intervention*. Notre Dame, IN: University of Notre Dame Press.

Holliday, G., et al. (2004) *EU Enlargement and Minority Rights*. Flensburg: ECMI.

Holzgrefe, J. L., and Keohane, R. O. (2003) *Humanitarian Intervention: Ethical, Legal and Political Dilemmas*. Cambridge: Cambridge University Press.

Horowitz, D. L. ([1985] 2000) *Ethnic Groups in Conflict*. Berkeley: University of California Press.

Horowitz, D. L. (1990) Ethnic conflict management for policymakers, in *Conflict and Peacemaking in Multiethnic Societies*, ed. J. V. Montville. Lexington, MA: Lexington Books.

Horowitz, D. L. (1991) *A Democratic South Africa? Constitutional Engineering in a Divided Society*. Berkeley: University of California Press.

Horowitz, D. L. (1993) Democracy in divided societies, *Journal of Democracy*, 4/4: 18–38.

Horowitz, D. L. (1998) Structure and strategy in ethnic conflict. Paper prepared for the Annual World Bank Conference on Development Economics, Washington, DC,

20–21 April; http://siteresources.worldbank.org/INTABCDEWASHINGTON1998/ Resources/horowitz.pdf.

Horowitz, D. L. (2002) Constitutional design: proposals versus processes, in *The Architecture of Democracy: Constitutional Design, Conflict Management and Democracy*, ed. A. Reynolds. Oxford: Oxford University Press.

Horowitz, D. L. (2003) Electoral systems and their goals: a primer for decision-makers, *Journal of Democracy*, 14/4: 115–27.

Horowitz, D. L. (2004) The Alternative Vote and interethnic moderation: a reply to Fraenkel and Grofman, *Public Choice*, 121/3–4: 507–17.

Horowitz, D. L. (2006) Strategy takes a holiday: Fraenkel and Grofman on the Alternative Vote, *Comparative Political Studies*, 39: 652–62.

Horowitz, D. L. (2007) The many uses of federalism. *Drake Law Review*, 55: 953–66.

Horowitz, D. L. (2008) Conciliatory institutions and constitutional processes in post-conflict states, *William and Mary Law Review*, 49: 1213–48.

Hughes, J., Sasse, G., and Gordon, C. (2004) *Europeanization and Regionalization in the EU's Enlargement to Central and Eastern Europe: The Myth of Conditionality*. Basingstoke: Palgrave Macmillan.

Human Rights Watch (2006) *The Impact of the Comprehensive Peace Agreement and the New Government of National Unity on Southern Sudan*. www.hrw.org/legacy/back grounder/africa/sudan0306/sudan0306.pdf.

Human Rights Watch (2007) Burma, in *World Report 2007*, www.hrw.org/legacy/ englishwr2k7/docs/2007/01/11/burma14865.htm.

ICG (International Crisis Group) (1998a) *Again, the Visible Hand: Slobodan Milošević's Manipulation of the Kosovo Dispute*. Brussels: ICG: www.crisisgroup.org/home/get file.cfm?id=418&tid=1747&type=pdf&l=1.

ICG (International Crisis Group) (1998b) *A View from Tirana: The Albanian Dimension of the Kosovo Crisis*. Brussels: ICG: www.crisisgroup.org/home/getfile.cfm?id=280 &tid=1602&type=pdf&l=1

ICG (International Crisis Group) (1998c) *The Albanian Question in Macedonia: Implications of the Kosovo Conflict on Inter-Ethnic Relations in Macedonia*. Brussels: ICG: www.crisisgroup.org/home/getfile.cfm?id=374&tid=1699&type=pdf&l=1

ICG (International Crisis Group) (2000) *Macedonia's Ethnic Albanians: Bridging the Gulf*. Brussels: ICG: www.crisisgroup.org/home/getfile.cfm?id=381&tid=1706&t ype=pdf&l=1.

ICG (International Crisis Group) (2001) *Macedonia: The Last Chance for Peace*. Brussels: ICG: www.crisisgroup.org/home/getfile.cfm?id=370&tid=1692&type=pdf&l=1.

ICG (International Crisis Group) (2004) *Georgia: Avoiding War in South Ossetia*. Brussels: ICF: www.crisisgroup.org/home/index.cfm?id=3128&l=1.

ICG (International Crisis Group) (2005) *Philippines Terrorism: The Role of Militant Islamic Converts*, Brussels: ICG: www.crisisgroup.org/home/getfile.cfm?id=2102& tid=3844&type=pdf&1=1.

ICG (International Crisis Group) (2008) *The Philippines: The Collapse of Peace in Mindanao*. Brussels: ICF: www.crisisgroup.org/home/getfile.cfm?id=3653&tid=5 740&type=pdf&1=1.

ICJ (International Court of Justice) (2007) *Judgment: Application of the Convention on the Prevention and Punishment of the Crime of Genocide (Bosnia and Herzegovina* v. *Serbia and Montenegro)*, www.icj-cij.org/docket/files/91/13685.pdf.

ICRC (International Committee of the Red Cross) (2005) Darfur suffering continues, solutions remain distant, www.icrc.org/web/eng/siteeng0.nsf/htmlall/darfur_future?opendocument.

ICRC (International Committee of the Red Cross) (2009) The ICRC in the Democratic Republic of the Congo, www.icrc.org/web/eng/siteeng0.nsf/htmlall/congo_kinshasa?opendocument.

IHFHR (International Helsinki Federation for Human Rights) (1993) *From Autonomy to Colonisation: Human Rights in Kosovo, 1989–1993*. Helsinki: IHFHR.

Ilievski, Z. (2007) *Ethnic Mobilization in Macedonia*. Bolzano: European Academy.

INCORE (2006) Electronic interview between Karl Cordell and representative from the Initiative on Conflict Resolution and Ethnicity, University of Ulster.

Janus, T. (2009) Interventions and conflict incentives, *Ethnopolitics*, 8/2: 191–208.

Jenne, E. (2007) *Ethnic Bargaining: The Paradox of Minority Empowerment*. Ithaca, NY: Cornell University Press.

Jervis, R. (1976) *Perception and Misperception in International Politics*. Princeton, NJ: Princeton University Press.

Jervis, R. (1978) Cooperation under the security dilemma. *World Politics*, 30/2: 167–214.

Kaldor, M. (2006) *New and Old Wars: Organized Violence in a Global Era*. 2nd edn, Cambridge: Polity.

Kaldor, M. (2007) *Human Security: Reflections on Globalization and Intervention*. Cambridge: Polity.

Kaufman, S. J. (1996) An 'international' theory of interethnic war, *Review of International Studies*, 22/2: 149–71.

Kaufman, S. J. (2001) *Modern Hatreds: The Symbolic Politics of Ethnic War*. Ithaca, NY: Cornell University Press.

Kaufmann, C. D. (1996a) Intervention in ethnic and ideological civil wars: why one can be done and the other one can't, *Security Studies*, 6/1: 62–100.

Kaufmann, C. D. (1996b) Possible and impossible solutions to ethnic civil wars, *International Security*, 20/4: 136–75.

Kaufmann, C. D. (1998) When all else fails: ethnic population transfers and partitions in the twentieth century, *International Security*, 23/2: 120–56.

Kedourie, E. (1960) *Nationalism*. Oxford: Blackwell.

Kelley, J. (2006) New wine in old wineskins: promoting political reforms through the new European Neighbourhood Policy. *Journal of Common Market Studies*, 44/1: 29–55.

Kemp, W. A. (ed.) (2001) *Quiet Diplomacy in Action: The OSCE High Commissioner on National Minorities*. The Hague, London and Boston: Kluwer Law International.

Keohane, R. O., and Nye, J. S. (1977) *Power and Interdependence: World Politics in Transition*. Boston: Little, Brown.

King, I., and Mason, W. (2006) *Peace at any Price: How the World Failed Kosovo*. Ithaca, NY: Cornell University Press.

Koinova, M. (2008) Kin-state intervention in ethnic conflicts: Albania and Turkey compared, *Ethnopolitics*, 7/4: 373–90.

Koufa, K., and Svolopoulos, C. (1991) The compulsory exchange of populations between Greece and Turkey: the settlement of minority questions at the

Conference of Lausanne and its impact on Greek–Turkish relations, in *Ethnic Groups in International Relations*, ed. P. Smith. Dartmouth: European Science Foundation.

Kramer, M. (2001) Introduction, in *Redrawing Nations: Ethnic Cleansing in East-Central Europe, 1944–1948*, ed. P. Ther and A Siljak. Lanham, MD: Rowman & Littlefield, pp. 1–41.

Krasner, S. D. (ed.) (1983) *International Regimes*. Ithaca, NY: Cornell University Press.

Kronenberger, V., and Wouters, J. (2004) *The European Union and Conflict Prevention: Policy and Legal Aspects*. The Hague: TMC Asser Press.

Kuperman, A. (2005) Suicidal rebellions and the moral hazard of humanitarian intervention, *Ethnopolitics*, 4/2: 150–73.

Kuperman, A. J. (2008) The moral hazard of humanitarian intervention: lessons from the Balkans, *International Studies Quarterly*, 52/1: 49–80.

Ladas, S. P. (1932) *The Exchange of Minorities: Bulgaria, Greece, and Turkey*. New York: Macmillan.

Laitin, D. (1998) *Identity in Formation: The Russian-Speaking Populations in the Near Abroad*. Ithaca, NY: Cornell University Press.

Laitin, D. (1999) Somalia: civil war and international intervention, in *Civil Wars, Insecurity and Intervention*, ed. B. Walter and J. Snyder. New York: Columbia University Press, pp. 146–80.

Lake, D. A., and Morgan, P. M. (1997) *Regional Orders: Building Security in a New World*. State College: Pennsylvania State University Press.

Lake, D., and Rothchild, D. (1996) Containing fear: the origins and management of ethnic conflict, *International Security*, 21/2: 41–75.

Lake, D., and Rothchild, D. (1998) Spreading fear: the genesis of transnational ethnic conflict, in *The International Spread of Ethnic Conflict: Fear, Diffusion, and Escalation*, ed. D. Lake and D. Rothchild. Princeton, NJ: Princeton University Press, pp. 3–32.

Lake, D., and Rothchild, D. (2001) Political decentralization and civil war settlements, Paper prepared for the 2001 Annual Meeting of the American Political Science Association, San Francisco.

Lang, A. F., Jr. (2003) *Just Intervention*. Washington, DC: Georgetown University Press.

Lapidoth, R. (1997) *Autonomy: Flexible Solutions for Ethnic Conflicts*. Washington, DC: United States Institute of Peace Press.

Levy, J. S. (2001) Theories of interstate and intrastate war: a levels-of-analysis approach, in *Turbulent Peace: The Challenges of Managing International Conflict*, ed. C. A. Crocker, F. O. Hampson and P. Aall. Washington, DC: United States Institute of Peace Press, pp. 3–27.

Lijphart, A. (1968) Typologies of democratic systems, *Comparative Political Studies*, 1/1: 3–44.

Lijphart, A. (1977) *Democracy in Plural Societies*. New Haven, CT, and London: Yale University Press.

Lijphart, A. (1985) *Power sharing in South Africa*. Berkeley: Institute of International Studies, University of California.

Lijphart, A. (1995) Self-determination versus pre-determination of ethnic minorities in power sharing systems, in *The Rights of Minority Cultures*, ed. W. Kymlicka. Oxford: Oxford University Press.

Lijphart, A. (2002a) Negotiation democracy versus consensus democracy: parallel conclusions and recommendations, *European Journal of Political Research*, 41: 107–13.

Lijphart, A. (2002b) The wave of power sharing democracy, in *The Architecture of Democracy: Constitutional Design, Conflict Management and Democracy*, ed. A. Reynolds. Oxford: Oxford University Press, pp. 37–54.

Lijphart, A. (2004) Constitutional design for divided societies, *Journal of Democracy*, 15/2: 96–109.

Lustick, I. D. (2000) Agent-based modelling of collective identity: testing constructivist theory, *Journal of Artificial Societies and Social Simulation*, 3/1; http://jasss.soc.surrey.ac.uk/3/1/1.html.

Lynch, D. (2004) *Engaging Eurasia's Separatist States: Unresolved Conflicts and the de facto States*. Washington, DC: United States Institute for Peace.

McGarry, J. (2006) Iraq: liberal consociation and conflict management, Draft working paper, MS in author's possession.

McGarry, J. (2007) Asymmetrical federal systems, *Ethnopolitics*, 6/1: 105–16.

McGarry, J., and Keating, M. (eds) (2006) *European Integration and the Nationalities Question*. London: Routledge.

McGarry, J. and O'Leary, B. (eds) (1993) *The Politics of Ethnic Conflict Regulation*. London: Routledge.

McGarry, J. and O'Leary, B. (2004) *The Northern Ireland Conflict: Consociational Engagements*. Oxford: Oxford University Press.

Magas, Branka (1993) *The Destruction of Yugoslavia*. London and New York: Verso.

Mahncke, D., Ambos, A., and Reynolds, C. (eds) (2004) *European Foreign Policy: From Rhetoric to Reality?* Oxford: Peter Lang.

Mango, A. (1999) *Atatürk*. London: John Murray.

Marko, J. (1999) Kosovo/a: a Gordian knot?, in *Gordischer Knoten Kosovo/a: Durchschlagen oder entwirren?*, ed. J. Marko. Baden-Baden: Nomos, pp. 261–80.

Marsh, S., and Mackenstein, H. (2005) *The International Relations of the European Union*. London: Longman.

Mearsheimer, J. J. (2001) *The Tragedy of Great Power Politics*. New York: Norton.

Mearsheimer, J. J., and Pape, R. A. (1993) The answer: a partition plan for Bosnia, *New Republic*, 14 June: 22–8.

Moffett, J. (1998) Yugoslavia: bishop says Kosovo peace prospects bleak under Milošević, *RFE/RL Features*, 16 September.

Montville, J. (1990) *Conflict and Peacemaking in Multiethnic Societies*. Lexington, MA: Lexington Books.

Moore, P. (1997) Balkan states: Crete summit points to more instability, *RFE/RL Features*, 6 November.

Muslim, M. A. (2003) Sustaining the constituency for Moro autonomy, in *Compromising on Autonomy: Mindanao in Transition*, ed. M. Stankovich. London: Conciliation Resources: www.c-r.org/our-work/accord/philippines-mindanao/sustaining-constituency.php.

Naimark, N. M. (2001) *Fires of Hatred: Ethnic Cleansing in Twentieth-Century Europe*. Cambridge, MA: Harvard University Press.

Noel, S. (ed.) (2005) *From Power Sharing to Democracy: Post-Conflict Institutions in Ethnically Divided Societies*. Montreal: McGill/Queen's University Press.

O'Flynn, I., and Russell, D. (eds) (2005) *Power Sharing: New Challenges for Divided Societies*. London: Pluto Press.

O'Leary, B. (2005a) Debating consociational politics: normative and explanatory arguments, in *From Powersharing to Democracy*, ed. S. Noel. Montreal and Kingston: McGill/Queen's University Press.

O'Leary, B. (2005b) Powersharing, pluralist federation, and federacy, in *The Future of Kurdistan in Iraq*, ed. B. O'Leary, J. McGarry and K. Salih. Philadelphia: University of Pennsylvania Press.

O'Leary, B. (2006) Debating partition: justifications, critiques, and evaluation, IBIS Working Paper No. 78. Dublin: Institute for British–Irish Studies.

O'Leary, B., Grofman, B. and Elklit, J. (2005) Divisor methods for sequential portfolio allocation in multi-party executive bodies: evidence from Northern Ireland and Denmark, *American Journal of Political Science*, 49/1: 198–211.

Otunnu, O. A., and Doyle, M. W. (eds) (1998) *Peacemaking and Peacekeeping for the New Century*. Lanham, MD: Rowman & Littlefield.

Paris, R. (2004) *At War's End*. Cambridge: Cambridge University Press.

Paris, R., and Sisk, T. D. (eds) (2008) *The Dilemmas of State-Building: Confronting the Contradictions of Postwar Peace Operations*. London: Routledge.

Pentzopoulos, D. (1962) *The Balkan Exchange of Minorities and its Impact upon Greece*. Paris and The Hague: Mouton.

Perry, D. M. (1992) Macedonia: a Balkan problem and a European dilemma. *RFE/RL Research Report*, 1/25.

Petritsch, W., Kaser, K., and Pichler, R. (1999) *Kosovo/Kosova: Mythen, Daten, Fakten*. Klagenfurt: Wieser.

Petroska-Beska, V., and Najcevska, M. (2004) *Macedonia: Understanding History, Preventing Future Conflict*. USIP Special Report 115. Washington, DC: United States Institute of Peace Press; www.usip.org/files/resources/sr115.pdf.]

Pettifer, J. (ed.) (2001) *The New Macedonian Question*. Basingstoke: Palgrave.

Posen, B. (1993) The security dilemma and ethnic conflict, *Survival*, 35/2: 27–47.

Poulton, H. (2000) *Who are the Macedonians?* London: Hurst.

Pugh, M., and Cooper, N. (2004) *War Economies in a Regional Context: Challenges of Transformation*. Boulder, CO: Lynne Rienner.

Pugh, M., and Sidhu, W. P. S. (eds) (2003) *The United Nations and Regional Security: Europe and Beyond*. Boulder, CO: Lynne Rienner.

Pushkina, D. (2006) A recipe for success? Ingredients of a successful peacekeeping mission, *International Peacekeeping*, 13/2: 133–49.

Quinn, D. (2008) Self-determination movements and their outcomes, in *Peace and Conflict 2008*, ed. J. J. Hewitt, J. Wilkenfeld and T. R. Gurr. Boulder, CO, and London: Paradigm, pp. 33–8.

Rabushka, A., and Shepsle, K. A. (1972) *Politics in Plural Societies: A Theory of Democratic Instability*. Columbus, OH: Merrill.

Reilly, B. (2001) *Democracy in Divided Societies: Electoral Engineering for Conflict Management*. Cambridge: Cambridge University Press.

Reilly, B. (2006) *Democracy and Diversity: Political Engineering in the Asia-Pacific*. Oxford: Oxford University Press.

Reuter, J. (1995) Albaniens Aussenpolitik: Balanceakt zwischen nationalen Sicherheitsinteressen und panalbanischen Träumen, *Südosteuropa*, 44/1–2: 95–102.

Reynolds, A. (ed.) (2002) *The Architecture of Democracy: Constitutional Design, Conflict Management and Democracy*. Oxford: Oxford University Press.

RFE/RL (1997) Balkan states: leaders seek to ease tensions, *RFE/RL Feature*, 6 November.

RFE/RL (2006) Putin urges 'universally applicable' solution for Kosovo, *Radio Free Europe/Radio Liberty*, 30 January; www.rferl.org/content/Article/1065240.html.

Roeder, P. G. (2005) Power dividing as an alternative to power sharing, in *Sustainable Peace: Power and Democracy after Civil Wars*, ed. P. G. Roeder and D. Rothchild. Ithaca, NY: Cornell University Press.

Roeder, P. G. and Rothchild, D. (eds) (2005) *Sustainable Peace: Power and Democracy after Civil Wars*. Ithaca, NY: Cornell University Press.

Romano, D. (2006) *The Kurdish Nationalist Movement: Opportunity, Mobilization and Identity*. Cambridge: Cambridge University Press.

Ross, M. H. (1993a) *The Culture of Conflict: Interpretations and Interests in Comparative Perspective*. New Haven, CT: Yale University Press.

Ross, M. H. (1993b) *The Management of Conflict: Interpretations and Interests in Comparative Perspective*. New Haven, CT: Yale University Press.

Ross, M. H. (2007) *Cultural Contestation in Ethnic Conflict*. Cambridge: Cambridge University Press.

Rotberg, R. I. (ed.) (2004) *When States Fail: Causes and Consequences*. Princeton, NJ: Princeton University Press.

Rothchild, D. (1997) *Managing Ethnic Conflict in Africa*. Washington, DC: Brookings Institution.

Roudometof, V. (ed.) (2000) *The Macedonian Question: Culture, Historiography, Politics*. Boulder, CO: East European Monographs.

Rubin, B. (2001) Regional approaches to conflict management in Africa, paper given at an IPA-sponsored meeting for the UN Security Council on Regional Approaches to Conflict Management in Africa; www.un.int/colombia/english/consejo_seguridad/IPA-RegAproAfricaBarnett%20R_%20RubinAug08-01.htm.

Sabanadze, N. (2002) *International Involvement in the South Caucasus*, www.ecmi.de/download/working_paper_15.pdf.

Safran, W. (2004) Ethnic conflict and third-party mediation: a critical review, in *Ethnonationalism in the Contemporary World: Walker and the Study of Nationalism*, ed. D. Conversi. London: Routledge, pp. 184–205.

Sambanis, N. (2000) Partition as a solution to ethnic war: an empirical critique of the theoretical literature, *World Politics*, 52/4: 437–83.

Sambanis, N. (2004) Using case studies to expand economic models of civil war, *Perspectives on Politics*, 2/2: 259–79.

Scherrer, C. P. (2003) *Structural Prevention of Ethnic Violence*. Basingstoke: Palgrave.

Schmidt, F. (2000) Generationskonflikte in Albaniens großen Parteien, *Südosteuropa*, 1–2: 32–52.

Schneckener, U. (2004) Models of ethnic conflict regulation: the politics of recognition, in *Managing and Settling Ethnic Conflicts: Perspectives on Successes and Failures from Africa, Asia, and Europe*, ed. U. Schneckener and S. Wolff. London: Hurst, pp. 18–39.

Schneckener, U., and Wolff, S. (eds) (2004) *Managing and Settling Ethnic Conflicts: Perspectives on Successes and Failures from Africa, Asia, and Europe.* New York and London: Hurst.

Sheffer, G. (2003) *Diaspora Politics: At Home Abroad.* Cambridge: Cambridge University Press.

Sherif, M., Harvey, O. J., White, B. J., Hood, W. R., and Sherif, C. W. (1954) *Intergroup Conflict and Cooperation: The Robbers Cave Experiment,* http://psychclassics.yorku.ca/Sherif/.

Singer, J. D. (1961) The level-of-analysis problem in international relations, *World Politics,* 14/1: 77–92.

Sisk, T. D. (1996) *Power Sharing and International Mediation in Ethnic Conflict.* Washington, DC: United States Institute of Peace Press.

Smith, A. D. (1971) *Theories of Nationalism.* New York: Harper & Row.

Smith, A. D. (1981) *The Ethnic Revival in the Modern World.* Cambridge: Cambridge University Press.

Smith, A. D. (1991) *National Identity.* London: Penguin.

Smith D. (2002) Framing the national question in Central and Eastern Europe: a quadratic nexus? *Ethnopolitics,* 2/1: 3–16; www.ethnopolitics.org/ethnopolitics/archive/volume_II/issue_1/smith.pdf.

Smith, H. (2002) *European Union Foreign Policy: What it Is and What it Does.* London: Pluto Press.

Smith, K. E. (2003) *European Union Foreign Policy in a Changing World.* Cambridge: Polity.

Smith, M. J. (1998) Humanitarian intervention: an overview of the ethical issues, *Ethics and International Affairs,* 12/December: 63–79.

Smith, M. J. (2004) *Europe's Foreign and Security Policy: The Institutionalization of Cooperation.* Cambridge, Cambridge University Press.

Smith, P. J. (2005) *Terrorism and Violence in Southeast Asia: Transnational Challenges to States and Regional Stability.* Armonk, NY: M. E. Sharpe.

Smith, S. (2005) Ceasefire negotiations in eastern Democratic Republic of Congo, in *Choosing to Engage: Armed Groups and Peace Processes,* ed. R. Ricigliano. London: Conciliation Resources; www.c-r.org/our-work/accord/engaging-groups/ceasefire-negotiations-drc.php.

Snyder, J., and Jervis, R. (1999) Civil war and the security dilemma, in *Civil Wars, Insecurity and Intervention,* ed. B. Walter and J. Snyder. New York: Columbia University Press, pp. 15–37.

Socor, V. (2006) Moscow on Kosovo: having its cake and eating it too, *Eurasia Daily Monitor,* 3/25; www.jamestown.org/single/?no_cache=1&tx_ttnews%5Btt_news%5D=31361.

Stankovich, M. (ed.) (2003) *Compromising on Autonomy: Mindanao in Transition.* London: Conciliation Resources: www.c-r.org/our-work/accord/philippines-mindanao/contents.php

State Failure Task Force (2000) *State Failure Task Force Report: Phase III Findings,* http://globalpolicy.gmu.edu/pitf/SFTF%20Phase%20III%20Report%20Final.pdf.

Steinberg, D. (2004) Feel-good US sanctions wrongheaded, *YaleGlobal,* 19 May; http://yaleglobal.yale.edu/display.article?id=3901.

Sunley, J. (1998) Kosovo's woes are Albania's too, *Wall Street Journal Europe,* 29 June.

Tajfel, H. (1981) *Human Groups and Social Categories: Studies in Social Psychology.* Cambridge: Cambridge University Press.

Tellis, A. J., Szayna, T. S., and Winnefeld, J. A. (1997) *Anticipating Ethnic Conflict.* Santa Monica, CA: RAND.

Thakur, R., and Schnabel, A. (eds) (2001) *United Nations Peacekeeping Operations: Ad Hoc Missions, Permanent Engagement.* Tokyo: United Nations University Press.

Thayer, B. (1999) Macedonia, in *The Costs of Conflict: Prevention and Cure in the Global Arena*, ed. M. E. Brown and R. N. Rosecrance. New York: Carnegie Commission on Preventing Deadly Conflict.

Tocci, N. (2007) *The EU's Role in Conflict Resolution: Promoting Peace in the European Neighbourhood.* London: Routledge.

Toggenburg, G. (ed.) (2005) *Minority Protection and the EU: The Way Forward.* Budapest: LGI, Open Society Institute.

UN Commission on Human Rights (1997) *Human Rights and Population Transfer.* Final Report of the Special Rapporteur (E/CN.4/Sub.2/1997/23).

UN Economic and Social Council (1996) Commission on Crime Prevention and Criminal Justice, Fifth Session, 21–31 May (Doc. E/CN.15/1996/2).

UNHCR (1975) *Report of the United Nations High Commissioner for Refugees*, Thirtieth Session, Supplement no. 12 (A/10012). New York: United Nations.

UNHCR (1976) *Report of the United Nations High Commissioner for Refugees*, Thirty-First Session, Supplement no. 12 (A/31/12). New York: United Nations.

UNHCR (1977) *Report of the United Nations High Commissioner for Refugees*, Thirty-Second Session, Supplement no. 12 (A/32/12). New York: United Nations.

UNHCR (1997) *Update on Regional Developments in the Former Yugoslavia.* New York: United Nations.

UNHCR (1998) *Update on Regional Developments in Central Asia, Southwest Asia, North Africa and the Middle East* (EC/48/SC/CRP.3). New York: United Nations.

UNHCR (2006) *The State of the World's Refugees 2006: Human Displacement in the New Millennium.* New York: United Nations.

UNPO (Unrepresented Nations and Peoples Organization) (2006) Electronic interview between Karl Cordell and M. Skeie.

UN Secretary General (1998) Report of the Secretary-General Prepared Pursuant to Resolutions 1160 (1998) and 1199 (1998) of the Security Council, S/1998/12.

UN Security Council (1998a) *Resolution 1160 (1998)*, S/RES/1160.

UN Security Council (1998b) *Resolution 1186 (1998)*, S/RES/1186.

UN Security Council (1998c) *Resolution 1199 (1998)*, S/RES/1199.

USAid (2006) Electronic interview between Karl Cordell and USAid representative.

US Department of Defense (1998) Bosnia Task Force Briefing, 9 September. Washington, DC.

US Department of Justice (1996) *NNICC Report 1996.* Washington, DC: Department of Justice.

US Department of Justice (1997) *NNICC Report 1997.* Washington, DC: Department of Justice.

USIP (United States Institute of Peace) (1998) *Serbia: Democratic Alternatives.* Washington, DC: United States Institute of Peace: www.usip.org/resources/serbia-democratic-alternatives.

Vachudova, M. A. (2005) *Europe Undivided: Democracy, Leverage, and Integration after Communism*. Oxford: Oxford University Press.

Valentino, B. A. (2004) *Final Solutions: Mass Killing and Genocide in the 20th Century*. Ithaca, NY: Cornell University Press.

Van Houten, P. (1998) The role of the minority's reference state in ethnic relations, *Archives européenes de sociologie*, 39/1: 110–46.

Van Houten, P. (2007) The World Bank's (post-)conflict agenda: the challenge of integrating development and security, *Cambridge Review of International Affairs*, 20/4: 639–57.

Volkan, V. (1979) *Cyprus: War and Adaptation: A Psychoanalytic History of Two Ethnic Groups in Conflict*. Charlottesville: University of Virginia Press.

Volkan, V. (1988) *The Need to Have Enemies & Allies: From Clinical Practice to International Relationships*. Northvale, NJ: Aronson.

Volkan, V. (1997) *Bloodlines: From Ethnic Pride to Ethnic Terrorism*. New York: Farrar, Straus, & Giroux.

Volkan, V. (2006) *Killing in the Name of Identity: A Study of Bloody Conflicts*. Los Angeles: Pitchstone.

Wallensteen, P. (2007) *Understanding Conflict Resolution*. 2nd edn, London: Sage.

Walter, B. (1999) Introduction, in *Civil Wars, Insecurity and Intervention*, ed. B. Walter and J. Snyder. New York: Columbia University Press, pp. 1–12.

Walter, B. F. (2002) *Committing to Peace: The Successful Settlement of Civil Wars*. Princeton, NJ: Princeton University Press.

Walter, B., and Snyder, J. (eds) (1999) *Civil Wars, Insecurity and Intervention*. New York: Columbia University Press.

Waltz, K. N. (1959) *Man, the State and War*. New York: Columbia University Press.

Waltz, K. N. (1979) *Theory of International Politics*. New York: McGraw Hill.

Walzer, M. (1977) *Just and Unjust Wars: A Moral Argument with Historical Illustrations*. New York: Basic Books.

Weiss, T. G. (2007) *Humanitarian Intervention*. Cambridge: Polity.

Weiss, T. G. (2008) *Humanitarian Intervention: Ideas in Action*. Cambridge: Polity.

Weissman, S. R. (1998) *Preventing Genocide in Burundi: Lessons from International Diplomacy*. Washington, DC: United States Institute of Peace Press; http://usip. forumone.com/files/resources/pwks22.pdf .

Weller, M. (1999) The Rambouillet Conference on Kosovo, *International Affairs* 75/2: 163–203.

Weller, M. (2005a) The self-determination trap, *Ethnopolitics*, 4/1: 3–28.

Weller, M. (2005b) Self-governance in interim settlements: the case of Sudan, in *Autonomy, Self-Governance and Conflict Resolution: Innovative Approaches to Institutional Design in Divided Societies*, ed. M. Weller and S. Wolff. London: Routledge.

Weller, M. and Wolff, S. (eds) (2005) *Autonomy, Self-Governance and Conflict Resolution: Innovative Approaches to Institutional Design in Divided Societies*. London: Routledge.

Weller, M., and Wolff, S. (2006) Bosnia and Herzegovina ten years after Dayton: Lessons for internationalized state building, *Ethnopolitics*, 5/1: 1–13.

Weller, M., and Wolff, S. eds (2008) *Institutions for the Management of Ethnopolitical Conflicts in Central and Eastern Europe*. Strasbourg: Council of Europe.

Wendt, A. (1992) Anarchy is what states make of it: the social construction of power politics. *International Organization*, 46/2: 391–425.

Wennmann, A. (2006) *Renewed Armed Conflict in Georgia*. PSIO Occasional Papers 3/2006. Geneva: Graduate Institute of International Studies.

Wheeler, N. (2000) *Saving Strangers: Humanitarian Intervention in International Society*. Oxford: Oxford University Press.

Williams, P. (2001) Transnational criminal enterprises, conflict and instability, in *Turbulent Peace: The Challenges of Managing International Conflict*, ed. C. A. Crocker, F. O. Hampson and P. Aall. Washington, DC: United States Institute of Peace Press, pp. 97–111.

Wimmer, A. (2003) Democracy and ethno-religious conflict in Iraq, *Survival*, 45/4: 111–34.

Wolff, S. (2000) *German Minorities in Europe: Ethnic Identity and Cultural Belonging*. Oxford and New York: Berghahn.

Wolff, S. (2001) *Disputed Territories: The Transnational Dynamics of Ethnic Conflict Resolution*. Oxford and New York: Berghahn.

Wolff, S. (2003a) *Disputed Territories: The Transnational Dynamics of Ethnic Conflict Settlement*. New York and Oxford: Berghahn.

Wolff, S. (2003b) *The German Question: An Analysis with Key Documents*. Westport, CT: Praeger.

Wolff, S. (2003c) The limits of non-military international intervention: a case study of the Kosovo conflict, in *Understanding the War in Kosovo*, ed. F. Bieber and Z. Daskalovski, London: Frank Cass, pp. 77–98.

Wolff, S. (2004a) Can forced population transfers resolve self-determination conflicts? A European perspective, *Journal for Contemporary European Studies*, 12/1: 11–29.

Wolff, S. (2004b) The institutional structure of regional consociations in Brussels, Northern Ireland, and South Tyrol, *Nationalism and Ethnic Politics*, 10/3: 387–414.

Wolff, S. (2004c) Settling an ethnic conflict through power sharing: South Tyrol, in *Managing and Settling Ethnic Conflicts: Perspectives on Success and Failures in Europe, Africa, and Asia*, ed. U. Schneckener and S. Wolff. London: Hurst, pp. 57–76.

Wolff, S. (2005) Electoral systems design and power sharing regimes, in *Powersharing: New Challenges for Divided Societies*, ed. I. O'Flynn and D. Russell. Ann Arbor: University of Michigan Press.

Wolff, S. (2006) *Ethnic Conflict: A Global Perspective*. Oxford: Oxford University Press.

Wolff, S. (2007a) Conflict resolution between power sharing and power dividing, or beyond? *Political Studies Review*, 5/3: 363–79.

Wolff, S. (2007b) Paradiplomacy: scope, opportunities and challenges, *Bologna Center Journal of International Affairs*, 10/spring: 141–50.

Wolff, S. (2008a) Complex power sharing as conflict resolution: South Tyrol in comparative perspective, in *Tolerance through Law: Self-Governance and Group Rights in South Tyrol*, ed. J. Woelk, F. Palermo and J. Marko. The Leiden and Boston: Martinus Nijhoff.

Wolff, S. (2008b) Learning the lessons of ethnic conflict management? Conditional recognition and international administration in the Western Balkans since the 1990s, *Nationalities Papers*, 36/3: 553–71.

Wolff, S. (2009) Complex power sharing and the centrality of territorial self-governance in contemporary conflict settlements, *Ethnopolitics*, 8/1: 27–45.

Wolff, S., and Van Houten, P. (2007) The dynamics of ethnopolitical conflict, *Review of International Affairs*, 20: 639–57.

Wolff, S., and Weller, M. (2005) Self-determination and autonomy: a conceptual introduction, in *Autonomy, Self-Governance and Conflict Resolution: Innovative Approaches to Institutional Design in Divided Societies*, ed. M. Weller and S. Wolff. London: Routledge.

Woodward, S. (1995) *Balkan Tragedy: Chaos and Dissolution after the Cold War*. Washington, DC: Brookings Institution.

Young, C. (1976) *The Politics of Cultural Pluralism*. Madison: University of Wisconsin Press.

Yugoslav Helsinki Committee (1998) *Report on Refugees from Kosovo Situated in Montenegro*. Belgrade.

Zaw, A. (2003) ASEAN–Burma relations, in *Challenges to Democratization in Burma: Perspectives on Multilateral and Bilateral Relations*. Stockholm: International Institute for Democracy and Electoral Assistance, pp. 37–56; www.idea.int/asia_pacific/burma/upload/challenges_to_democratization_in_burma.pdf.

Index

Page numbers in *italics* refer to tables.